# POCKET
# WORLD
# ATLAS

Published in Great Britain in 2004 by Philip's,
a division of Octopus Publishing Group Limited,
2–4 Heron Quays, London E14 4JP

Copyright © 2004 Philip's

Cartography by Philip's

ISBN-13   978-0-540-08694-8
ISBN-10   0-540-08694-0

A CIP catalogue record for this book is available from
the British Library.

Printed in Hong Kong

Details of other Philip's titles and services can be found
on our website at: www.philips-maps.co.uk

Philip's World Atlases are published in association
with The Royal Geographical Society (with The
Institute of British Geographers).
  The Society was founded in 1830 and given a
Royal Charter in 1859 for 'the advancement of
geographical science'. Today it is a leading world
centre for geographical learning – supporting
education, teaching, research and expeditions, and
promoting public understanding of the subject.
  Further information about the Society and how to
join may be found on its website at: www.rgs.org

# PHILIP'S

# POCKET
# WORLD
# ATLAS

IN ASSOCIATION WITH
THE ROYAL GEOGRAPHICAL SOCIETY
WITH THE INSTITUTE OF BRITISH GEOGRAPHERS

# Contents

vi–ix      World Statistics

x–xi       Time Zones

xii–xiii   Flight Paths

xiv–xv     Climate

xvi–xvii   Wealth

xviii–xix  International Organizations

xx–xxiv    World Gazetteer


**WORLD MAPS**

I          World Maps –
           general reference

2–3        Northern hemisphere
           1:133.3M

4–5        Southern hemisphere
           1:133.3M


**EUROPE**

6–7        Europe 1:26.7M

8–9        Scandinavia and the
           Baltic Lands 1:13.3M

10–11      British Isles 1:6.7M

12–13      France 1:6.7M

14–15      Germany and Benelux
           1:6.7M

16–17      Central Europe 1:6.7M

18–19      Spain and Portugal 1:6.7M

20–21      Italy and the Adriatic 1:6.7M

22–23      Greece and the Balkans
           1:6.7M

24–25      Eastern Europe 1:13.3M


**ASIA**

26–27      Asia 1:67M

28–29      Western Russia and
           Central Asia 1:26.7M

30–31      Eastern Siberia 1:26.7M

32–33      Japan 1:8.5M

34–35      China 1:26.7M

36–37      Philippines and Eastern
           Indonesia 1:16.7M

38–39      South-east Asia 1:16.7M

40–41      Eastern India, Bangladesh
           and Burma 1:13.3M

42–43      Western India and
           Pakistan 1:13.3M

44–45      Iran, the Gulf and
           Afghanistan 1:13.3M

46–47      The Middle East and
           Turkey 1:13.3M

| | |
|---|---|
| **48–49** | Arabia and the Horn of Africa 1:20M |

## AFRICA

| | |
|---|---|
| **50–51** | Africa 1:56M |
| **52–53** | North-west Africa 1:20M |
| **54–55** | North-east Africa 1:20M |
| **56–57** | Central Africa 1:20M |
| **58–59** | Southern Africa 1:20M |

## AUSTRALASIA

| | |
|---|---|
| **60–61** | Australia 1:26.7M |
| **62–63** | South-east Australia 1:10.7M |
| **64–65** | New Zealand 1:8M Central and South-west Pacific |

## NORTH AMERICA

| | |
|---|---|
| **66–67** | North America 1:46.7M |
| **68–69** | Western Canada 1:20M |
| **70–71** | Eastern Canada 1:20M |
| **72–73** | North-west USA 1:8M |
| **74–75** | North-central USA 1:8M |
| **76–77** | North-east USA 1:8M |
| **78–79** | South-west USA 1:8M |
| **80–81** | Southern USA 1:8M |
| **82–83** | South-east USA 1:8M |
| **84–85** | Mexico 1:20M |
| **86–87** | Caribbean and Central America 1:20M |

## SOUTH AMERICA

| | |
|---|---|
| **88–89** | South America 1:46.7M |
| **90–91** | South America North-west 1:21.3M |
| **92–93** | South America – North-east 1:21.3M |
| **94–95** | South America – South 1:21.3M |

## POLAR REGIONS

| | |
|---|---|
| **96** | Antarctica 1:46.7M |

## INDEX

| | |
|---|---|
| **97–120** | Index to World Maps |

# WORLD STATISTICS

| Country/Territory | Area (1,000 sq km) | Area (1,000 sq miles) | Population (1,000s) | Capital City | Annual Income US$ |
|---|---|---|---|---|---|
| Afghanistan | 652 | 252 | 28,717 | Kabul | 700 |
| Albania | 28.7 | 11.1 | 3,582 | Tirana | 4,400 |
| Algeria | 2,382 | 920 | 32,819 | Algiers | 5,400 |
| American Samoa (US) | 0.20 | 0.08 | 70 | Pago Pago | 8,000 |
| Andorra | 0.47 | 0.18 | 69 | Andorra La Vella | 19,000 |
| Angola | 1,247 | 481 | 10,766 | Luanda | 1,700 |
| Anguilla (UK) | 0.10 | 0.04 | 13 | The Valley | 8,600 |
| Antigua & Barbuda | 0.44 | 0.17 | 68 | St John's | 11,000 |
| Argentina | 2,780 | 1,074 | 38,741 | Buenos Aires | 10,500 |
| Armenia | 29.8 | 11.5 | 3,326 | Yerevan | 3,600 |
| Aruba (Netherlands) | 0.19 | 0.07 | 71 | Oranjestad | 28,000 |
| Australia | 7,741 | 2,989 | 19,732 | Canberra | 26,900 |
| Austria | 83.9 | 32.4 | 8,188 | Vienna | 27,900 |
| Azerbaijan | 86.6 | 33.4 | 7,831 | Baku | 3,700 |
| Azores (Portugal) | 2.2 | 0.86 | 236 | Ponta Delgada | 15,000 |
| Bahamas | 13.9 | 5.4 | 297 | Nassau | 15,300 |
| Bahrain | 0.69 | 0.27 | 667 | Manama | 15,100 |
| Bangladesh | 144 | 55.6 | 138,448 | Dhaka | 1,800 |
| Barbados | 0.43 | 0.17 | 277 | Bridgetown | 15,000 |
| Belarus | 208 | 80.2 | 10,322 | Minsk | 8,700 |
| Belgium | 30.5 | 11.8 | 10,289 | Brussels | 29,200 |
| Belize | 23.0 | 8.9 | 266 | Belmopan | 4,900 |
| Benin | 113 | 43.5 | 7,041 | Porto-Novo | 1,100 |
| Bermuda (UK) | 0.05 | 0.02 | 64 | Hamilton | 35,200 |
| Bhutan | 47.0 | 18.1 | 2,140 | Thimphu | 1,300 |
| Bolivia | 1,099 | 424 | 8,586 | La Paz/Sucre | 2,500 |
| Bosnia-Herzegovina | 51.2 | 19.8 | 3,989 | Sarajevo | 1,900 |
| Botswana | 582 | 225 | 1,573 | Gaborone | 8,500 |
| Brazil | 8,514 | 3,287 | 182,033 | Brasília | 7,600 |
| Brunei | 5.8 | 2.2 | 358 | Bandar Seri Begawan | 18,600 |
| Bulgaria | 111 | 42.8 | 7,538 | Sofia | 6,500 |
| Burkina Faso | 274 | 106 | 13,228 | Ouagadougou | 1,100 |
| Burma (= Myanmar) | 677 | 261 | 42,511 | Rangoon | 1,700 |
| Burundi | 27.8 | 10.7 | 6,096 | Bujumbura | 500 |
| Cambodia | 181 | 69.9 | 13,125 | Phnom Penh | 1,600 |
| Cameroon | 475 | 184 | 15,746 | Yaoundé | 1,700 |
| Canada | 9,971 | 3,850 | 32,207 | Ottawa | 29,300 |
| Canary Is. (Spain) | 7.2 | 2.8 | 1,682 | Las Palmas/Santa Cruz | 19,900 |
| Cape Verde Is. | 4.0 | 1.6 | 412 | Praia | 1,400 |
| Cayman Is. (UK) | 0.26 | 0.10 | 42 | George Town | 35,000 |
| Central African Republic | 623 | 241 | 3,684 | Bangui | 1,200 |
| Chad | 1,284 | 496 | 9,253 | Ndjaména | 1,000 |
| Chile | 757 | 292 | 15,665 | Santiago | 10,100 |
| China | 9,597 | 3,705 | 1,286,975 | Beijing | 4,700 |
| Colombia | 1,139 | 440 | 41,662 | Bogotá | 6,100 |
| Comoros | 2.2 | 0.86 | 633 | Moroni | 700 |
| Congo | 342 | 132 | 2,954 | Brazzaville | 900 |
| Congo (Dem. Rep. of the) | 2,345 | 905 | 56,625 | Kinshasa | 600 |
| Cook Is. (NZ) | 0.24 | 0.09 | 21 | Avarua | 5,000 |
| Costa Rica | 51.1 | 19.7 | 3,896 | San José | 8,300 |
| Croatia | 56.5 | 21.8 | 4,422 | Zagreb | 9,800 |
| Cuba | 111 | 42.8 | 11,263 | Havana | 2,700 |
| Cyprus | 9.3 | 3.6 | 772 | Nicosia | 13,200 |
| Czech Republic | 78.9 | 30.5 | 10,249 | Prague | 15,300 |

Listed above are the principal countries of the world; the more important territories are also included. If a territory is not completely independent, then the country it is associated with is named. The area figures give the total area of land, inland water and ice. The population figures are 2003 estimates where available. The annual income is the Gross Domestic Product per capita in US dollars. [Gross Domestic Product per capita has been measured using the

| Country/Territory | Area (1,000 sq km) | Area (1,000 sq miles) | Population (1,000s) | Capital City | Annual Income US$ |
|---|---|---|---|---|---|
| **Denmark** | 43.1 | 16.6 | 5,384 | Copenhagen | 28,900 |
| **Djibouti** | 23.2 | 9.0 | 457 | Djibouti | 1,300 |
| **Dominica** | 0.75 | 0.29 | 70 | Roseau | 5,400 |
| **Dominican Republic** | 48.5 | 18.7 | 8,716 | Santo Domingo | 6,300 |
| **East Timor** | 14.9 | 5.7 | 998 | Dili | 500 |
| **Ecuador** | 284 | 109 | 13,710 | Quito | 3,200 |
| **Egypt** | 1,001 | 387 | 74,719 | Cairo | 4,000 |
| **El Salvador** | 21.0 | 8.1 | 6,470 | San Salvador | 4,600 |
| **Equatorial Guinea** | 28.1 | 10.8 | 510 | Malabo | 2,700 |
| **Eritrea** | 118 | 45.4 | 4,362 | Asmara | 700 |
| **Estonia** | 45.1 | 17.4 | 1,409 | Tallinn | 11,000 |
| **Ethiopia** | 1,104 | 426 | 66,558 | Addis Ababa | 700 |
| **Færoe Is. (Denmark)** | 1.4 | 0.54 | 46 | Tórshavn | 22,000 |
| **Fiji Islands** | 18.3 | 7.1 | 869 | Suva | 5,600 |
| **Finland** | 338 | 131 | 5,191 | Helsinki | 25,800 |
| **France** | 552 | 213 | 60,181 | Paris | 26,000 |
| **French Guiana (France)** | 90.0 | 34.7 | 187 | Cayenne | 14,400 |
| **French Polynesia (France)** | 4.0 | 1.5 | 262 | Papeete | 5,000 |
| **Gabon** | 268 | 103 | 1,322 | Libreville | 6,500 |
| **Gambia, The** | 11.3 | 4.4 | 1,501 | Banjul | 1,800 |
| **Gaza Strip (OPT)\*** | 0.36 | 0.14 | 1,275 | – | 600 |
| **Georgia** | 69.7 | 26.9 | 4,934 | Tbilisi | 3,200 |
| **Germany** | 357 | 138 | 82,398 | Berlin | 26,200 |
| **Ghana** | 239 | 92.1 | 20,468 | Accra | 2,000 |
| **Gibraltar (UK)** | 0.006 | 0.002 | 28 | Gibraltar Town | 17,500 |
| **Greece** | 132 | 50.9 | 10,666 | Athens | 19,100 |
| **Greenland (Denmark)** | 2,176 | 840 | 56 | Nuuk (Godthåb) | 20,000 |
| **Grenada** | 0.34 | 0.13 | 89 | St George's | 5,000 |
| **Guadeloupe (France)** | 1.7 | 0.66 | 440 | Basse Terre | 9,000 |
| **Guam (US)** | 0.55 | 0.21 | 164 | Agana | 21,000 |
| **Guatemala** | 109 | 42.0 | 13,909 | Guatemala City | 3,900 |
| **Guinea** | 246 | 94.9 | 9,030 | Conakry | 2,100 |
| **Guinea-Bissau** | 36.1 | 13.9 | 1,361 | Bissau | 700 |
| **Guyana** | 215 | 83.0 | 702 | Georgetown | 3,800 |
| **Haiti** | 27.8 | 10.7 | 7,528 | Port-au-Prince | 1,400 |
| **Honduras** | 112 | 43.3 | 6,670 | Tegucigalpa | 2,500 |
| **Hong Kong (China)** | 1.1 | 0.42 | 7,394 | – | 27,200 |
| **Hungary** | 93.0 | 35.9 | 10,045 | Budapest | 13,300 |
| **Iceland** | 103 | 39.8 | 281 | Reykjavik | 30,200 |
| **India** | 3,287 | 1,269 | 1,049,700 | New Delhi | 2,600 |
| **Indonesia** | 1,905 | 735 | 234,893 | Jakarta | 3,100 |
| **Iran** | 1,648 | 636 | 68,279 | Tehran | 6,000 |
| **Iraq** | 438 | 169 | 24,683 | Baghdad | 2,400 |
| **Ireland** | 70.3 | 27.1 | 3,924 | Dublin | 29,300 |
| **Israel** | 20.6 | 8.0 | 6,117 | Jerusalem | 19,500 |
| **Italy** | 301 | 116 | 57,998 | Rome | 25,100 |
| **Ivory Coast (= Côte d'Ivoire)** | 322 | 125 | 16,962 | Yamoussoukro | 1,400 |
| **Jamaica** | 11.0 | 4.2 | 2,696 | Kingston | 3,800 |
| **Japan** | 378 | 146 | 127,214 | Tokyo | 28,700 |
| **Jordan** | 89.3 | 34.5 | 5,460 | Amman | 4,300 |
| **Kazakhstan** | 2,725 | 1,052 | 16,764 | Astana | 7,200 |
| **Kenya** | 580 | 224 | 31,639 | Nairobi | 1,100 |
| **Kiribati** | 0.73 | 0.28 | 99 | Tarawa | 800 |
| **Korea, North** | 121 | 46.5 | 22,466 | Pyŏngyang | 1,000 |

purchasing-power parity method. This enables comparisons to be made between countries through their purchasing power (in US dollars), showing real price levels of goods and services.] The figures are the latest available, usually 2002 estimates.

\*OPT = Occupied Palestinian Territory     N/A = Not available

# WORLD STATISTICS

| Country/Territory | Area (1,000 sq km) | Area (1,000 sq miles) | Population (1,000s) | Capital City | Annual Income US$ |
|---|---|---|---|---|---|
| **Korea, South** | 99.3 | 38.3 | 48,289 | Seoul | 19,600 |
| **Kuwait** | 17.8 | 6.9 | 2,183 | Kuwait City | 17,500 |
| **Kyrgyzstan** | 200 | 77.2 | 4,893 | Bishkek | 2,900 |
| **Laos** | 237 | 91.4 | 5,922 | Vientiane | 1,800 |
| **Latvia** | 64.6 | 24.9 | 2,349 | Riga | 8,900 |
| **Lebanon** | 10.4 | 4.0 | 3,728 | Beirut | 4,800 |
| **Lesotho** | 30.4 | 11.7 | 1,862 | Maseru | 2,700 |
| **Liberia** | 111 | 43.0 | 3,317 | Monrovia | 1,000 |
| **Libya** | 1,760 | 679 | 5,499 | Tripoli | 6,200 |
| **Liechtenstein** | 0.16 | 0.06 | 33 | Vaduz | 25,000 |
| **Lithuania** | 65.2 | 25.2 | 3,593 | Vilnius | 8,400 |
| **Luxembourg** | 2.6 | 1.0 | 454 | Luxembourg | 48,900 |
| **Macau (China)** | 0.02 | 0.007 | 470 | – | 18,500 |
| **Macedonia (FYROM)** | 25.7 | 9.9 | 2,063 | Skopje | 5,100 |
| **Madagascar** | 587 | 227 | 16,980 | Antananarivo | 800 |
| **Madeira (Portugal)** | 0.78 | 0.30 | 241 | Funchal | 22,700 |
| **Malawi** | 118 | 45.7 | 11,651 | Lilongwe | 600 |
| **Malaysia** | 330 | 127 | 23,093 | Kuala Lumpur/Putrajaya | 8,800 |
| **Maldives** | 0.30 | 0.12 | 330 | Malé | 3,900 |
| **Mali** | 1,240 | 479 | 11,626 | Bamako | 900 |
| **Malta** | 0.32 | 0.12 | 400 | Valletta | 17,200 |
| **Marshall Is.** | 0.18 | 0.07 | 56 | Majuro | 1,600 |
| **Martinique (France)** | 1.1 | 0.43 | 426 | Fort-de-France | 10,700 |
| **Mauritania** | 1,026 | 396 | 2,913 | Nouakchott | 1,700 |
| **Mauritius** | 2.0 | 0.79 | 1,210 | Port Louis | 10,100 |
| **Mayotte (France)** | 0.37 | 0.14 | 178 | Mamoundzou | 600 |
| **Mexico** | 1,958 | 756 | 104,908 | Mexico City | 8,900 |
| **Micronesia, Fed. States of** | 0.70 | 0.27 | 108 | Palikir | 2,000 |
| **Moldova** | 33.9 | 13.1 | 4,440 | Chişinău | 2,600 |
| **Monaco** | 0.001 | 0.0004 | 32 | Monaco | 27,000 |
| **Mongolia** | 1,567 | 605 | 2,712 | Ulan Bator | 1,900 |
| **Montserrat (UK)** | 0.10 | 0.04 | 9 | Plymouth | 3,400 |
| **Morocco** | 447 | 172 | 31,689 | Rabat | 3,900 |
| **Mozambique** | 802 | 309 | 17,479 | Maputo | 1,100 |
| **Namibia** | 824 | 318 | 1,927 | Windhoek | 6,900 |
| **Nauru** | 0.02 | 0.008 | 13 | Yaren District | 5,000 |
| **Nepal** | 147 | 56.8 | 26,470 | Katmandu | 1,400 |
| **Netherlands** | 41.5 | 16.0 | 16,151 | Amsterdam/The Hague | 27,200 |
| **Netherlands Antilles (Neths)** | 0.80 | 0.31 | 216 | Willemstad | 11,400 |
| **New Caledonia (France)** | 18.6 | 7.2 | 211 | Nouméa | 14,000 |
| **New Zealand** | 271 | 104 | 3,951 | Wellington | 20,100 |
| **Nicaragua** | 130 | 50.2 | 5,129 | Managua | 2,200 |
| **Niger** | 1,267 | 489 | 11,059 | Niamey | 800 |
| **Nigeria** | 924 | 357 | 133,882 | Abuja | 900 |
| **Northern Mariana Is. (US)** | 0.46 | 0.18 | 80 | Saipan | 12,500 |
| **Norway** | 324 | 125 | 4,546 | Oslo | 33,000 |
| **Oman** | 310 | 119 | 2,807 | Muscat | 8,300 |
| **Pakistan** | 796 | 307 | 150,695 | Islamabad | 2,000 |
| **Palau** | 0.46 | 0.18 | 20 | Koror | 9,000 |
| **Panama** | 75.5 | 29.2 | 2,961 | Panamá | 6,200 |
| **Papua New Guinea** | 463 | 179 | 5,296 | Port Moresby | 2,100 |
| **Paraguay** | 407 | 157 | 6,037 | Asunción | 4,300 |
| **Peru** | 1,285 | 496 | 28,410 | Lima | 5,000 |
| **Philippines** | 300 | 116 | 84,620 | Manila | 4,600 |
| **Poland** | 323 | 125 | 38,623 | Warsaw | 9,700 |
| **Portugal** | 88.8 | 34.3 | 10,102 | Lisbon | 19,400 |
| **Puerto Rico (US)** | 8.9 | 3.4 | 3,886 | San Juan | 11,100 |
| **Qatar** | 11.0 | 4.2 | 817 | Doha | 20,100 |
| **Réunion (France)** | 2.5 | 0.97 | 755 | St-Denis | 5,600 |

| Country/Territory | Area (1,000 sq km) | Area (1,000 sq miles) | Population (1,000s) | Capital City | Annual Income US$ |
|---|---|---|---|---|---|
| Romania | 238 | 92.0 | 22,272 | Bucharest | 7,600 |
| Russia | 17,075 | 6,593 | 144,526 | Moscow | 9,700 |
| Rwanda | 26.3 | 10.2 | 7,810 | Kigali | 1,200 |
| St Kitts & Nevis | 0.26 | 0.10 | 39 | Basseterre | 8,800 |
| St Lucia | 0.54 | 0.21 | 162 | Castries | 5,400 |
| St Vincent & Grenadines | 0.39 | 0.15 | 117 | Kingstown | 2,900 |
| Samoa | 2.8 | 1.1 | 178 | Apia | 5,600 |
| San Marino | 0.06 | 0.02 | 28 | San Marino | 34,600 |
| São Tomé & Príncipe | 0.96 | 0.37 | 176 | São Tomé | 1,200 |
| Saudi Arabia | 2,150 | 830 | 24,294 | Riyadh | 11,400 |
| | | | | | |
| Senegal | 197 | 76.0 | 10,580 | Dakar | 1,500 |
| Serbia & Montenegro | 102 | 39.4 | 10,656 | Belgrade | 2,200 |
| Seychelles | 0.46 | 0.18 | 80 | Victoria | 7,800 |
| Sierra Leone | 71.7 | 27.7 | 5,733 | Freetown | 500 |
| Singapore | 0.68 | 0.26 | 4,609 | Singapore | 25,200 |
| Slovak Republic | 49.0 | 18.9 | 5,430 | Bratislava | 12,400 |
| Slovenia | 20.3 | 7.8 | 1,936 | Ljubljana | 19,200 |
| Solomon Is. | 28.9 | 11.2 | 509 | Honiara | 1,700 |
| Somalia | 638 | 246 | 8,025 | Mogadishu | 600 |
| South Africa | 1,221 | 471 | 42,769 | C. Town/Pretoria/Bloem. | 10,000 |
| | | | | | |
| Spain | 498 | 192 | 40,217 | Madrid | 21,200 |
| Sri Lanka | 65.6 | 25.3 | 19,742 | Colombo | 3,700 |
| Sudan | 2,506 | 967 | 38,114 | Khartoum | 1,400 |
| Suriname | 163 | 63.0 | 435 | Paramaribo | 3,400 |
| Swaziland | 17.4 | 6.7 | 1,161 | Mbabane | 4,800 |
| Sweden | 450 | 174 | 8,878 | Stockholm | 26,000 |
| Switzerland | 41.3 | 15.9 | 7,319 | Bern | 32,000 |
| Syria | 185 | 71.5 | 17,586 | Damascus | 3,700 |
| Taiwan | 36.0 | 13.9 | 22,603 | Taipei | 18,000 |
| Tajikistan | 143 | 55.3 | 6,864 | Dushanbe | 1,300 |
| | | | | | |
| Tanzania | 945 | 365 | 35,922 | Dodoma | 600 |
| Thailand | 513 | 198 | 64,265 | Bangkok | 7,000 |
| Togo | 56.8 | 21.9 | 5,429 | Lomé | 1,400 |
| Tonga | 0.65 | 0.25 | 108 | Nuku'alofa | 2,200 |
| Trinidad & Tobago | 5.1 | 2.0 | 1,104 | Port of Spain | 10,000 |
| Tunisia | 164 | 63.2 | 9,925 | Tunis | 6,800 |
| Turkey | 775 | 299 | 68,109 | Ankara | 7,300 |
| Turkmenistan | 488 | 188 | 4,776 | Ashkhabad | 6,700 |
| Turks & Caicos Is. (UK) | 0.43 | 0.17 | 19 | Cockburn Town | 9,600 |
| Tuvalu | 0.03 | 0.01 | 11 | Fongafale | 1,100 |
| | | | | | |
| Uganda | 241 | 93.1 | 25,633 | Kampala | 1,200 |
| Ukraine | 604 | 233 | 48,055 | Kiev | 4,500 |
| United Arab Emirates | 83.6 | 32.3 | 2,485 | Abu Dhabi | 22,100 |
| United Kingdom | 242 | 93.4 | 60,095 | London | 25,500 |
| United States of America | 9,629 | 3,718 | 290,343 | Washington, DC | 36,300 |
| Uruguay | 175 | 67.6 | 3,413 | Montevideo | 7,900 |
| Uzbekistan | 447 | 173 | 25,982 | Tashkent | 2,600 |
| Vanuatu | 12.2 | 4.7 | 199 | Port-Vila | 2,900 |
| Vatican City | 0.0004 | 0.0002 | 1 | Vatican City | N/A |
| Venezuela | 912 | 352 | 24,655 | Caracas | 5,400 |
| | | | | | |
| Vietnam | 332 | 128 | 81,625 | Hanoi | 2,300 |
| Virgin Is. (UK) | 0.15 | 0.06 | 22 | Road Town | 16,000 |
| Virgin Is. (US) | 0.35 | 0.13 | 125 | Charlotte Amalie | 19,000 |
| Wallis & Futuna Is. (France) | 0.20 | 0.08 | 16 | Mata-Utu | 2,000 |
| West Bank (OPT)* | 5.9 | 2.3 | 2,237 | – | 800 |
| Western Sahara | 266 | 103 | 262 | El Aaiún | N/A |
| Yemen | 528 | 204 | 19,350 | Sana | 800 |
| Zambia | 753 | 291 | 10,307 | Lusaka | 800 |
| Zimbabwe | 391 | 151 | 12,577 | Harare | 2,100 |

# TIME ZONES

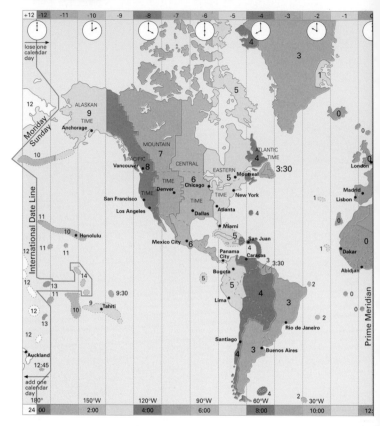

The world is divided into 24 time zones, each centred on meridians at 15° intervals, which is the longitudinal distance the sun travels every hour. The meridian running through Greenwich in London, England, passes through the middle of the first time zone. Zones to the east of Greenwich are ahead of Greenwich Mean Time (GMT) by one hour for every 15° of longitude, while zones to the west are behind GMT by one hour.

When it is 12 noon at the Greenwich meridian, 180° east it is midnight of the same day, while at 180° west the day is only just beginning. To overcome this, the International Date Line was established in 1883 – an imaginary line which approximately follows the 180th meridian. Therefore, if one travelled eastwards from Japan (140° East) towards Samoa (170° West), one would pass from Sunday night straight into Sunday morning.

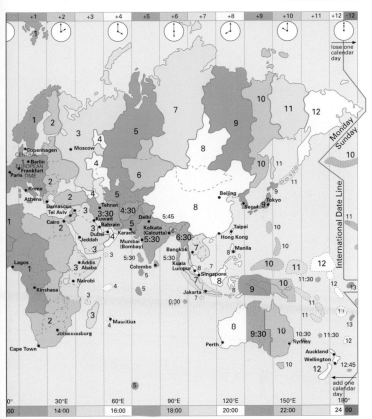

## TIME DIFFERENCES FROM GMT (LONDON)

| | | | |
|---|---|---|---|
| BEIJING | +8 | BANGKOK | +7 |
| CHICAGO | −6 | DELHI | +5.30 |
| JO'BURG | +2 | LAGOS | +1 |
| LOS ANGELES | −8 | MEXICO CITY | −6 |
| MOSCOW | +3 | NEW YORK | −5 |
| PARIS | +1 | ROME | +1 |
| SYDNEY | +10 | TEHRAN | +3.30 |
| TOKYO | +9 | TORONTO | −5 |

## KEY TO TIME ZONES MAP

**10** Hours slow or fast of UT or Co-ordinated Universal Time

Zones using UT (GMT)

Zones slow of UT (GMT)

- - - - International boundaries

Actual Solar Time, when time at Greenwich is 12:00 (noon)

Zones fast of UT (GMT)

Half-hour zones

——— Time zone boundaries

——— International Date Line

**Note:** Certain time zones are affected by the incidence of 'Summer Time' in countries where it is adopted.

# FLIGHT PATHS

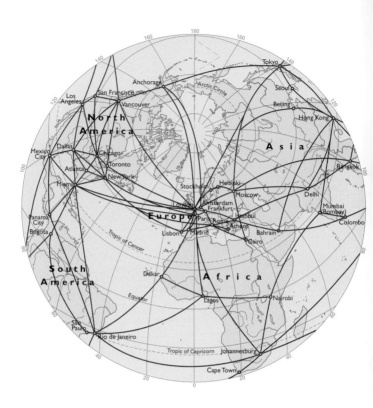

The flight paths shown on the maps above usually follow the shortest, most direct route from A to B, known as the *great-circle route*. A great circle is any circle that divides the globe into equal halves. Aircraft do not always fly along great-circle routes, however. Lack of search and rescue and emergency landing provisions, together with limits on fuel consumption and minimum flying altitudes, mean that commercial aircraft do not usually fly across Antarctica.

# FLIGHT PATHS

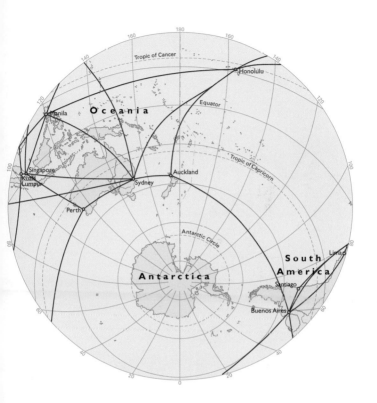

| FLIGHT TIMES FROM LONDON | | |
|---|---|---|
| ATHENS | 4hrs | 05mins |
| AUCKLAND | 24hrs | 20mins |
| BANGKOK | 14hrs | 30mins |
| BUENOS AIRES | 14hrs | 20mins |
| HONG KONG | 14hrs | 10mins |
| LOS ANGELES | 12hrs | 00mins |
| MOSCOW | 3hrs | 50mins |
| MUMBAI (BOMBAY) | 11hrs | 15mins |
| NEW YORK | 6hrs | 50mins |

| FLIGHT TIMES FROM NEW YORK | | |
|---|---|---|
| FRANKFURT | 8hrs | 35mins |
| JOHANNESBURG | 17hrs | 45mins |
| MEXICO CITY | 5hrs | 45mins |
| PARIS | 8hrs | 15mins |
| ROME | 9hrs | 35mins |
| SANTIAGO | 12hrs | 55mins |
| SINGAPORE | 23hrs | 10mins |
| TOKYO | 14hrs | 35mins |
| VANCOUVER | 7hrs | 25mins |

# CLIMATE

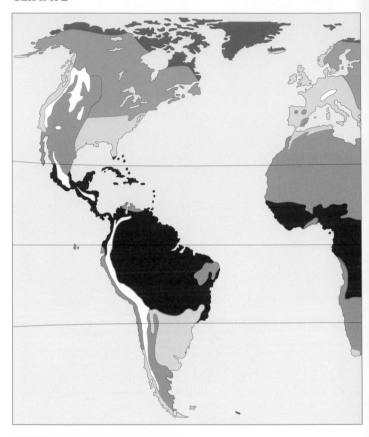

## SEASONAL WEATHER EXTREMES

- **Caribbean**
  Hurricanes – August to October

- **Northern Latitudes**
  Blizzards – November to March

- **Southern Asia**
  Cyclones and typhoons – June to November

- **Southern Asia**
  Monsoon rains – July to October

Climate is weather in the long term: the seasonal pattern of temperature and precipitation averaged over a period of time. Temperature roughly follows latitude, warmest near the equator and coldest near the poles. The interplay of various factors, however, namely the differential heating of land and sea, the influence of landmasses and mountain ranges on winds and ocean currents, and the effect of vegetation,

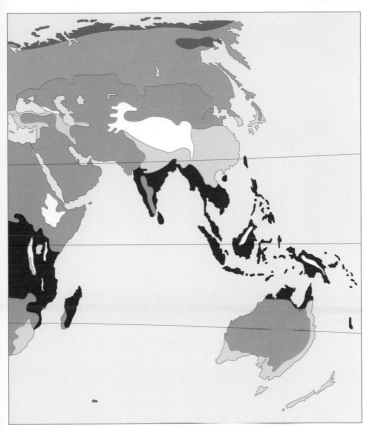

combine to add complexity. Thus New York, Naples and the Gobi Desert share almost the same latitude, but their resulting climates are very different.

Most scientists are now in agreement that the world's climate is changing, due partly to atmospheric pollution. By the year 2050 average world temperatures are predicted to rise by 1.5–2.8°C to make it hotter than at any time during the last 120,000 years.

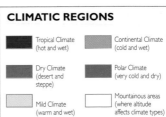

## CLIMATIC REGIONS

Tropical Climate (hot and wet)

Dry Climate (desert and steppe)

Mild Climate (warm and wet)

Continental Climate (cold and wet)

Polar Climate (very cold and dry)

Mountainous areas (where altitude affects climate types)

Note: Climate comprises a description of the condition of the atmosphere over a considerable area for a long time (at least 30 years).

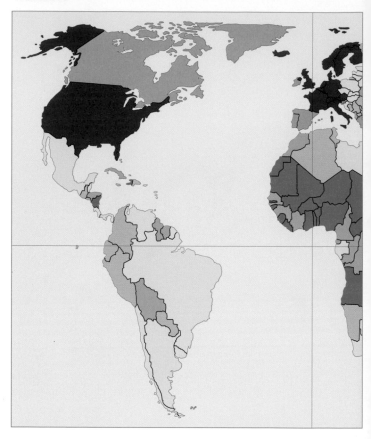

The most commonly used method of classifying countries according to economic well-being is to calculate the Gross National Product (GNP) per capita. The World Bank identifies three main groups according to GNP: high-income, middle-income and low-income economies. Sometimes low- and middle-income economies are referred to as developing countries. Per capita GNPs are a measure of the total goods and services produced by a country divided by the population, and converted into US$. Though useful indicators of a country's prosperity, like all statistics they must be treated with care. For example, the prices for goods and services in China are far cheaper than they are in the USA. China's per capita GNP in 1999 was $750 (compared with $29,340 in the US), but the ppp (purchasing-power parity) estimate of China's per capita GNP was considerably higher at $3,570.

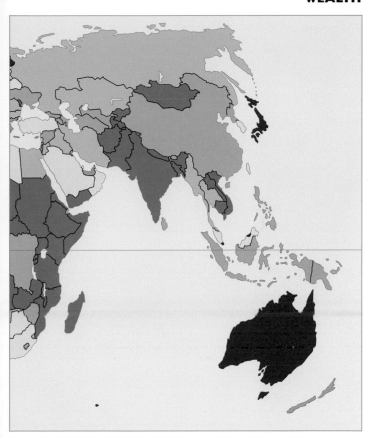

## EXCHANGE RATES, MID-2004

(UNITS PER US$)

| | | | |
|---|---|---|---|
| AUSTRALIA | 1.43 | INDONESIA | 9,420 |
| BRAZIL | 3.11 | ISRAEL | 4.49 |
| CANADA | 1.35 | JAPAN | 108 |
| DENMARK | 6.11 | NORWAY | 6.83 |
| EGYPT | 6.19 | S. AFRICA | 6.27 |
| EURO | 0.82 | SWEDEN | 7.52 |
| HONG KONG | 7.80 | SWITZERLAND | 1.25 |
| INDIA | 45.94 | UK | 0.55 |

## LEVELS OF INCOME

Gross National Product per capita: the value
of total production divided by the population
(latest available year)

| | |
|---|---|
| Over 400% of world average | 50 – 100% |
| 200 – 400% | 25 – 50% |
| 100 – 200% | 10 – 25% |
| | Under 10% |

[World average wealth per person US$4,890]

# INTERNATIONAL ORGANIZATIONS

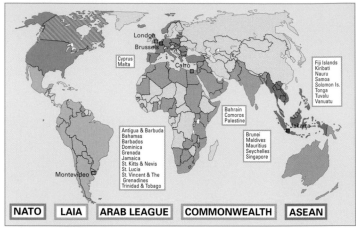

London
Brussels
Cyprus
Malta
Cairo

Fiji Islands
Kiribati
Nauru
Samoa
Solomon Is.
Tonga
Tuvalu
Vanuatu

Bahrain
Comoros
Palestine

Brunei
Maldives
Mauritius
Seychelles
Singapore

Jakarta

Antigua & Barbuda
Bahamas
Barbados
Dominica
Grenada
Jamaica
St. Kitts & Nevis
St. Lucia
St. Vincent & The
Grenadines
Trinidad & Tobago

Montevideo

| NATO | LAIA | ARAB LEAGUE | COMMONWEALTH | ASEAN |

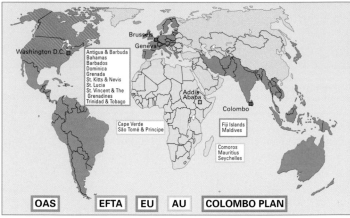

Brussels
Geneva
Washington D.C.

Antigua & Barbuda
Bahamas
Barbados
Dominica
Grenada
St. Kitts & Nevis
St. Lucia
St. Vincent & The
Grenadines
Trinidad & Tobago

Cape Verde
São Tomé & Principe

Addis
Ababa

Colombo

Fiji Islands
Maldives

Comoros
Mauritius
Seychelles

| OAS | EFTA | EU | AU | COLOMBO PLAN |

## GLOSSARY OF ACRONYMS

| | | | |
|---|---|---|---|
| ACP | African-Caribbean-Pacific | LAIA | Latin American Integration Association |
| ASEAN | Association of South-east Asian Nations | NATO | North Atlantic Treaty Organization |
| AU | African Union | OAS | Organization of American States |
| CIS | Commonwealth of Nations | OECD | Organization for Economic Co-operation and Development |
| EFTA | European Free Trade Association | | |
| EU | European Union | OPEC | Organization for Petroleum Exporting Countries |
| G8 | Group of 'Eight' | | |

# INTERNATIONAL ORGANIZATIONS

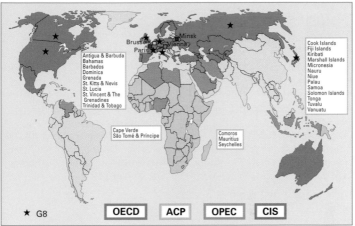

Antigua & Barbuda
Bahamas
Barbados
Dominica
Grenada
St. Kitts & Nevis
St. Lucia
St. Vincent & The
    Grenadines
Trinidad & Tobago

Cape Verde
São Tomé & Príncipe

Comoros
Mauritius
Seychelles

Cook Islands
Fiji Islands
Kiribati
Marshall Islands
Micronesia
Nauru
Niue
Palau
Samoa
Solomon Islands
Tonga
Tuvalu
Vanuatu

★ G8

| OECD | ACP | OPEC | CIS |

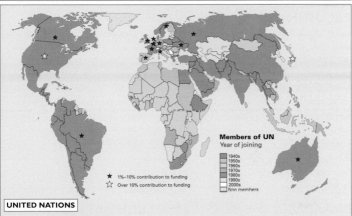

**Members of UN**
Year of joining

1940s
1950s
1960s
1970s
1980s
1990s
2000s
Non members

★ 1%–10% contribution to funding
☆ Over 10% contribution to funding

UNITED NATIONS

## THE UNITED NATIONS

Created in 1945 to promote peace and co-operation and based in New York, the UN is the world's largest international organization. The UN regular budget for 2002 was US$1.3 billion. Contributions are assessed by the members' ability to pay, with the maximum 22% of the total (USA's share), and the minimum 0.01%. The European Union pays over 37% of the budget. From the original 51, membership of the UN has now grown to 191. Recent additions include East Timor and Switzerland. There are only two independent states which are not members – Taiwan and the Vatican City.

## AUSTRALIA

**AREA** 7,741,220 sq km / 2,988,885 sq miles
**POPULATION** 19,732,000
**CAPITAL** Canberra
**GOVERNMENT** Federal constitutional monarchy
**LANGUAGES** English (official)
**CURRENCY** Australian dollar = 100 cents
**EMPLOYMENT** Agriculture 5%, industry 21%, services 74%

## CANADA

**AREA** 9,970,610 sq km / 3,849,653 sq miles
**POPULATION** 32,207,000
**CAPITAL** Ottawa
**GOVERNMENT** Federal multiparty constitutional monarchy
**LANGUAGES** English and French (official)
**CURRENCY** Canadian dollar = 100 cents
**EMPLOYMENT** Agriculture 3%, industry 23%, services 74%

## BELGIUM

**AREA** 30,528 sq km / 11,787 sq miles
**POPULATION** 10,289,000
**CAPITAL** Brussels
**GOVERNMENT** Constitutional monarchy
**LANGUAGES** Dutch, French, German (all official)
**CURRENCY** Euro = 100 cents
**EMPLOYMENT** Agriculture 2%, industry 27%, services 71%

## CHINA

**AREA** 9,596,961 sq km / 3,705,387 sq miles
**POPULATION** 1,286,975,000
**CAPITAL** Beijing (Peking)
**GOVERNMENT** Single-party Communist republic
**LANGUAGES** Mandarin Chinese (official)
**CURRENCY** Renminbi yuan = 10 jiao
**EMPLOYMENT** Agriculture 50%, industry 23%, services 27%

## BRAZIL

**AREA** 8,514,215 sq km / 3,287,338 sq miles
**POPULATION** 182,033,000
**CAPITAL** Brasília
**GOVERNMENT** Federal multiparty republic
**LANGUAGES** Portuguese (official)
**CURRENCY** Real = 100 centavos
**EMPLOYMENT** Agriculture 24%, industry 19%, services 57%

## CZECH REPUBLIC

**AREA** 78,866 sq km / 30,450 sq miles
**POPULATION** 10,249,000
**CAPITAL** Prague
**GOVERNMENT** Multiparty democratic republic
**LANGUAGES** Czech (official)
**CURRENCY** Czech koruna = 100 haler
**EMPLOYMENT** Agriculture 5%, industry 40%, services 55%

## DENMARK

**AREA** 43,094 sq km/16,639 sq miles
**POPULATION** 5,384,000
**CAPITAL** Copenhagen
**GOVERNMENT** Parliamentary monarchy
**LANGUAGES** Danish (official), English
**CURRENCY** Danish krone = 100 øre
**EMPLOYMENT** Agriculture 3%, industry 20%, services 77%

## GERMANY

**AREA** 357,022 sq km/137,846 sq miles
**POPULATION** 82,398,000
**CAPITAL** Berlin
**GOVERNMENT** Federal multiparty republic
**LANGUAGES** German (official)
**CURRENCY** Euro = 100 cents
**EMPLOYMENT** Agriculture 3%, industry 33%, services 65%

## EGYPT

**AREA** 1,001,449 sq km/386,659 sq miles
**POPULATION** 74,719,000
**CAPITAL** Cairo (El Qâhira)
**GOVERNMENT** Multiparty republic
**LANGUAGES** Arabic (official), French, English
**CURRENCY** Egyptian pound = 100 piastres
**EMPLOYMENT** Agriculture 30%, industry 22%, services 48%

## GREECE

**AREA** 131,957 sq km/50,949 sq miles
**POPULATION** 10,666,000
**CAPITAL** Athens
**GOVERNMENT** Multiparty republic
**LANGUAGES** Greek (official), English, French
**CURRENCY** Euro = 100 cents
**EMPLOYMENT** Agriculture 16%, industry 23%, services 61%

## FRANCE

**AREA** 551,500 sq km/212,934 sq miles
**POPULATION** 60,181,000
**CAPITAL** Paris
**GOVERNMENT** Multiparty republic
**LANGUAGES** French (official), Breton, Occitan
**CURRENCY** Euro = 100 cents
**EMPLOYMENT** Agriculture 1%, industry 25%, services 74%

## HUNGARY

**AREA** 93,032 sq km/35,920 sq miles
**POPULATION** 10,045,000
**CAPITAL** Budapest
**GOVERNMENT** Multiparty democratic republic
**LANGUAGES** Hungarian (official)
**CURRENCY** Forint = 100 fillér
**EMPLOYMENT** Agriculture 6%, industry 35%, services 59%

## INDIA

**AREA** 3,287,263 sq km/1,269,212 sq miles
**POPULATION** 1,049,700,000
**CAPITAL** New Delhi
**GOVERNMENT** Multiparty federal republic
**LANGUAGES** Hindi, English, Telugu, Bengali, Marathi, Urdu, Tamil, Gujarati and others
**CURRENCY** Indian rupee = 100 paisa
**EMPLOYMENT** Agriculture 67%, industry 12%, services 21%

## JAPAN

**AREA** 377,829 sq km/145,880 sq miles
**POPULATION** 127,214,000
**CAPITAL** Tokyo
**GOVERNMENT** Democratic constitutional monarchy
**LANGUAGES** Japanese (official)
**CURRENCY** Yen = 100 sen
**EMPLOYMENT** Agriculture 5%, industry 31%, services 64%

## IRELAND

**AREA** 70,273 sq km/27,132 sq miles
**POPULATION** 3,924,000
**CAPITAL** Dublin
**GOVERNMENT** Multiparty democratic republic
**LANGUAGES** Irish and English (both official)
**CURRENCY** Euro = 100 cents
**EMPLOYMENT** Agriculture 7%, industry 29%, services 64%

## MEXICO

**AREA** 1,958,201 sq km/756,061 sq miles
**POPULATION** 104,908,000
**CAPITAL** Mexico City
**GOVERNMENT** Multiparty federal republic
**LANGUAGES** Spanish (official)
**CURRENCY** Mexican peso = 100 centavos
**EMPLOYMENT** Agriculture 18%, industry 27%, services 55%

## ITALY

**AREA** 301,318 sq km/116,339 sq miles
**POPULATION** 57,998,000
**CAPITAL** Rome
**GOVERNMENT** Multiparty republic
**LANGUAGES** Italian (official), German, French, Slovene
**CURRENCY** Euro = 100 cents
**EMPLOYMENT** Agriculture 5%, industry 32%, services 63%

## NETHERLANDS

**AREA** 41,526 sq km/16,033 sq miles
**POPULATION** 16,151,000
**CAPITAL** Amsterdam; The Hague (seat of government)
**GOVERNMENT** Constitutional monarchy
**LANGUAGES** Dutch (official), Frisian
**CURRENCY** Euro = 100 cents
**EMPLOYMENT** Agriculture 3%, industry 17%, services 80%

## NEW ZEALAND

**AREA** 270,534 sq km/104,453 sq miles
**POPULATION** 3,951,000
**CAPITAL** Wellington
**GOVERNMENT** Constitutional monarchy
**LANGUAGES** English and Maori (both official)
**CURRENCY** New Zealand dollar = 100 cents
**EMPLOYMENT** Agriculture 9%, industry 23%, services 68%

## RUSSIA

**AREA** 17,075,400 sq km/6,592,812 sq miles
**POPULATION** 144,526,000
**CAPITAL** Moscow
**GOVERNMENT** Federal multiparty republic
**LANGUAGES** Russian (official), many others
**CURRENCY** Russian ruble = 100 kopeks
**EMPLOYMENT** Agriculture 12%, industry 29%, services 59%

## NIGERIA

**AREA** 923,768 sq km/356,667 sq miles
**POPULATION** 133,882,000
**CAPITAL** Abuja
**GOVERNMENT** Federal multiparty republic
**LANGUAGES** English (official), Hausa, Yoruba, Ibo
**CURRENCY** Naira = 100 kobo
**EMPLOYMENT** Agriculture 3%, industry 22%, services 75%

## SAUDI ARABIA

**AREA** 2,149,690 sq km/829,995 sq miles
**POPULATION** 24,294,000
**CAPITAL** Riyadh
**GOVERNMENT** Absolute monarchy with consultative assembly
**LANGUAGES** Arabic (official)
**CURRENCY** Saudi riyal = 100 halalas
**EMPLOYMENT** Agriculture 5%, industry 26%, services 69%

## POLAND

**AREA** 323,250 sq km/124,807 sq miles
**POPULATION** 38,623,000
**CAPITAL** Warsaw
**GOVERNMENT** Multiparty democratic republic
**LANGUAGES** Polish (official)
**CURRENCY** Zloty = 100 groszy
**EMPLOYMENT** Agriculture 19%, industry 31%, services 50%

## SINGAPORE

**AREA** 683 sq km/264 sq miles
**POPULATION** 4,609,000
**CAPITAL** Singapore
**GOVERNMENT** Multiparty republic
**LANGUAGES** Chinese, Malay, Tamil and English (all official)
**CURRENCY** Singapore dollar = 100 cents
**EMPLOYMENT** Agriculture 0%, industry 26%, services 74%

## SOUTH AFRICA
**AREA** 1,221,037 sq km/471,442 sq miles
**POPULATION** 42,769,000
**CAPITAL** Cape Town (legislative)/
Pretoria (admin.)/Bloemfontein (judiciary)
**GOVERNMENT** Multiparty republic
**LANGUAGES** Afrikaans, English, others
**CURRENCY** Rand = 100 cents
**EMPLOYMENT** Agriculture 6%, industry
24%, services 70%

## SWITZERLAND
**AREA** 41,284 sq km/15,940 sq miles
**POPULATION** 7,319,000
**CAPITAL** Bern
**GOVERNMENT** Federal republic
**LANGUAGES** French, German, Italian and
Romansch (all official)
**CURRENCY** Swiss franc = 100 centimes
**EMPLOYMENT** Agriculture 4%, industry
26%, services 70%

## SPAIN
**AREA** 497,548 sq km/192,103 sq miles
**POPULATION** 40,217,000
**CAPITAL** Madrid
**GOVERNMENT** Constitutional monarchy
**LANGUAGES** Castilian Spanish (official),
Catalan, Galician, Basque
**CURRENCY** Euro = 100 cents
**EMPLOYMENT** Agriculture 7%, industry
31%, services 62%

## UNITED KINGDOM
**AREA** 241,857 sq km/93,381 sq miles
**POPULATION** 60,095,000
**CAPITAL** London
**GOVERNMENT** Constitutional monarchy
**LANGUAGES** English (official), Welsh,
Gaelic
**CURRENCY** Pound sterling = 100 pence
**EMPLOYMENT** Agriculture 1%, industry
25%, services 74%

## SWEDEN
**AREA** 449,964 sq km/173,731 sq miles
**POPULATION** 8,878,000
**CAPITAL** Stockholm
**GOVERNMENT** Democratic constitutional
monarchy
**LANGUAGES** Swedish (official), Finnish
**CURRENCY** Swedish krona = 100 öre
**EMPLOYMENT** Agriculture 2%, industry
24%, services 74%

## UNITED STATES
**AREA** 9,629,091 sq km/3,717,792 sq miles
**POPULATION** 290,343,000
**CAPITAL** Washington, DC
**GOVERNMENT** Federal republic
**LANGUAGES** English (official), Spanish,
more than 30 others
**CURRENCY** US dollar = 100 cents
**EMPLOYMENT** Agriculture 2%, industry
23%, services 75%

# WORLD MAPS – GENERAL REFERENCE

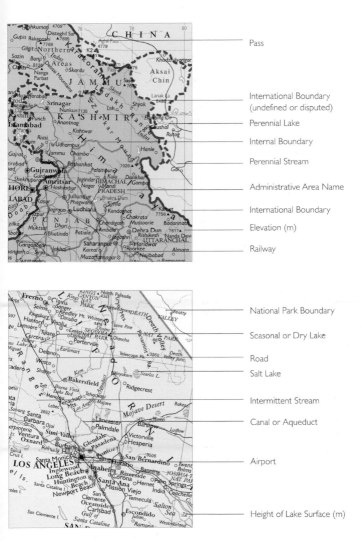

Pass

International Boundary
(undefined or disputed)

Perennial Lake

Internal Boundary

Perennial Stream

Administrative Area Name

International Boundary

Elevation (m)

Railway

National Park Boundary

Seasonal or Dry Lake

Road

Salt Lake

Intermittent Stream

Canal or Aqueduct

Airport

Height of Lake Surface (m)

Settlements

Settlement symbols and type styles vary
according to the scale of each map and
indicate the importance of towns rather
than speciific population figures.

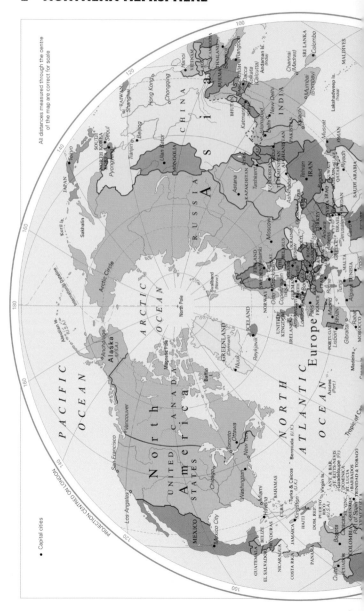

All distances measured through the centre of the map are correct for scale

PROJECTION CENTRED ON LONDON

• Capital cities

**3**

OCEAN

Chagos Arch. (U.K.)

SEYCHELLES

MAURITIUS

Réunion (Fra.)

Antananarivo

MADAGASCAR

COMOROS

Mayotte

MOZAMBIQUE

ETHIOPIA

DJIBOUTI

SOMALIA

Mogadishu

KENYA

Nairobi

UGANDA

TANZANIA

Dodoma

SUDAN

Khartoum

RWANDA

BURUNDI

MALAWI

ZAMBIA

Lusaka

Harare

ZIMBABWE

Maputo

Pretoria

Johannesburg

SWAZILAND

LESOTHO

SOUTH AFRICA

CHAD

NIGER

Niamey

N'djamena

CENTRAL AFRICAN REPUBLIC

Bangui

Yaoundé

CAMEROON

EQUAT. GUINEA

GABON

Libreville

CONGO

Brazzaville

DEM. REP. OF THE CONGO

ANGOLA

Luanda

NAMIBIA

Windhoek

Gaborone

BOTSWANA

Cape Town

NIGERIA

Abuja

BENIN

TOGO

GHANA

Accra

CÔTE D'IVOIRE

Monrovia

LIBERIA

SIERRA LEONE

Freetown

GUINEA

Conakry

Bissau

GUINEA BISSAU

Banjul

THE GAMBIA

Dakar

SENEGAL

MALI

MAURITANIA

Nouakchott

SÃO TOMÉ & P.

St. Helena (U.K.)

Ascension (U.K.)

CAPE VERDE IS.

**A f r i c a**

**OCEAN**

**SOUTH**

**ATLANTIC**

**OCEAN**

Tropic of Capricorn

Equator

0 East from Greenwich

0 West from Greenwich

20

40

80

**S o u t h  A m e r i c a**

GUYANA

SURINAM

FRENCH GUIANA

Georgetown

Paramaribo

Cayenne

BRAZIL

Brasília

São Paulo

Rio de Janeiro

BOLIVIA

## TIME ZONES

Zones using Greenwich Mean Time

Zones fast of Greenwich Mean Time

Zones slow of Greenwich Mean Time

Standard Time not the Zone hour

No Official Time

### PROJECTION CENTRED ON CAPE TOWN

-8.00 +7.00 +8.00

+5.30 +4.30 +4.00

+3.00 +2.00 +1.00

Greenwich 0.00

+1.00 +2.00 +3.00

-3.00 -3.30 -4.00 -5.00 -6.00

+ South Pole

**Cape Town**

30 60 90 120 150 180

COPYRIGHT PHILIP'S

### PROJECTION CENTRED ON SAN FRANCISCO

-3.30 -3.00 -4.00 -5.00 -6.00

+9.00 +8.00 +7.00 +6.00 +5.00 +4.00 +3.00

+12.00 +11.00 +10.00 +9.00 +8.00 +7.00

-3.00

Greenwich 0.0

-7.00 -8.00 -9.00 -10.00

**San Francisco**

+ North Pole

International Date Line

30 60 90 120 150 180

West from Greenwich

East from Greenwich

Projection: Oblique Azimuthal Equidistant

**5**

PROJECTION CENTRED ON SHANGHAI

-10.00

-8.00

-6.00

-9.00

International Dateline

+12.00

+11.00

+10.00

+12.00

North Pole

+5.00

+6.00

-3.00

+7.00

-1.00

+8.00

Shanghai

+9.00

+10.00

+8.30

+8.00

+9.00

+8.00

-7.00

+5.30

+4.30

+4.00

+3.30

+5.30

+1.00

+2.00

+3.00

+4.00

+2.00

-3.00

+1.00

East from Greenwich

COPYRIGHT PHILIP'S

South America

CHILE

BOLIVIA

Santiago

PARAGUAY

ARGENTINA

ASUNCION

URUGUAY

BRAZIL

Buenos Aires

MONTEVIDEO

Montevideo

Falkland Is. (U.K.)

South Georgia (U.K.)

South Sandwich Is. (U.K.)

SOUTH ATLANTIC OCEAN

** Pr. Edward I. (S. Africa)

Bouvet I. (Norw.)

Antarctica

Byrd Lanc

Ellsworth Land

South Pole

Queen Maud Land

Enderby Land

Wilkes Land

Heard I. (Austral.)

* Crozet I. (Fr.)

Kerguelen (Fr.)

**TIME ZONES**

Zones using Greenwich Mean Time

Zones fast of Greenwich Mean Time

Zones slow of Greenwich Mean Time

Standard Time not the Zone hour

PROJECTION CENTRED ON CAIRO

+8.00

+9.00

+9.30

+10.30

-9.00

+10.00

+11.00

North Pole

+8.00

-7.00

+9.00

+7.00

+3.00

+8.00

+6.30

+5.30

+4.00

+5.00

+2.30

+4.00

+3.00

-4.00

+2.00

+3.00

Cairo

+3.00

+3.00

Greenwich

0.00

+2.00

+1.00

0.00

-2.00

-3.00

-5.00

-3.30

-4.00

-6.00

-7.00

-1.00

-3.00

-3.30

West from Greenwich

Projection: Oblique Azimuthal Equidistant

Projection: Oblique Azimuthal Equidistant

■ LONDON Capital Cities

**7**

100 0 100 200 300 400 500 600 700 800 km

100 0 100 200 300 400 500 miles

Hammerfest

Murmansk

*White Sea*

Ob

Kiruna

Luleå

Arkhangelsk

N. Dvina

Kotlas

Perm

Nizhniy Tagil

Vaasa

FINLAND

L. Onega

Yekaterinburg

Tampere

L. Ladoga

Vyborg

Vologda

Kirov

Chelyabinsk

Turku

Helsinki

ST. PETERSBURG

Rybinsk Res.

Kostroma

Ufa

Magnitogorsk

Tallinn

ESTONIA

L. Chudskoye

R U S S I A

Yaroslavl

Ivanovo

Nizhniy Novgorod

Kazan

Sea

LATVIA

Riga

MOSCOW

Simbirsk

Samara

Orenburg

W. Dvina

LITHUANIA

Vitebsk

Smolensk

Tula

Penza

Volga

Uralsk

50

Kaunas

Kaliningrad

(Russia)

Vilnius

Mogilev

Minsk

Orel

Tambov

Saratov

K A Z A K H S T A N

Białystok

BELARUS

Gomel

Pripet

Kursk

Voronezh

Volgograd

Atyrau

ND

Warsaw

Chernigov

Dnepr

Kharkov

Don

45

Lublin

Zhitomir

Kiev

Astrakhan

Caspian

Kraków

Lvov

U K R A I N E

Dnepropetrovsk

Donetsk

Rostov

Sea

AK RER

Dniester

Bug

Krivoy Rog

Zaporozhye

Taganrog

Miskolc

MOLDOVA

Nikolayev

Kherson

Debrecen

Cluj-Napoca

Kishinev

Odessa

Stavropol

Makhachkala

RY

ROMANIA

Crimea

Krasnodar

Timișoara

Brașov

Galați

40

Belgrade

Ploiești

Sevastopol

GEORGIA

Tbilisi

AZERBAIJAN

Baku

SERBIA &

Bucharest

Constanța

*Black Sea*

ARMENIA

MONTENEGRO

Danube

BULGARIA

Varna

Yerevan

Araks

MACEDONIA

Skopje

Sofia

Plovdiv

Bosporus

ISTANBUL

Samsun

Erzurum

Tabriz

IA T

Thessaloniki

Bursa

Ankara

T U R K E Y

Diyarbakır

I R A N

GREECE

İzmir

Kayseri

A s i a

35

Patrai

Athens

Konya

Adana

Aleppo

Baghdad

IRAQ

Rhodes

Antalya

SYRIA

Euphrates

Tigris

Baghdad

Crete

CYPRUS

Nicosia

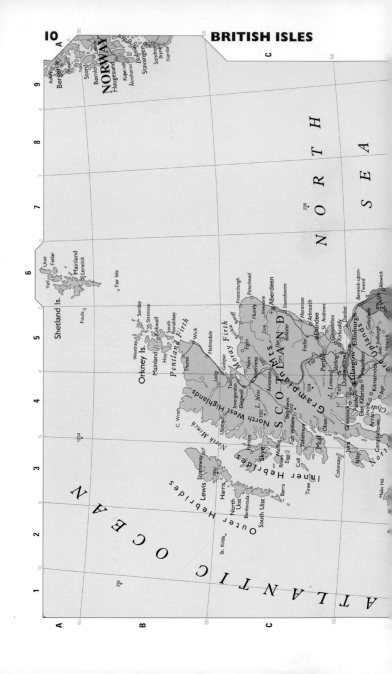

ATLANTIC OCEAN

NORTH SEA

NORWAY

Askøy
Bergen
Stord
Bømlo
Haugesund
Leirvik
Kopervik
Åkrehamn
Bønes
Stavanger
Sandnes
Bryne
Nærbø

SCOTLAND

Shetland Is.
Unst
Fetlar
Yell
Mainland
Lerwick

Foula

Fair Isle

Orkney Is.
Westray
Sanday
Stronsay
Hoy
Kirkwall
Mainland
South Ronaldsay

Pentland Firth
Wick
Thurso
Helmsdale

C. Wrath
Ullapool
North West Highlands
Dingwall
Dornoch
Lairg
Golspie
Tain
Nairn
Elgin
Moray Firth
Inverness
Aviemore
L. Ness
Ben Nevis 1343
Fort William
Tomintoul
Banff
Fraserburgh
Peterhead
Aberdeen
Don
Inverurie
Huntly
Stonehaven
Ballater
Montrose
Arbroath
Dundee
St. Andrews
Forfar
Perth
Glenrothes
Kirkcaldy
Dunfermline
Stirling
Dunbar
Edinburgh
Galashiels
Berwick-upon-Tweed

North Minch
1224
Lewis
Stornoway
795
Harris
North Uist
Benbecula
South Uist
Barra
St. Kilda
336

Inner Hebrides
Skye
Rhum
Eigg
Portree
Mallaig
Coll
Tiree
Mull
Tobermory
Oban
Jura
Colonsay
Islay
Campbeltown

Outer Hebrides

Grampian Mts.
1311
Blair Atholl

L. Lomond
1174
Greenock
Paisley
Glasgow
Dumbarton
East Kilbride
Kilmarnock
Irvine
Ayr
Arran
Clyde
North
Main Hill

Southern Uplands
Hawick
Jedburgh
Alnwick

238

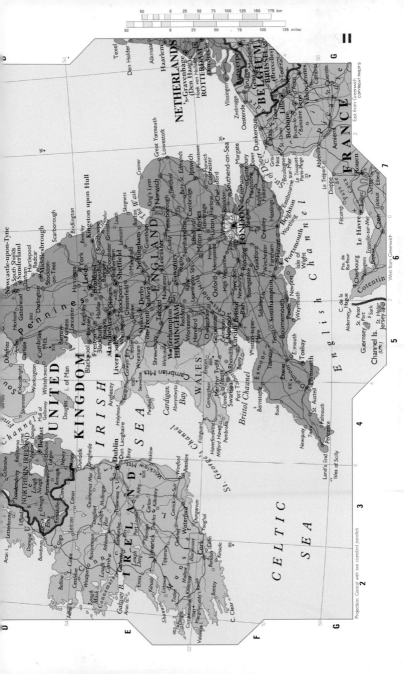

**BELGIUM**

**GERMANY**

**LUXEMBOURG**

**SWITZERLAND**

**ITALY**

**AUSTRIA**

**LIECHTENSTEIN**

**MONACO**

**Massif Central**

**MEDITERRANEAN SEA**

**Golfe du Lion**

**Corse (Corsica)**

Brussel (Bruxelles), Gent, Mechelen, Leuven, Heerlen, Maastricht, Aachen, Bonn, Giessen, Vogelsberg 774, Wasserkuppe 950, Fulda, Suhl, Coburg, Kissingen, Bad

Kortrijk, Roubaix, Tournai, Mons, Namur, Liège, Verviers, Düren, Köln, Limburg, Lahn, Wetzlar, Taunus, Frankfurt, Hanau, Aschaffenburg, Würzburg, Schweinfurt, Bamberg

Lille, Lens, Arras, Cambrai, St-Quentin, Charleroi, Maubeuge, Dinant, Bastogne, Koblenz, Rheinland, Wiesbaden, Mainz, Offenbach, Darmstadt, Nürnberg

Douai, Valenciennes, Charleville-Mézières, Sedan, LUXEMBOURG, Trier, Idar-Oberstein, Ludwigshafen, Mannheim, Ansbach

Reims, Verdun, Metz, Thionville, Hagondange, Saarbrücken, Kaiserslautern, Neustadt, Speyer, Heidelberg, Heilbronn, Crailsheim, Aalen

Châlons-en-Champagne, Bar-le-Duc, Nancy, Lunéville, Sarreguemines, Haguenau, Pirmasens, Karlsruhe, Pforzheim, Baden-Baden, Stuttgart, Esslingen, Göppingen, Augsburg

Épernay, Marne, St-Dizier, Toul, Chaumont, Épinal, Strasbourg, Colmar, Tübingen, Reutlingen, Württemberg, Rottweil, Donau, Ulm, Memmingen

Provins, Melun, Seine, Troyes, Sens, Langres, Plateau de Langres, Vesoul, Belfort, Mulhouse, Freiburg, Schwenningen, Villingen, Schaffhausen, Konstanz, Biberach, Ravensburg, Friedrichshafen, Kempten

Montargis, Auxerre, Avallon, Dijon, Besançon, Montbéliard, Basel, Winterthur, Sankt Gallen, Feldkirch, Dornbirn, Bregenz

NIVERNAIS, Nevers, Autun, Beaune, Chalon-sur-Saône, Dole, La Chaux-de-Fonds, Neuchâtel, Biel, Solothurn, Luzern, Zürich, Schwyz 3247, Chur, LIECHTENSTEIN

Le Creuset, Montceau-les-Mines, Charolles, Mâcon, Pontarlier, Lac de Neuchâtel, Fribourg, Bern, Thun, SWITZERLAND, Engadin

Moulins, Bourbonnais, Montluçon, Vichy, Roanne, Bourg-en-Bresse, Lons-le-Saunier, Genève, Lausanne, Montreux, Jura, Interlaken 4158, Gotthard, 3402, Sankt Moritz, 3439, 3899

Clermont-Ferrand, Puy de Dôme 1886, Thiers, Annecy, Aix-les-Bains, Chambéry, Mont Blanc 4807, Aosta, Matterhorn, Monte Rosa 4634, Domodossola, Verbania, di Como, Lecco, Bérgamo, Brescia

St-Étienne, St-Chamond, Voiron, Grenoble, Bourg-St-Maurice 3852, Ivrea, Biella, Novara, Vigevano, Busto Arsizio, MILANO, Monza, Créma, Cremona

Issoire, St-Flour, Le Puy-en-Velay, Tournon, Romans-sur-Isère, Modane, Lanslebourg, Massif du Pelvoux 4103, Briançon, Pinerolo, TORINO (Turin), Rivoli, Asti, Alessandria, Novi Ligure, Vogherá, Piacenza, Parma

Mézenc 1754, Plomb du Cantal 1858, Privas, Valence, Gap, Embrun, Viso 3841, Col di Tenda 1870, Cúneo, Mondovì, Savona, Génova, Riviera di Levante, La Spézia, Massa

Mende, Mt. Mézenc 1754, Montélimar, Digne-les-Bains, Alpes Maritimes, San Remo, Mónaco, Monte-Carlo, Menton

Rodez, Millau, Alès, Orange, Mt. Ventoux 1912, Carpentras, Avignon, Salon-de-Provence, Aix-en-Provence, Draguignan, Grasse, Cannes, Antibes, Nice, Riviera di Ponente, Chiávari

Nîmes, Aigues-Mortes, Arles, Istres, Martigues, Aubagne, Fréjus, St-Tropez, Côte d'Azur

Montpellier, Béziers, Sète, MARSEILLE, Toulon, La Seyne-sur-Mer, Hyères, Iles d'Hyères 2580

Narbonne, Agde, Port-Vendres, Port Bou, C. de Creus, Figueres

C. Corse, Calvi, Bastia, Mte. Cinto 2710, Corte, Mte. Rotondo 2625, Ajaccio, Porto-Vecchio, Bonifacio

# 14 GERMANY AND BENELUX

Projection: Conical with two standard parallels

*Zatoka Gdańska*

Wejherowo  Rumia  Gdynia  Baltiysk  Kaliningrad (Russia)

Słupsk  Lębork  Gvardeysk  Chernyakhovsk

Darłowo  Sopot  Tczew  Elbląg  Bagrationovsk

Kołobrzeg  Koszalin  Bytów  Gdańsk  Malbork  Kętrzyn  Giżyck

**A**

Usedom  Wolin  Świnoujście  Białogard  Szczecinek  Chojnice  Starogard  Kwidzyn  Iława  Ostróda  Olsztyn  *Pojezierze Mazursk*

Świecie  Grudziądz

Neubrandenburg  Police  Goleniów  Stargard Szczeciński  Wałcz  Piła  Chełmno  Brodnica  Mława  Dzialdowo  Ostrołęka  Ostr

**B**

Schwedt  Gorzów Wielkopolski  *Noteć*  Bydgoszcz  Toruń  Rypin  Ciechanów  Pułtusk  Soko

Eberswalde-Finow  Kostrzyn  Inowrocław  Włocławek  Płock  Legionowo  Mińsk Mazowiecki

**BERLIN**  Frankfurt  Świebodzin  Międzychód  *Warta*  Poznań  Gniezno  Września  Koło  Kutno  **WARSZAWA** (Warsaw)  Otwock

Fürstenwalde  Nowy Tomyśl  Łęczyca  *Vistula*  Łowicz  Pruszków  Grójec  Skierniewice

**GERMANY**  Cottbus  Forst  Zielona Góra  Nowa Sól  Leszno  Kościan  Śrem  Konin  Turek  Kalisz  Zduńska Wola  Sieradz  Tomaszów Mazowiecki  Radom

Lauchhammer  Żary  Zagań  *Odra*  Głogów  Lubin  Krotoszyn  Ostrów Wielkopolski  Pabianice  Piotrków Trybunalski  Końskie  Skarżysko-Kamienna  Starachowice

**C**  Hoyerswerda  Bautzen  Bolesławiec  Wieluń  Radomsko  Ostrowiec-Świętokrzyski  Kielce

Dresden  Görlitz  Zgorzelec  Legnica  Wrocław  Kluczbork  Częstochowa  Jędrzejów  Pińczów  Tarnobr

Chemnitz  Děčín  Liberec  Jelenia Góra  Świdnica  Oława  Opole  Myszków  Zawiercie  *Wisła*  Miele

*Erzgebirge*  Ústí nad Labem  Jablonec  Wałbrzych  Śnieżka  Dzierżoniów  Kłodzko  Nysa  Tarnowskie Góry  Bytom  Sosnowiec  Tychy

Most  Mladá Boleslav  Trutnov  Gliwice  Zabrze  Chorzów  Katowice  Oświęcim  Kraków  Tarnów

Karlovy Vary  Kladno  Hradec Králové  Pardubice  Racibórz  Opava  Karviná  Bielsko-Biała  Bochnia

Cheb  **PRAHA** (Prague)  Beroun  Kolín  Šumperk  Ostrava  Frýdek-Místek  Cieszyn  Żywiec  Jasło  Nowy Sącz

Plzeň  Příbram  Vrchovina  Olomouc  Havířov  Czarny  *Západné Beskydy*  Nowy Targ  Zakopane  Bardejov

**CZECH REP.**  Tábor  Havlíčkův Brod  Prostějov  Přerov  Povážská Bystrica  Žilina  *Tatry*  Ružomberok  Poprad  Prešov  Hum

Klatovy  Písek  Českomoravská  Jihlava  Vyškov  Zlín  Martin  *Nízke Tatry*  Banská Bystrica  Sátoraljaújhely  Koš

**D**  *Böhmer wald*  České Budějovice  Jindřichův Hradec  Třebíč  **Brno**  Hodonín  Bielé Karpaty  Trenčín  Prievidza  Zvolen  *Slovenské Rudohorie*  Ožd  Miskolc

Grosser Arber  Třeboň  Znojmo  Malé Karpaty  Topoľčany  Nitra  Levice  Lučenec  Salgótarján  Eger  Mezőkövesd  Hajdúbös

Passau  *Donau* (Danube)  Freistadt  Zwettl  Horn  Stockerau  Trnava  Nové Zámky  Komárno  Vác  Gyöngyös  Hatvan  Mezőkövesd  Debrecen

**SLOVAK REP.**

Linz  Ried  Wels  Melk  Krems  Sankt Pölten  **WIEN** (Vienna)  Bratislava  Esztergom  Dunakeszi  Józsefváros  Korçag

Steyr  Amstetten  Wiener Neustadt  *Neusiedler See*  Sopron  Győr  Tatabánya  Erd  **BUDAPEST**  Székesfehérvár  Cegléd  Szolnok  Mezőtúr

**AUSTRIA**  Eisenerz  Kapfenberg  Mürzzuschlag  Bruck an der Mur  Szombathely  Pápa  *Bakony*  Nagykőrös  Kecskemét  Mezőtúr

**E**  Leoben  Graz  *Steiermark*  **HUNGARY**  Kiskunfélegyháza  Kiskőrös  Csongrád  Békéscsaba  Szentes  Oroszháza  Gyula  Hódmezővásárhely

Wolfsberg  Zalaegerszeg  *Balaton*  Siófok  Kecskemét  Kiskunhalas  Szeged  Makó

*Kärnten*  Klagenfurt  Nagykanizsa  Kaposvár  Szekszárd  Baja  Kalocsa  Subotica  Kikinda

Villach  *Drava*  Maribor  Pécs  Mohács  Sombor  Senta  *Sinnicolau Mare*

Triglav  *Karawanken*  Celje  Koprivnica  Zagreb  Bjelovar  Virovitica  Osijek  *Voivodina*  Zrenjanin  Timişoa

**SLOVENIA**  Ljubljana  Novo Mesto  Varaždin  *Drava*  Vukovar  Novi Sad

**F**  Trieste  Postojna  **CROATIA**  Karlovac  Osijek

Rijeka

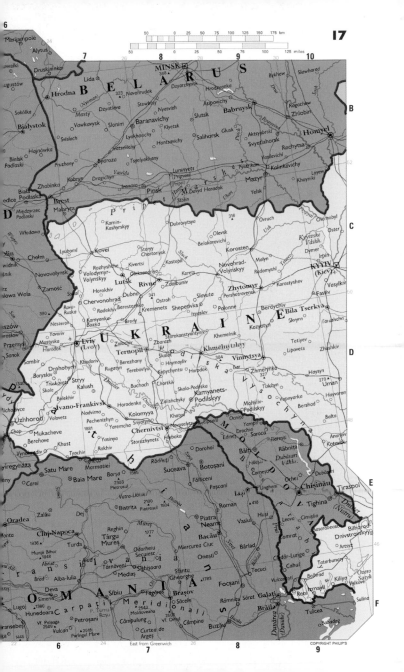

Projection: Conical with two standard parallels

**50  0  25  50  75  100  125  150  175 km**
**50  0  25  50  75  100  125 miles**

**5**  **6**  **7**  **8**

## FRANCE

Gascogne

Graulhet
Arles
Montpellier
Camargue

Guernica y Luno
Biarritz
Dax
Orthez
Auch
Toulouse
Castres
Béziers
Sète
Agde

Bilbao
Eibar
Bayonne
Tarbes
Pamiers
Carcassonne
Narbonne

Donostia
San Sebastián
Béarn
Lourdes
St-Gaudens
Foix
Limoux

**A**

Vitoria-Gasteiz
Pamplona
Pyrénées
2872
Rico de
Aneto
3080
Sierra
Mt. Canigou
Perpignan
Port-Vendres

*Golfe du Lion*

Logroño
Navarra
Puerto de
Somport
Jaca
3355
Mte. Perdido
3404
ANDORRA
La Seu d'Urgell
Ripoll
2785
Olot
Figueres
Port Bou
C. de Creus

*G. de Roses*

Calahorra
Tudela
Huesca
Barbastro
Tremp
Berga
Vic
Girona
Sant Feliu de Guixols
42

Rioja
Tarazona
Ebro
Monzón
1677
Balaguer
Cervera
Manresa
Terrassa
Granollers
Lloret de Mar
Costa Brava

Sierra de Moncayo
2316
**Zaragoza**
Lleida
Igualada
Sabadell
Mataró

Almazán
Calatayud
Caspe
Reus
**L'Hospitalet de Llobregat**
**BARCELONA**
Santa Coloma de Gramenet

**B**

Soria
Sigüenza
Calamocha
Montalbán
Alcañiz
Valls
Sitges
El Prat de Llobregat
Badalona

Henares
Aragón
Teruel
2019
Morella
Tortosa
*G. de Sant Jordi*
C. de Tortosa
Vilanova i la Geltrú
Tarragona
*Costa Dorada*

2410

alajara
El Maestrazgo
Vinaròs
40

Cuenca
Castelló de la Plana
*Baleares*
Menorca
C. de Formentor
Maó
(Mahón)

Villarrobledo
Onda
La Vall d'Uixó
Vila-real de los Infantes
1700
Sóller
1445
Inca
Mancor
Mallorca

La Roda
Llíria
Sagunt
*Golfo de*
Palma de Mallorca
Calvià
Lluchmayor

**C**

Albacete
Torrent
**Valencia**
L'Albufera
*Valencia*
B. de Palma

Almansa
Algemesí
Sueca
Xúquer
Cullera
Gandia
Sant Antoni Abat
Eivissa (Ibiza)
Cabrera

Yecla
Xàtiva
Alzira
Eivissa (Ibiza)

Villena
Alcoy
1558
Denia
C. de la Nao
Formentera

Jumilla
Elda
Altea

Cieza
Benidorm
Villajoyosa

Caravaca de la Cruz
Mula
Elche
Orihuela
**Alicante**
*Costa Blanca*

2001
Murcia

**D**

2381
Alcantarilla
Torrevieja

Vélez Rubio
Lorca
Cartagena
*Mar Menor*
C. de Palos

Baza
Almanzora
Mazarrón

Cuevas del
Almanzora
Aguilas

Almería
38

Roquetas de Mar
C. de Gata
2700

*MEDITERRANEAN SEA*

*Córdj d'Kifan*
**ALGER**
Birkhadem
Aïn Benian
Koléa
C. de Ténès
Damous
Ténès
Cherchell
Gouraya
Bou Ismael
Boufarik
Blida
El Arba
Maïnou
Bordj Menaïel

**D**

36

C. Kramis
Beni-Haoua
Miliana
Djendel
Medéa
Berrouaghia
Sour el Ghozlane
Sidi-Aïssa

Massif de Dahra
Khemis Miliana
Ksar el Boukhari
Theniet el Had
Aïn Oussera
Zahrez Chergui

Mostaganem
Aïn Tédelès
O. Chéliff
Oued Rhiou
1985
Relizane
Tissemsilt
Hamadia
Chabounia

**E**

Oran
Arzew
**ALGERIA**
Tiaret
Ksar Chellala
Souguer

C. Falcon
Sig
Mohammadia
Mascara

Melilla (Sp.)
Beni Saf
Hammam Bouhadjar
Aïn Témouchent

Ghazaouet
Remchi

**5**  **6**  **7**

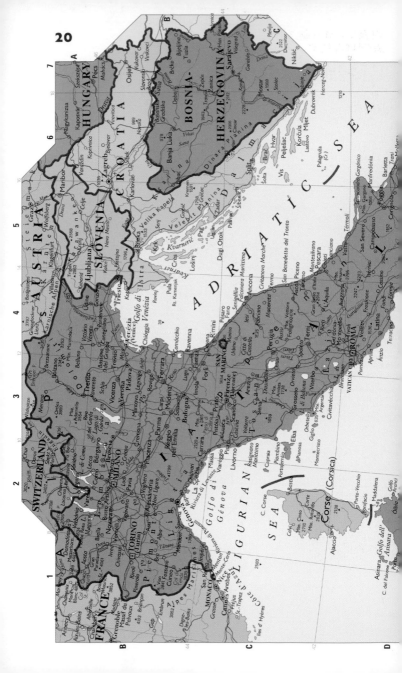

50   0   25   50   75   100   125   150   175 km

50   0   25   50   75   100   125 miles

East from Greenwich

Lecce
Galatina
Brindisi
Gallipoli   Otranto
Nardò
Francavilla   Fontana
Fasano
Martina   Franca
Putignano
Altamura
Matera
Taranto   Golfo di   Táranto
Metaponto
Potenza
Laterza
Sala Consilina
Avellino
Ostuni

IONIAN   SEA

Rossano
Corigliano Calabro
Cosenza
Nicastro
Catanzaro
Crotone
C. Rizzuto
Cetraro

Paola
Lamezia
Vibo Valentia
Palmi
C. Spartivento

Reggio di Calabria
C. Peloro
Str. di Messina

Messina
Giarre
Acireale
Catánia
Augusta
Siracusa
Avola
C. Passero

Taormina
Etna

NÁPOLI
Pozzuoli
Ischia   Torre del Greco
Castellammare di Stabia
Capri

Ponza
Ventotene

Strómboli
Isole Eólie
Lípari
Vulcano
Salina

Milazzo
Barcellona
Pozzo di Gotto
Adrano
Enna
Caltanissetta
Caltagirone
Ragusa
Módica
Vittoria
Gela

Palermo
Termini Imerese
Cefalù
Monti Nébrodi
Petralia
Corleone

Castelvetrano
Sciacca
Agrigento
Canicattì
Licata

Ústica
(Italy)

Érice
Trápani
Marsala
Mazzara del Vallo

Isole Égadi
Favignana

Pantelleria
(Italy)

Isole Pelágie
(Italy)
Lampione
Lampedusa
J. Rossa
Linosa

TYRRHENIAN   SEA

Gozo
Valletta
MALTA
Rabat

Sardegna (Sardinia)
C. Comino
C. di Monte Santu
Arbatax
Tortolì
Sant' Elena
Oristano
G. di Oristano
Quartu
Carbonara
Cágliari
G. di Cágliari
C. Spartivento
C. Carbonara

San Pietro
Sant' Antíoco
Carbónia
Iglésias
Portoscuso
G. di Pálmas

Alghero
Bosa
C. Marráyu

C. Blanc

Golfe de   Hammamet
Mahdia
Monastir
Moknine
Ksar-Hellal
Sousse

Bizerte
Menzel-Bourguiba
Tunis
Golfe de Tunis
C. Bon
Kélibia
Ras Mostefa
Menzel-Temime
Korba
Nabeul
Hammamet
Soliman

Manouba
Tébourba
Béja
Medjerda

Kairouan

TUNISIA

Maktar
Thala

Kasserine
Hadjeb El Aïoun
Sbeïtla
Sidi Bou   Ali

Teboursouk
El Kef
Siliana
Zaghouan

Bou Salem
Jendouba
Ghardimaou

Souk-Ahras
Annaba

Guelma
Sedrata
Aïn Beïda
Tébessa

ALGERIA

Is. de la Galite
(Tunisia)

Projection: Conical with two standard parallels

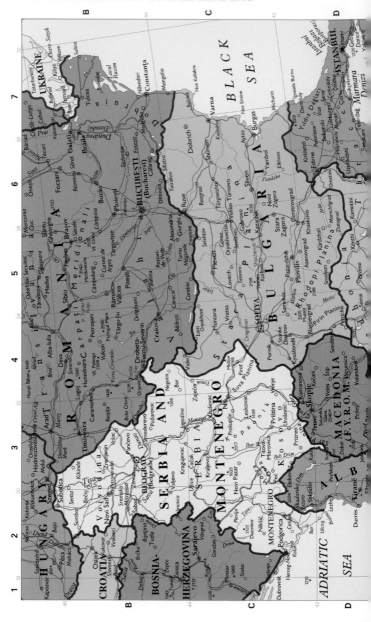

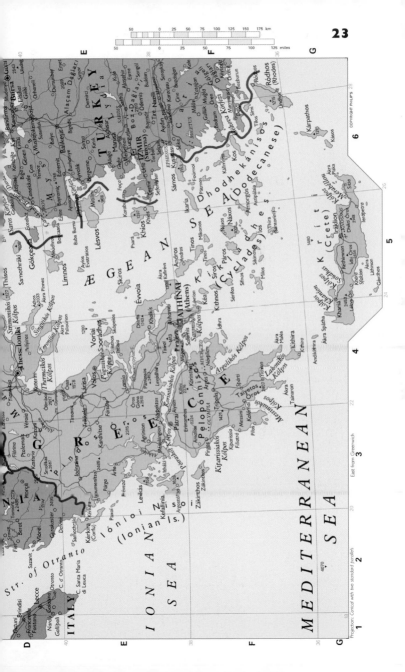

**23**

MEDITERRANEAN SEA

ÆGEAN SEA

IONIAN SEA

Str. of Otranto

TURKEY

GREECE

ITALY

Kríti (Crete)

Peloponnísos

Dhodhekánisos (Dodecanese)

Kikládhes (Cyclades)

Iónioi (Ionian Is.)

ATHINAI (Athens)

ÍZMIR (Smyrna)

Thessaloníki

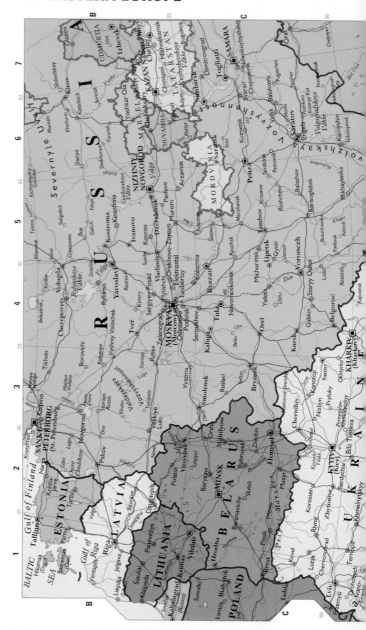

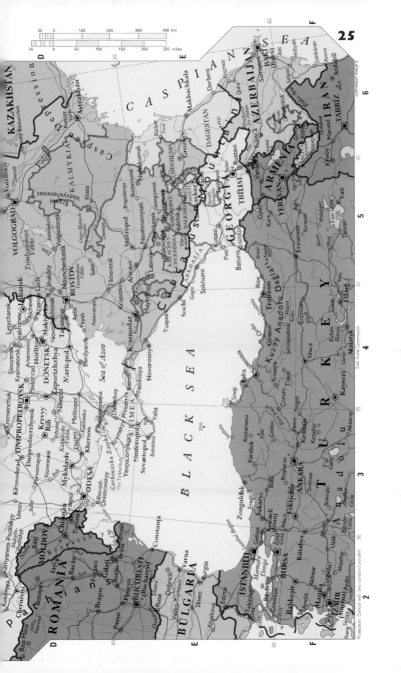

CASPIAN SEA

KAZAKHSTAN

Caspian Depression

VOLGOGRAD (Volzhsky)

Astrakhan

Volga

KALMYKIA

Vozyshennost

Elista

DAGESTAN

Makhachkala

Derbent

Qızıl

AZERBAIJAN

BAKI (Baku)

CHECHENYA

Grozhny

Neftegorsk

Mountains

IRAN

TABRIZ

ARMENIA

YEREVAN

Caucasus

GEORGIA

TBILISI

Rustavi

Kutaisi

AJARIA

Batumi

Poti

Sukhumi

ABKHAZIA

VOLGOGRAD

ROSTOV

Novocherkassk

Shakhty

DONETSK

Makiivka

Taganrog

Sea of Azoe

Novorossiysk

Sochi

Rize

Trabzon

Giresun

TURKEY

ANKARA

BLACK SEA

CRIMEA

Sevastopol

Simferopol

Yalta

ODESA

DNIPROPETROVSK

MOLDOVA

Chisinau

ROMANIA

BUCURESTI (Bucharest)

BULGARIA

Varna

Burgas

ISTANBUL

BURSA

İZMİR

Anadolu

Kayseri

Malatya

Erzurum

Projection: Conical with two standard parallels

COPYRIGHT PHILIP'S

50 0 100 200 300 400 km
50 0 50 100 150 200 250 miles

ATLANTIC OCEAN

ARCTIC

GREENLAND

Svalbard

ICELAND

Arctic Circle

Barents Sea

Novaya Zemlya

Kara Sea

NORWAY

UNITED KINGDOM

North Sea

LONDON

Murmansk

White Sea

Vorkuta

Salekhard

Ob'

Yenisey

SWEDEN

FINLAND

ST.PETERSBURG

FRANCE

PARIS

GERMANY

Berlin

Warsaw

Nizhniy Novgorod

Perm

Yekaterinburg

Irtysh

R U

Tomsk

Prague

Vienna

UKRAINE

MOSCOW

Kazan

Ufa

Chelyabinsk

Omsk

Novosibirsk

ITALY

Rome

Belgrade

Danube

Odessa

Rostov

Volgograd

Volga

Don

Samara

Astana

Pavlodar

Semey

Athens

Black Sea

ISTANBUL

GEORGIA

Tbilisi

Aral Sea

Syrdar'ya

KAZAKHSTAN

Qaraghandy

L. Balkhash

Bursa

İzmir

Ankara

TURKEY

Adana

ARMENIA

AZERBAIJAN

Baku

Caspian Sea

Tabriz

UZBEKISTAN

Tashkent

Samarkand

Bishkek

KYRGYZSTAN

Almaty

SIN

CYPRUS

Nicosia

Aleppo

SYRIA

Mosul

Mashhad

TURKMENISTAN

Ashkhabad

TAJIKISTAN

Dushanbe

Kashi

Hotan

UIG

Mediterranean Sea

LEBANON

Beirut

Damascus

Amman

IRAQ

Baghdad

Tehrān

IRAN

Herāt

Kābul

Islamabad

JAMMU & KASHMIR

Alexandria

CAIRO

ISRAEL

Jerusalem

JORDAN

Basra

Esfahān

Qandahār

AFGHANISTAN

Faisalabad

Lahore

T

LIBYA

EGYPT

Suez

KUWAIT

Kuwait

Shiraz

Zāhedān

DELHI

New Delhi

Lucknow

Aswān

BAHRAIN

Manāmah

The Gulf

Doha

PAKISTAN

Jaipur

Kanpur

Varanasi

INDI

Red Sea

Medina

Riyadh

QATAR

UNITED ARAB EMIRATES

Abu Dhabi

G. of Oman

KARACHI

Indus

Ahmadabad

Bhopal

Nagpur

SUDAN

SAUDI ARABIA

Jedda

Mecca

Muscat

Vadodara

Indore

Surat

MUMBAI (Bombay)

Pune

Hyderabad

Port Sudan

ERITREA

OMAN

Khartoum

YEMEN

Sana

G. of Aden

Arabian Sea

Bangalore

CHENNA (Madras)

DJIBOUTI

Socotra (Yemen)

Lakshadweep Is. (India)

Madurai

SR

Addis Ababa

SOMALI REP.

ETHIOPIA

Colombo

UGANDA

L. Victoria

KENYA

a

Mogadishu

MALDIVES

Male

CONGO

Nairobi

Equator

INDIAN

OC

DEM. REP. OF THE

Dodoma

Mombasa

TANZANIA

SEYCHELLES

Victoria

ZAMBIA

MALAWI

Dar es Salaam

Aldabra Is. (Seychelles)

Amirante Is. (Seychelles)

Chagos Arch. (U.K.)

500   0   250   500   750   1000   1250   1500   1750 km
500        0      250      500      750     1000     1250 miles

B                    C                    D

OCEAN
Severnaya
Zemlya
Laptev Sea          New
                    Siberian
                    Is.        Wrangel I.        ALASKA
                                                 (USA)        Bering
Khatanga        Verkhoyansk                                   Sea
                                          Gizhiga
Norilsk                                                   Aleutian Is.
                    Lena                  Magadan          (USA)
            Yakutsk                                     Petropavlovsk-
Angara                          Okhotsk                 Kamchatskiy        E
    Bratsk    L. Baikal                   Sea of
Krasnoyarsk                               Okhotsk
                        Chita                                              50
Novokuznetsk    Irkutsk  Ulan Ude  Blagoveshchensk   Komsomolsk  Sakhalin
                                          Khabarovsk
                                                      Yuzhno-              F
                                                      Sakhalinsk          40
                    Hailar   Qiqihar    Harbin   Vladivostok   Kurils
Ürümqi                                Changchun  Jilin        Hokkaidō
ANG   Hami            Ulan Bator                              Sapporo
'AR                  MONGOLIA   SHENYANG  Anshan NORTH         Honshū      G
                              Jinzhou  Dalian  KOREA  Japan    TŌKYŌ      30
        Baotou     BEIJING  TIANJIN      PYONGYANG Sea of  Nagoya Yokohama
Yumen              Taiyuan  Jinan        SEOUL SOUTH  Kyōto  Osaka  JAPAN
Lanzhou                     Yellow  Pusan KOREA  Hiroshima
UR                  Huang-ho        Sea          Kyūshū
BET                 Yellow          Shanghai
        Chengdu    CHINA            SHANGHAI      East     Volcano Is.     H
Lhasa                      Wuhan  Nanjing  HANGZHOU  China  (Japan)        20
        CHONGQING  Yangtze  Nanchang  Sea  RYUKYU   Tropic of Cancer
BHUTAN   Kunming  Changsha  Fuzhou
Thimphu            GUANGZHOU  Taipei  TAIWAN              PACIFIC          GUAM
BANGLADESH BURMA   Si Kiang  HONG KONG                                    (USA)  J
Patna  DACCA  Chittagong  Macau                         FED. STATES
KOLKATA (MYANMAR)                 Hainan               OF MICRONESIA
(Calcutta)         Hanoi  Haiphong         Luzon        PALAU
        LAOS                               MANILA  PHILIPPINES
Bay of   VIETNAM                           Mindanao                       0
Bengal  Rangoon THAILAND  CAMBODIA  Ho Chi Minh  Sulu  Davao
Andaman Is. BANGKOK  Phnom Penh         Sea   Zamboanga
(India)            G. of                Palawan
ANKA Nicobar Is.  Thailand   BRUNEI SABAH  Celebes  Manado  Halmahera    K
     (India)      PEN.  Bandar Seri Begawan  Sea                          10
EAN      Str. of Malacca MALAYSIA SARAWAK   Celebes  Ambon  Ceram
     Medan        Kuala Lumpur              Borneo
                  MALAYSIA                  Ujung Pandang  Banda Sea  Arafura Sea
                  SINGAPORE                            EAST
     Sumatra      Banjarmasin   INDONESIA  DILI TIMOR               AUSTRALIA  L
     Palembang             Semarang  Flores  Timor  Sumba  Timor Sea
     JAKARTA Bandung  Java  Surabaya
12        13        14        15        16        17
90        100       110       120       130   COPYRIGHT PHILIP'S

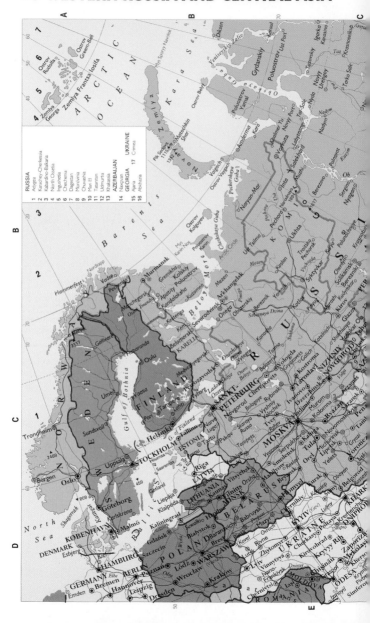

RUSSIA
1 Adygea
2 Karachay-Cherkessia
3 Kabardino-Balkaria
4 North Ossetia
5 Ingushetia
6 Chechenia
7 Dagestan
8 Mordovia
9 Chuvashia
10 Mari El
11 Tatarstan
12 Udmurtia
13 Khakassia

AZERBAIJAN
14 Naxçıvan

GEORGIA
15 Ajaria
16 Abkhazia

UKRAINE
17 Crimea

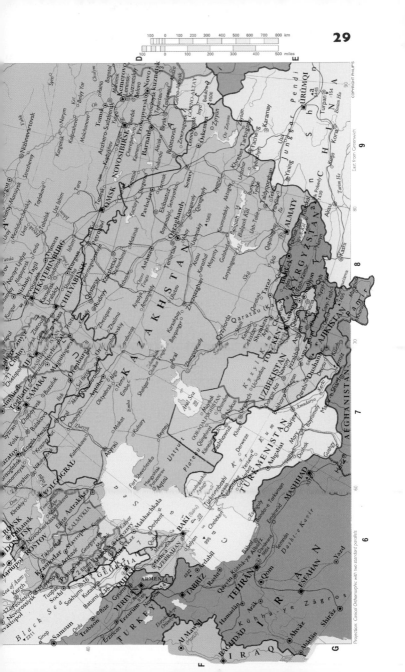

A

1  2  3  4  5  6  7  8  9  10  11  12

40  50  60  70  80  90  100  110  120  130  140  150

Zemlya George
Ostrov Rudolfa
Ostrov Green-Bell
Zemlya Frantsa Iosifa

Mys Arkticheskiy

Ostrov Shmidta
Ostrov Komsomolets
Ostrov Pioner
Ostrov Oktyabrskoy Revolyutsii
Ostrov Bolshevik

A R C T I C    O C E A N

965
Severnaya Zemlya

B

Z e m l y a
Mys Spony Navolok
K a r a   S e a
Proliv Vilkitskogo
Mys Chelyuskin

L a p t e v   S e a

Ostrov Novos
Ostrov Belkovsky
Ostrov Kot
Ostrov Stolb

Matochkin Shar
Ostrov Belyy

Byrranga
Gory
P o l u o s t r o v  1146
T a y m y r
Nordvik

Ostrov Bolshoy Begichev
Oz. Taymyr

Anderma
Kara
Poluostrov Yamal
O
b
s
k
a
y
a
G
u
b
a
Dikson
Mys Zhelte

Novorybnoye
Kheta
Khatanga
Khatanga

Ust Olenek
Olenek
Tit-Ary  Tik
Bulun

70

Kholmer Yu
Novy Porto
Yar-Sale
Labytnangi
Salekhard
Gydanskiy
Poluostrov Ust Port
Karaul

Volochanka
Kheta

Saskylakh
Anabar

Zhilinda

Kyus

C

Nadym
Nyda
Novy
Tazovskiy
Dudinka
Norilsk
Gory Putorana 1701

Igarka
Karasina

Kureyka

Yessey

Olenek

Kystatyan
Zhigan

962

Arctic Circle

Novy Urengoy
Tarko Sale
Krasnoselkup
Turukhansk

Noginsk
Tura

Nizhnaya Tunguska

Vilyuy

S

Verkhnevilyu
Nyurt
Mirnyy

Noyabrsk
Vakh
Podkamennaya Tunguska
Yuktao
Chernyshevskiy

Yerbogachen

C

Surgut
Strezhevoy
Nizhnevartovsk
Yenisey
Sym
Yartsevo
1104
Severo-Yeniseyskiy
Kuyumba  Mutoray
R
Vanavara
U

Lensk  S
Vitim
Boday

Taylakova
Kargasok  Narym
Kolpashevo
Belyy Yar
Ket
Yeniseysk
Angara
Boguchany
Kezhma
Chuna
Makarovo
Ust-Ilimsk
Korshunovo
Kirensk
Mama
Karaion

Tara
Molchanovo
Chulym
Asino
Bogotol
Achinsk
Kansk
Kondratyevo
Ust-Kut
Magistralnyy

D

Om
Tatarsk
Kuybyshev
Yurga
Tomsk
Anzhero-Sudzhensk
Mariinsk
Ilanskiy
Zheleznogorsk-Ilimskiy
Tayshet
Nizhneangarsk

2840  Bogd

NOVOSIBIRSK
Kalaiol
Leninsk
Kemerovo
Krasnoyarsk
Bratsk
Nizhneudinsk

Barguzin

Karasuk
Kamen
Cherepanovo
Berdsk
Prokopyevsk
Novo-
kuznetsk
Belovo
Leninsk-Kuznetskiy
Artemovsk
Tulun
Zima
Cheremkhovo

Slovgorod
Novoaltaysk
Tashtagol
Chernogorsk
Minusinsk
Abaza
Abakan

Angarsk  1620
Ulan Ude
Khilok

Pavlodar
Barnaul
KHAKASSIA
Vostochnyy Sayan
Munku-Sardyk 3491
Irkutsk
Petrovsk-Zabaykalsky

Kulunda
Aleiska
Biysk
Tomirtau
Zapadno
Toora-Khem
Slyudyanka

Gusinoozersk
Kyakhta
Khopcherang

Semipalatinsk
Semey
Rubtsovsk
Zmeinogorsk
Gorno-Altaysk
GORNO-ALTAY
Turan
Chadan
Kyzyl
Hovsgol Nuur
Zakamensk
Darhan
Hentiyn

E

Öskemen
Leninogorsk
Inya
Belukha 4506
TUVA
Samagaltay
Hatgal

Zyryan
Uliastay
Erzin

50

Projection: Conical Orthomorphic with two standard parallels

6  7  100  8  110

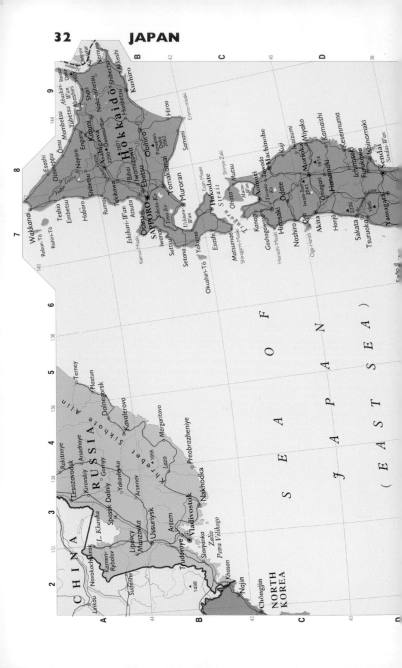

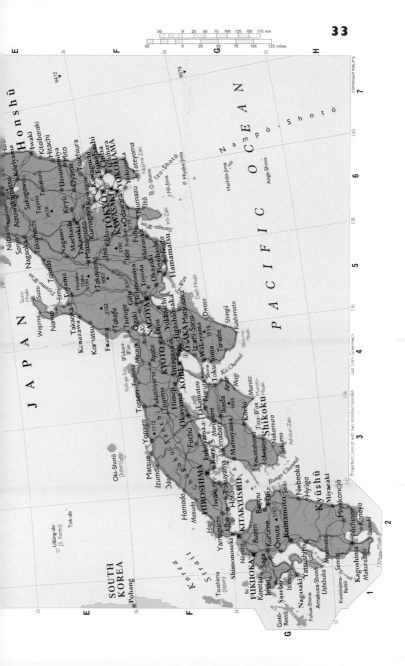

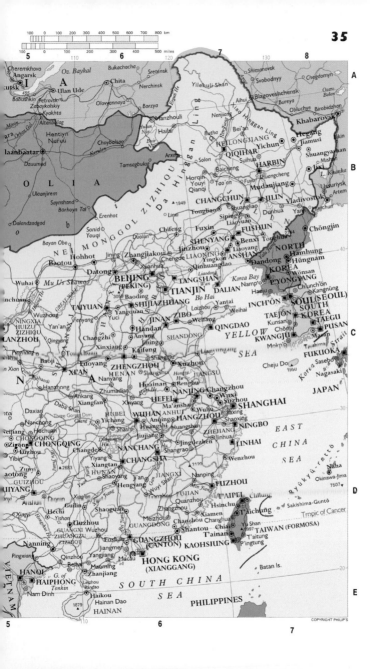

100  0    100  200  300  400  500  600  700  800 km
100  0       100    200     300      400     500 miles

A

**I A**
Cheremkhovo
Angarsk
Oz. Baykal
Bukachacha
Sretensk
Shimonovsk
Svobodnyy
Chegdomyn
kutsk
455
Babushkin
Ulan Ude
Chita
Nerchinsk
Yilehuli Shan
Aihui
Blagoveshchensk
Ozero
Bolon
Petrovsk
Zabaykalskiy
Olovyannaya
Borzya
Obluchye
Birobidzhan
Kyakhta
Altanbulag
Da  Hinggan Ling
Nenjiang
Bei'an
Bureya
Khabarovsk
ara
Orhon Gol
aanbaatar
Hentiyn
Nuruu
Manzhouli
Hulun
Nur
Hailar
Butha
Qi
HEILONGJIANG
Solon
Yichun
Suihua
Jiamusi
Hegang
kin
Dzuumod
Choybalsan
Arxan
QIQIHAR
Baicheng
HARBIN
Shuangyashan
Jixi
Tamsagbulag
Horqin
Youyi
Qianqi
Tao'an
Fuyu
Shuangcheng
Mishan
L. Khanka
Ussuriysk
**O L I A**
Ulaanjirem
Saynshand
Borhoyn Tal
Erenhot
i
1949
Linxi
CHANGCHUN
Tongliao
Shuangliao
JILIN
Mudanjiang
Vladivostok
Artem
b
Dalandzadgad
Bayan Obo
Sonid
Youqi
Chifeng
Fuxin
Liaoyuan
Siping
Dunhua
Yanji
Chŏngjin
NORTH
Wuhai
Mu Us Shamo
NEI  MONGGOL  ZIZHIQU
Obotun
SHENYANG
FUSHUN
Benxi
Tonghua
Hohhot
Jining
Zhangjiakou
Jinzhou
LIAONING
Liaoyang
ANSHAN
KOREA
Hamhŭng
Hŭngnam
Baotou
Datong
Xuanhua
Chengde
Yingkou
Qinhuangdao
Dandong
PYONGYANG
40
Wuzhong
NINGXIA
HUIZU
ZIZHIQU
3058
**BEIJING**
(PEKING)
Baoding
**TANGSHAN**
Liaodong
Korea Bay
Nampo
Haeju
Ch'unch'on
Kangnŭng
nchuan
ANZHOU
Pingliang
TAIYUAN
Yangquan
**TIANJIN**
Yuci
**SHIJIAZHUANG**
**DALIAN**
Bo Hai
Laizhou
Yantai
Weihai
INCH'ON
SŎUL(SEOUL)
SOUTH
i Xian
Qingyang
Yan'an
Fenyang
**JINAN**
**ZIBO**
Weifang
QINGDAO
TAEJŎN
KOREA
TAEGU
**N**
Changzhi
Handan
SHANDONG
Chŏlju
Kunsan
PUSAN
Baoji
Tongchuan
Xinxiang
Anyang
Jining
KWANGJU
Mokp'o
Tsushima Strait
Yinchuan
**XI'AN**
Qingyang
**LUOYANG**
Kaifeng
Shangqiu
Xuzhou
Lianyungang
YELLOW
Cheju Do
1950
Korea
Strait
FUKUOKA
Sasebo
HENAN
Nanyang
Shangshui
JIANGSU
Nagasaki
i Xian
Ankang
Hanzhong
Zhumadian
Huaiyin
Bengbu
NANJING
Changzhou
Wuxi
SHANGHAI
SEA
JAPAN
Daxian
Nanchong
Xiangfan
Three Gorges Dam
Xinyang
**HEFEI**
Ma'anshan
Suzhou
Weijiang
Hechuan
Yichang
HUBEI
**WUHAN**
ANHUI
Anqing
**HANGZHOU**
Wuhu
Jiaxing
Shaoxing
NINGBO
EAST
Zigong
**CHONGQING**
Shashi
Huangshi
Huanggang
Jiujiang
Jingdezhen
Jinhua
ZHEJIANG
CHINA
Yibin
NANCHANG
Hu
Shangrao
LINHAI
aotong
CHANGSHA
Xiangtan
JIANGXI
Wenzhou
SEA
UIYANG
GUIZHOU
Zunyi
2683
HUNAN
Ji'an
Nanping
Anshun
Ji'an
Shaoyang
Hengyang
Wuyi Shan
FUJIAN
FUZHOU
ü
Duyun
Guilin
Ji'an
Shaoguan
Min Jiang
TAIPEI
Xingyi
Hechi
Yishan
Meizhou
GUANGDONG
Zhangzhou
Quanzhou
Hsinchu
Chilung
D
GUANGXI
ZHUANGZU
ZIZHIQU
Wuzhou
Zhangjiang
Changhua
T'aichung
Xiamen
Shantou
Chiai
Tropic of Cancer
Sakishima-Guntō
Pingxiang
Nanning
Foshan
GUANGZHOU
(CANTON)
KAOHSIUNG
T'ainan
Yü Shan
3997
TAIWAN (FORMOSA)
T'aitung
P'ingtung
Qinzhou
Yangjiang
Maoming
Macau
HONG KONG
(XIANGGANG)
Batan Is.
HANOI
G. of
Beihai
Zhanjiang
SOUTH  CHINA
HAIPHONG
Tonkin
BANDAO
Nam Dinh
1879
Haikou
SEA
PHILIPPINES
VIETNAM
Hainan Dao
HAINAN

E

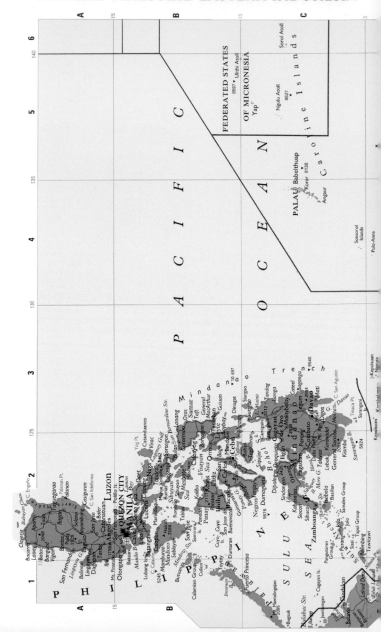

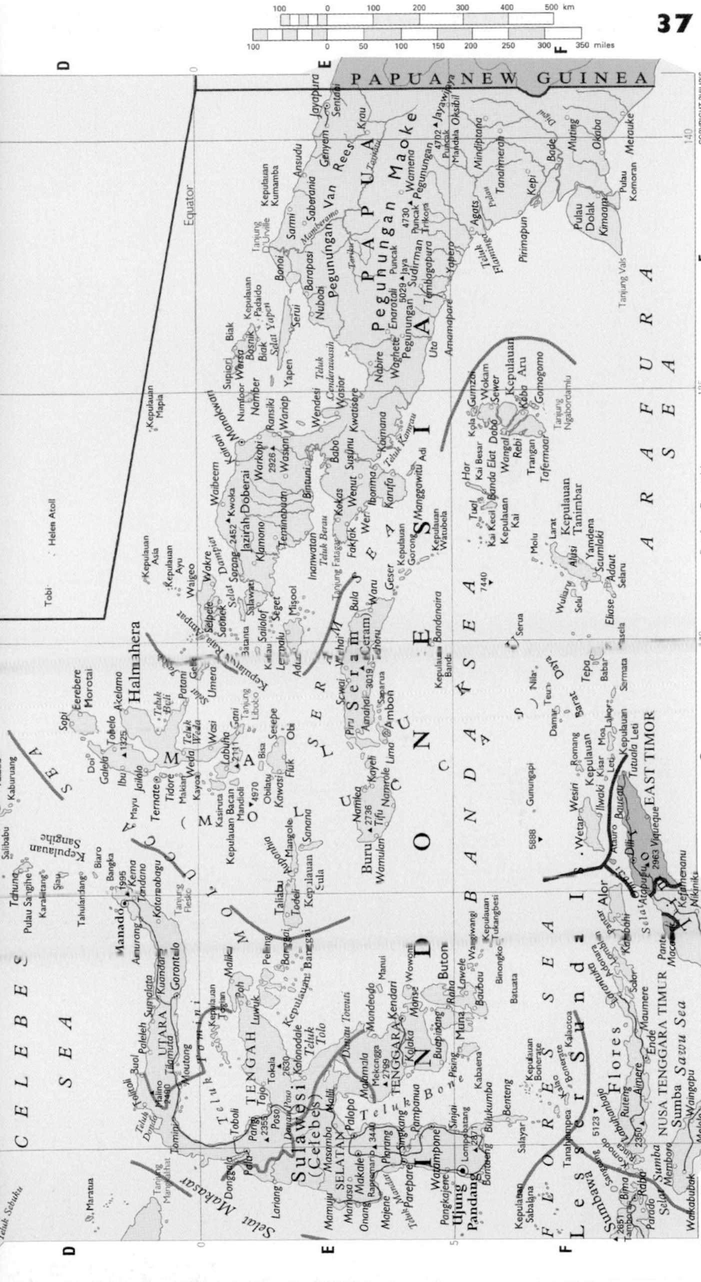

PAPUA NEW GUINEA

INDONESIA

CELEBES SEA

Sulawesi (Celebes)

Halmahera

MALUKU

SERAM SEA

BANDA SEA

FLORES SEA

Flores

NUSA TENGGARA TIMUR

EAST TIMOR

Sumba

Sumbawa

ARAFURA SEA

Pegunungan Maoke

Equator

100 0 100 200 300 400 500 km
100 0 50 100 150 200 250 300 350 miles

East from Greenwich

Projection Mercator

COPYRIGHT PHILIP'S

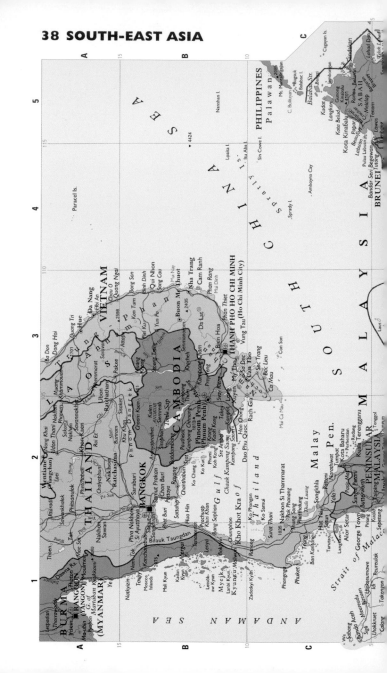

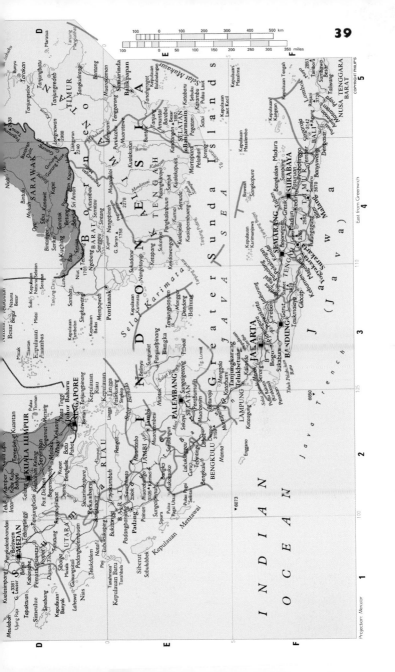

**39**

Projection: Mercator

COPYRIGHT PHILIP'S

East from Greenwich

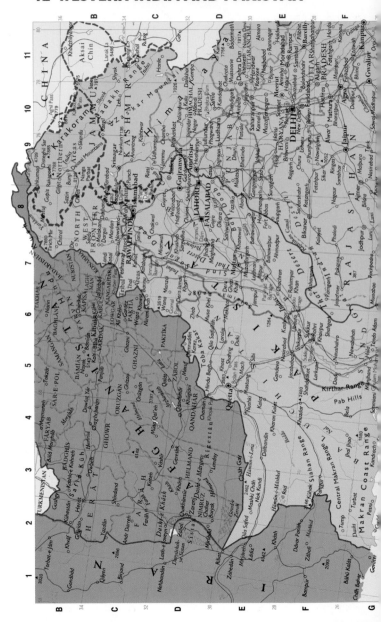

**43**

COPYRIGHT PHILIPS

Continuation Southwards on same scale

Projection: Conical with two standard parallels

# 44 IRAN, THE GULF AND AFGHANISTAN

Projection: Conical Orthomorphic with two standard parallels

East from Greenwich

50  0  100  200  300  400 km
50  0  50  100  150  200  250 miles

**B**

**C**

**D**

**E**

**F**

UZBEKISTAN
Bukhoro
Qarshi
Shakhrisabz
Dushanbe
Ordzhonikidzeabad
TAJIKISTAN
Kŭlob
Pamir
Chärjew
Guzar
Sherabad
Qŭrghonteppa
Khorugh
Pamir
Ishkuman
Rakaposhi
Kerki
Termiz
Qarävo
Feyzabad
Eshkamesh
Mastuj
Gupis
Gilgit
Sazin
Chilas
Andkhvoy
Shebberghān
Mazar-e
Sharīf
BALKH
Kholm
Qondūz
Khānābād
Jorm
TAKHAR BADAKHSHĀN
Tirich Mir
Chitral
Dir
JOWZJĀN
SAMANGĀN
Narin
Baghlān
BAGHLĀN
NŪRISTĀN
North
Dargai
Dārban
Mardan
Nowshera
Peshawar
RAWALPINDI
Meymaneh
Band-e Torkestān
Sayghan
Bāmiān
PARVĀN
Chārikār
KĀPĪSĀ
LAGHMĀN
Jalālābād
KUNARHA
Khyber Pass
FĀRYĀB
SAR-E
POL
Kohi-Baba
Kābul
KĀBUL-NANGARHĀR
Dowlat Yār
Nowak
VARDAK
LOWGAR
WEST
Jhand
Chakwal
BĀDGHĪS
Kosh-e
Kohneh
Owbeh
Hamūn
Chaghcharān
Panjab
Gardēz
Khwest
Thal
Kohat
Bannu
Mianwali
Khushab
Herāt
Darreh-ye
Namakzar
Yazdān
HERĀT
GHOWR
Teyvareh
ORUZGĀN
Ghaznī
GHAZNĪ
PAKTĪĀ
Manzai
Sargodha
Chiniot
Torbat-e
Jām
Khvāf
Tūlak
Shindand
Mūsá Qal'eh
Qalāt
ZĀBOL
PAKTĪKĀ
Gomal
Pass
Dera Ismail Khan
Zhob
Jhang
Maghiana
Khanewal
FARĀH
Chakhānsūr
Gereshk
Khūgīānī
Qandahār
QANDAHĀR
Ma'rūf
Toba Kakar
Musa Khel
Loralai
Fort
Munro
Dera Ghazi
Khan
Jampur
Bahawalpur
Multan
Muzaffargarh
Ahmadpur
Rahimyar
Khan
NĪMRŪZ
HELMAND
Dasht-e Mārgow
Rīgestān
Khojak Pass
Chaman
Quetta
Hindu Bagh
Shahrig
Duki
Bolan Pass
Mach
Sibi
Dasht-e Khāsh
Lash-e
Joveyn
Zorah
Zāhedān
Mushki Chāh
Nok Kundi
Dālbandin
Kharan Kalat
Khuzdar
Nushki
Kalat
Gandava
Jacobabad
Ubauro
Kashmor
Sukkur
Rohri
Khairpur
Ranigarh
Shahdadkot
Larkana
Shahdadpur
Naushahro
Jaisalmer
INDIA
SĪSTĀN VA
BALŪCHESTĀN
Ladiz
Kūh-e
Tattan
Khāsh
Rod
Hāmūn-i-Māshkel
Kūhak
Siahan Range
Panjgur
Dadu
Nawabshah
INDUS
Great Indian Desert
Bampūr
Irānshahr
Māshkid
Jhal Jhao
Bela
Pab Hills
Manjhand
Hala
Tando Adam
Mirpur Khas
Thar Desert
Munabao
Umarkot
Mashkel
Qasr-e Qand
Sarbāz
Central Makran Range
Turbat
Kharan
Kirthar Range
Khuzdar
Ghulam Mohammad
Barrage
Kotri
Hyderabad
Nagar
Parkar
Bent
Nīkshahr
Pīshīn
Tump
Makran Coast Range
Kandrach
Sonmiani
Hab Nadi Chauki
Ghulam Mohammad
Tatta
Badin
Rann of Kachchh
Lakhpat
Khavda
Kharan
Chāh Bahār
Gavāter
Gwādar
Pasni
Ormara
Ras Mūari
KARACHI
Mandvi
Kandla
Gulf of Kachchh
Mouths of the Indus
Jamnagar
Gop
Porbandar
of Oman
Tropic of Cancer
ARABIAN
Matraḥ
Masqat (Muscat)
Al Qurayyāt
Dwarka
SEA
'Ibrī
Tiwi
Sūr
Ras al Hadd
As Suwayḥ
Al Kāmil
Al Ashkhara

**AFGHANISTAN**

**PAKISTAN**

**Hindu Kush**

**BALUCHISTAN**

COPYRIGHT PHILIP'S

5    6    7    8

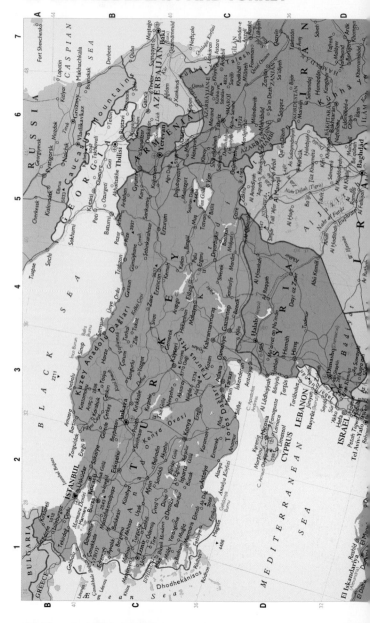

**47**

Projection: Conical Orthomorphic with two standard parallels

COPYRIGHT PHILIPS

THE GULF

KUWAIT

SAUDI ARABIA

Al Kuwayt (Kuwayt)

Mesopotamia

IRAQ

JORDAN

El QÂHIRA

EGYPT

SUDAN

RED SEA

Es Sahrâ' Nûbiya

An Nafûd

Jabal Shammar

Dahnâ

Al 'Aramah

Es Sahrâ' esh Sharqiya

THEBES

PYRAMIDS

Es Sînâ

Khalîg el Suweis

Khalîg Suez

Suez Canal

Dead Sea

Jerusalem

Gebel

Wâdi Halfa

Bahairet en Nâsir (Lake Nasser)

50   0   100   200   300   400 km
50   0   50   100   150   200   250 miles

East from Greenwich

Al Jafûrah

Ad Dahnâ'

Harrat al Kishb

Harrat Nawâsif

'Urûq Subay'

Sahl Rakbah

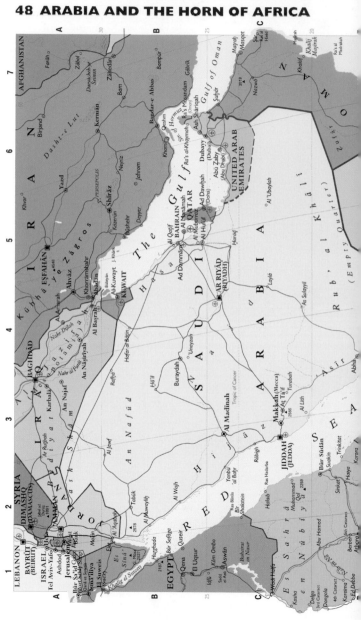

49

Projection: Sinusoidal

**INDIAN**

**OCEAN**

Mirbat

Socotra (Yemen)

Hadiboh

Ras Faruk

Sayhut

Abd al Kuri

Ras Asir

Bereda

Xaafuun

El Gal

Bender Bella

Gardo

El

Obbia

Bosaso

Garoe

Erigavo

Galcaio

2408

El Dere

Sinadogo

MUQDISHO (MOGADISHU)

Merca

Bar Acabo

Bardera

Baidoa

Lugh Ganana

Belet Uen

Ferfer

Kebri Dehar

Las Anod

Burao

Hargeisa

Berbera

Karin

Zeila

Djibouti

Tajura

Harer

Dire Dawa

Gode

Dolo

Doi

El Wak

Wajir

Moyale

Marsabit

**KENYA**

Mega

Negele

Kbre Mengist

Dilla

Yrga Alem

Goba

Mt. Batu 4307

Ginir

Imi

Awash

Shashemene

Asela

Nazret

Debre Zeit

**ADDIS ABEBA**

Debre Markos

Debre Birhan

Nekemte

Jima

Gore

Netta

**ETHIOPIA**

Dembidolo

Gambela

Pibor Post

Malakal

Sobat

Bor

**SUDAN**

Juba

Yei

Torit

Kapoeta

**UGANDA**

Moroto

Lira

Soroti

Mbale

Tororo

L. Turkana

L. Shamo

L. Abaya

Cheu Bahir

Lokitaung

Lodwar

Kitale

3202

3398

Metu

E. Tana

Bure

Bahir Dar

Debre Tabor

Gonder

1830

Alem

Mekele

Lalibela

4120

Ras Dashen 4620

Adigrat

Aksum

Adwa

Asmera

**ERITREA**

Akordat

Keren

Massawa

Zula

Dahlak Kebir

Nakfa

Kassala

Gedaref

Khashm el Girba

Wad Medani

Ed Dueim

Kosti

Gezira

El Obeid

**Khartoum**

Omdurman

Shendi

Wad Hamid

Ed Damazin

Umm Ruwaba

Sennar

Ras Furak

**YEMEN**

Sana'

Ta'izz

Al Mukalla

Shibam

Aden (Al' Adan)

Mukha

Bab el Mandeb

Assab

Al Hudaydah

Kamaran

Al Luhayyah

Farasan

Jizan

Khamir

Najib

Shaqra

Zinjibar

Bir Ali

**Hadramawt**

Jihal Thamar 3350

Jihal 2469

**Gulf of Aden**

**Danakil Desert**

L. Abhe

1599

3381

Tendaho

Dese

Kombolcha

Weldiya

**Ogaden**

Fafen

Shebele

Genale

Dawa

Juba

**S O M A L I A**

**Nahr 'Atbara**

Nile (Nahr el Abiad)

Bahr el Azraq

**Sudd**

Bahr el Jebel

Victoria Nile

L. Albert

Murchison Falls

L. Kyoga

Bida

Gulu

Pakwach

Masindi

Kajo Kaji

Kaga

Nile

East from Greenwich

100   0   100   200   300   400   500   600 km
100   0   100   200   300          400 miles

15   E   10   E   5   F   G

6   5   50   45   40   35   15   10   5   1

E   F   G

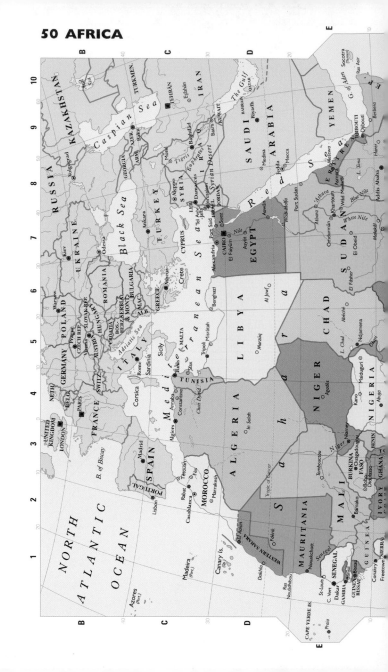

**51**

200 0 200 400 600 800 1000 1200 1400 1600 1800 km

200 0 200 400 600 800 1000 1200 miles

SEYCHELLES

INDIAN OCEAN

SOMALI

Mogadishu

Kismayu

Mombasa

Zanzibar

Dar es Salaam

C. Delgado

COMOROS

Moroni

Mayotte (Fr.)

Mamoudzou

Aldabra Is.

MAURITIUS

Réunion (Fr.)

St-Denis

Port Louis

MADAGASCAR

Antsiranana

Mahajanga

Toamasina

Antananarivo

Fianarantsoa

Toliara

Mozambique Channel

KENYA

UGANDA

Nairobi

Kisumu

Kampala

TANZANIA

Dodoma

Tabora

L. Malawi

MOZAMBIQUE

Mozambique

Beira

Maputo

MALAWI

Lilongwe

Blantyre

Zambezi

RWANDA

BURUNDI

Bujumbura

Kigali

L. Victoria

L. Edward

L. Kivu

L. Tanganyika

CONGO (DEM. REP. OF THE) (Zaïre)

Kisangani

Lualaba

Mbandaka

Kananga

Likasi

Lubumbashi

Kolwezi

ZAMBIA

Lusaka

Ndola

Kitwe

ZIMBABWE

Harare

Bulawayo

Ludovyo

Gweru

Livingstone

BOTSWANA

Gaborone

Windhoek

NAMIBIA

Cubango

Cunene

ANGOLA

Luanda

Lobito

Namibe

Huambo

Cuango

Kasai

Cuanza

Congo

Kinshasa

Matadi

Brazzaville

Pointe Noire

CABINDA (Angola)

GABON

Libreville

C. Lopez

CONGO

Annobón

SÃO TOMÉ & PRÍNCIPE

EQUATORIAL GUINEA

CAMEROON

Yaoundé

Douala

Malabo

CENTRAL AFRICAN REP.

Bangui

Ubangi

Congo

Sangha

Ogooué

LIBERIA

Monrovia

Port Harcourt

Lagos

Porto Novo

Accra

Sekondi-Takoradi

Abidjan

Gulf of Guinea

Bight of Benin

SOUTH AFRICA

Johannesburg

Pretoria

Kimberley

Mbabane

SWAZILAND

Maseru

LESOTHO

Durban

East London

Port Elizabeth

Cape Town

C. of Good Hope

C. Agulhas

Vaal

Orange

Limpopo

Ascension I. (U.K.)

St. Helena (U.K.)

SOUTH ATLANTIC OCEAN

Tristan da Cunha (U.K.)

Tropic of Capricorn

Equator

Projection: Azimuthal Equidistant

West from Greenwich   East from Greenwich

● Dakar Capital Cities

COPYRIGHT PHILIP'S

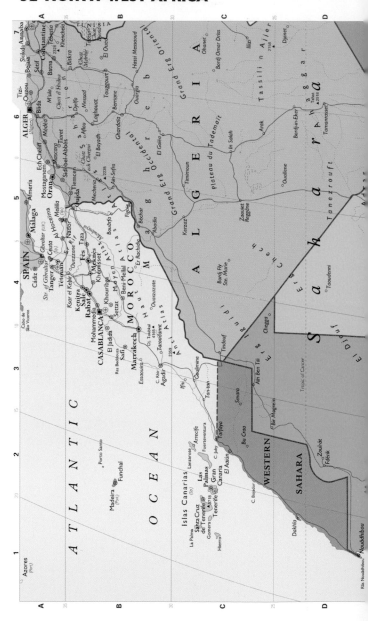

**53**

Projection: Sanson–Flamsteed's Sinusoidal

100   0   100   200   300   400   500   600 km
100   0   100   200   300   400 miles

E   F   G   H

**MAURITANIA**

Nouakchott
St. Louis
Akjoujt
Rás Timerist
C. Vert
DAKAR
SENEGAL
Thiès
Diourbel
Kaolack
Banjul
GAMBIA
Bignona
Ziguinchor
Bissau
GUINEA
BISSAU
Arq. dos
Bijagós

Rosso
Mbout
Louga
Linguère
Matam
Bakel
Kédougou
Tambacounda
Kolda
Labé
Dalaba
Mamou
Kindia
Conakry
Boké
Dubréka
Fouta
Djalon

SIERRA
LEONE
Freetown
Port Loko
Makeni
Bo
Bonthe
Sherbro I.

Aleg
Kaédi
Kaédi
Kayes
Nioro du Sahel

**M**
Kiffa
Ayoûn el Atroûs
Néma

Rachid
Tidjikja
**A o u k â r**

**d e s   I f o r a s**

**Aïr**
Iférouâne
Agadez
1900

**NIGER**
Arlit
In-Gall
Teguidda
Tanout
Zinder
Hadejia
Azare

**S a h e l**

Tombouctou
Gao
Ansongo
Menaka
Filingué
Niamey
Dosso
Gaya

Kidal
Bourem

**M A L I**
Bamako
Ségou
Sikasso
Bougouni

Kayes
Nara
Nioro du Sahel
Didiéni
Diéma

Bafoulabé
Siguiri
Kouroussa
Kankan
Faranah
Kissidougou

**GUINEA**
Beyla
Macenta
Nzérékoré

Mopti
Niafunké
Douentza
San
Koutiala
Koro
Tougan
Ouahigouya

Hombori

**BURKINA**
Ouagadougou
Koudougou
Kaya
Dori

**FASO**
Bobo-
Dioulasso
Banfora
Gaoua
Bouna

Tamale
Bolgatanga
Wa
Bole
Tumu
Wenchi
Salaga
Yendi

**GHANA**
Kumasi
Obuasi
Sekondi-Takoradi
Accra
Tema
Cape Coast

**Gold Coast**
C. Three Points

Fada-
Ngourma
Diapaga

**BENIN**
Natitingou
Djougou
Parakou
Savé
Abomey

**TOGO**
Sokodé
Kpalimé
Atakpamé
Lomé

Porto-Novo
Cotonou

**Slave Coast**
**Bight of Benin**

Dapango
Kara
Sansanné-
Mango

Lake
Volta

**NIGERIA**
Sokoto
Birnin Kebbi
Gusau
Kano
Katsina
Maradi

Zaria
Kaduna
Funtua
Bida
Minna
Abuja
Keffi
Lafia
Jos
Bauchi
Gombe
Wukari
Shendam

Kontagora
Kainji
Res.
Kandi

Kishi
Oyo
Iwo
Ilorin
Offa
Oshogbo
Ilesha
Ede
Ogbomosho
**IBADAN**
Iwo
Abeokuta
Ife
Ondo
Owo
Akure
Benin
City
Sapele
Warri
Forcados
**LAGOS**
Ijebu-Ode

Makurdi
Enugu
Onitsha
Aba
Owerri
Aba
Port Harcourt
Uyo
Calabar

**CAMEROUN**
Bamenda
Nkongsamba
Kumba
Buea
Mt. Cameroun
Mamfe
Mbalmayo
Douala
Limbe
**Bioko**

Rey Malabo

**IVORY**
Odienné
Korhogo
Ferkéssédougou
Kong
Séguéla
Katiola
Bouaké
Bouaflé
Daloa
Gagnoa
Lakota
Divo
Dabou
**ABIDJAN**
Grand
Bassam
Aboisso

**COAST**
Man
L. de
Kossou
Yamoussoukro
Agboville
Adzopé
Abengourou
Bondoukou
Agnibilékrou
Bouna

**LIBERIA**
Monrovia
Buchanan
Greenville
Harper
C. Palmas

Tabou
San Pédro
Sassandra

**Grain Coast**
**Ivory Coast**

Sanniquellie
Tapeta
Zwedru

Guéckédou
Macenta
Danané

Lac. Volta

Black Volta

White Volta

Black Volta

3   10   4   5   6   7

West from Greenwich   0   East from Greenwich

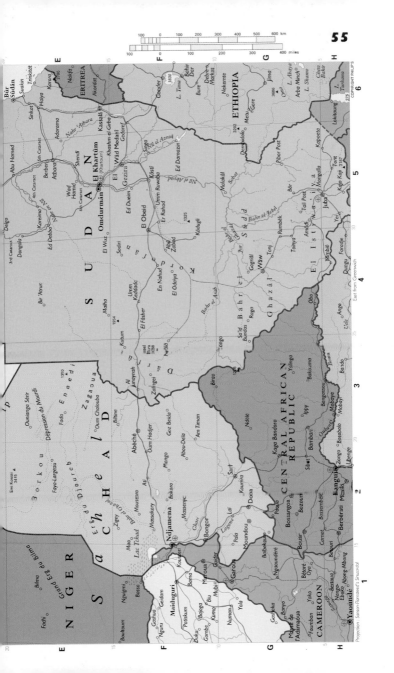

55

100   0   100   200   300   400   500   600 km
100    0      100      200      300      400 miles

**E**

Bûr
Sudân
Suakin
Trinkitat
Karora
Nakfa
2780
ERITREA
Akordat
Sinkat
Haiya
Adarama
Nahr Atbara
Kassala
Bahir
Dar
L. Tana
Gonder
1830

Abu Hamed
Berber
5th Cataract
Atbara
Khashm el Girba
Gedaref
Sennar
Nil el Azraq
Ed Damazin
Bure
Debre
Markos
Nekemte

Delgo
Wad
Hamid
4th Cataract
KHARTÛM
(Khartoum)
Omdurmân
El
Gezira
Wâd Medani
Kôsti
Metu
Gore
2202
Dembidolo
3696
Oni
Jima

3rd Cataract
Dongola
Ed Debba
Kareima
El Wâd
Ed Dueim
Umm Ruwaba
Nil el Abiad
Sobat
Malakâl
L. Abaya
L. Shamo
Arba Minch

S   U   D   A   N
El Obeid
Er Rahad
1325
Abu
Zabad
Kâdugli
Fur
River
Bahr
el
Sobat
Akobo
Pibor Post
Kapoeta
Lokitaung
375

Bîr Atrun
Sodiri
K   o   r   d   o   f   a   n
En Nahud
El Odaiya
Sûd
Bahir al Arab
Gogrial
Wâw
Tonj
Rumbek
Tall Post
Bôr
Amâdi
Yei
Yambio
Mongalla
Juba
L.
Turkana

Malha
1954
Kutum
El Fâsher
Nyala
D   a   r   f   u   r
Jabal Marra
3088
Zalingei
Nyala
Radom
Tembura
Rafa
Bahr el Ghazâl
Bahr
el
Ghazâl
Forodje
Dungu
Uele
3187

Emi Koussi
3415
Foyé-Largeau
E   n   n   e   d   i
Fada
Oum Chalouba
1310
Z   a   g   a   w   a
Biltine
Abéché
Oum Hadjer
Am Timan
Birao
Ndélé
Bokaranga
Ouaka
Mobaye
Mobayi

Ouanianga Sérir
Dépression du Mourdi
B   o   r   k   o   u
E   r   d   i
T   i   b   e   s   t   i
Zaghawa

N   I   G   E   R
Fachi
Bilma
Grand Erg de Bilma
Boultoum
Nguigmi
Bosso
Ngel
Geidam
Potiskum
Diku
Gombe
Biu
Mubi
Kumo
Numan
Yola

C   H   A   D
Mao
Lac Tchad
Bol
Ati
Moussoro
Bahr el Ghazâl
Massakory
Bokoro
Mongo
Gaz Beïda
Abou-Deïa
Salt

Ndjamena
Bongor
Kousséri
Maroua
Maiduguri
Bama
Guider
Garoua
Mbi
Bokoro
Moussoro
Lai
Bongor
Lagone
Moundou
Palo
Doba
Koumra
Baïbokoum
Bozoum
Bouar
Garoua
Carnot
Berbérati
Bossangoa
Bossembélé
Poala
Mbaïki
Bangui
Zongo
Ubengi
Bosobolo
Bambari
Sibut
Ippy
Bakouma
Yalinga
Kaga Bandoro

CENTRAL   AFRICAN
REPUBLIC

CAMEROON
Yaoundé
Abong-Mbang
Bertoua
Batouri
Ngaoundéré
Ngaoundaba
Massif de l'Adamaoua
Foumban
Yoko
Garoua
Banyo
Mbe

Projection: Sanson-Flamsteed's Sinusoidal

Tourist
Copyright Philips

**F**          **G**          **H**

East from Greenwich

1   2   3   4   5   6

A

15 | NIGER
Tanout
Zinder
Boultoum
Nguigmi
Lac Tchad
Mao
Zigey
Bilma El Ghazal
Moussoro
Abéché
Biltine
Al Junaynah
Oum Chalouba
Kutum
jebel Ma

B
Gumel
Kano
Azare
Hadeja
Potiskum
Geidam
Maiduguri
Kousseri
Ndjamena
Bokoro
Bama
Massakory
Massenya
Mongo
Gaz Beida
Abou-Deia
CHAD
Am Timan
Birao
Songo
Sarh
Nya
Jebel Ma

10
Bauchi
Gombe
Kumo
Biu
Mubi
Maroua
Guider
Bongor
Lai
Koumra
Ndélé
Mt Toussoro
1226
Sa'i
Jos
Shendam
Numan
Yola
Garoua
Pala
Moundou
Doba

C
Lafia
Makurdi
Wukari
Oturkpo
Gashaka
Banyo
Baïbokoum
Ngaoundéré
Poqua
Kaga Bandoro
CENTRAL AFRICAN
REPUBLIC
Yalinga
NIGERIA
Massif de
l'Adamaoua
Bétaré
Oya
Bossangoa
Bozoum
Sibut
Bambari
Ippy
Bakouma
Bamenda
Bafoussam
Foumban
Yoko
Bouar
Carnot
Bessembélé
Bangassou
Bomu

5
Calabar
Kumba
Mt Cameroun
4070
Limbe
Douala
Bioko
B. of Bon
Nkongsamba
Yaoundé
Simana
Bertoua
Nanga-
Eboko
Abang-Mbang
Mbalmayo
Yokadouma
Batouri
Nola
Berbérati
Mbaïki
Bangui
Zongo
Libenge
Bosobolo
Gemena
Businga
Mobaye
Mobayi
Bondo
Aketi
Congo

D
EQUATORIAL
GUINEA
Bata
Rio Muni
Libreville
Kribi
Ebolowa
Sangmélima
Djoum
Oyem
Souanké
Ouesso
Impfondo
Budjala
Bombome
Lisala
Busu Djanoa
Yahuma
Yangambi
Congo
Djolu
Opala

0
C. Lopez
Port-
Gentil
Omboué
GABON
Lambaréné
Koula Moutou
Booué
Makokou
Abalo
CONGO
Mbandaka
Bokote
Boende
Ikela
Monkoto
Lomela
Basin
CON
(DEM.

E
Tchibanga
Mouila
Mayumba
Mbigou
Lastoursville
Franceville
Gamboma
Ewo
Djambala
Owando
Bolobo
Bikoro
L. Tumba
Inongo
L.
Mai-Ndombe
Kutu
Mushie
Oshwe
Lukenii
Bandundu
Dekese
Kasai
Sankuru
Lodja
Lubumbashi
OF THE

5
Pointe-Noire
Cabinda
Cabinda
(Angola)
Loubomo
Madingou
Sibiti
Massendjo
Kinkala
Brazzaville
KINSHASA
Tshela
Kimpese
Mbanza Ngungu
Kenge
Kikwit
Idiofa
Dibaya-
Lubue
Ilebo
Mweka
Lusambo
Kananga
Mbuji-
Mayi
Kabinda

F
ATLANTIC
OCEAN
Matadi
Boma
Mbanza
Congo
Nzeto
Songo
Uíge
N'Gage
Ambriz
LUANDA
Quibaxi
Ndalatando
Maquela
do Zomba
Damba
Massango
Carnabatela
Calulo
Gunza
Gabela
Sumbe
Andulo
Malanje
Cambundi-
Catembo
Kasongo Lunda
Popokabaka
Luachimo
Tshikapa
Luachimo
Cacólo
Saurimo
Luau
Dilolo
Kasai
Cuango
Luremo
Caungula
Capenda
Camulemba
Lucapa
Kapanga
Sandoa
Mwene
Ditu
Gandajika
Lubilash
Luiza
Luilu
ANGOLA
K

East from Greenwich

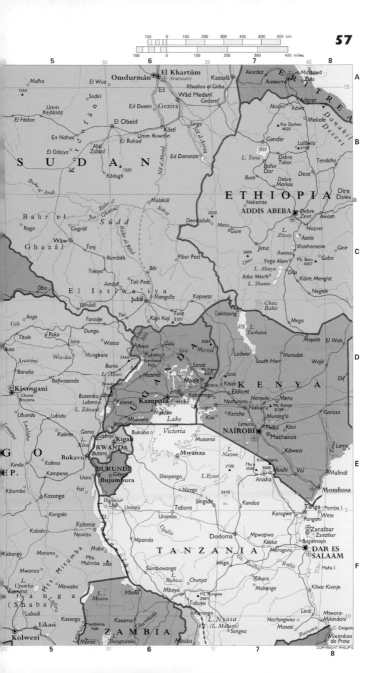

**57**

100 0 100 200 300 400 500 600 km
100 0 100 200 300 400 miles

5    30    6    35    7    40    8

Malha
1954
Umm Keddada
El Fâsher
En Nahud
El Odaiya
Abu Zabad

Sodiri
El Wuz
El Obeid
Umm Ruwaba
Er Rahad
1325
Kâdugli

Omdurmân
El Khartûm
(Khartoum)
El
Wâd Medanî
Gezira
Kôstî
Singa
Nîl el Azraq
Ed Damazin

Kassalâ
Khashm el Girba
Gedaref

Akordat
Asmera
Zula
Massawa

Aksum
Adwa
Adigrat
Mekele

**SUDAN**

Kordofan
Bahr ra Arab
Bahr el Ghazal
Jur
Gogrial
Tonj
Bahr el Abad
Malakâl
Sobat

Raga
Wâw
Ghazâl

Rumbêk
Toinya
Amadi
Tali Post
El Istiwa'iya
Bôr
Pibor Post

Obo
Yambiô
Juba
Mongalla
Kapoeta

Ras Dashen
4620
Gonder
Lalibela
4193
L. Tana
Bahir
Dar
Debre
Tabor
Bure
Debre
Markos
Nekemte
**ADDIS ABEBA**
Debre
Zeyit
Metu
Dembidolo
Gore
3202
Jima
Omo
Yirga Alem
Arba Minch
Dila
Kibre Mengist
L. Abaya
L. Shamo
Negele

**ETHIOPIA**
Dire
Dawa
Awash
Nazret
L.
Zway
Asela
Shashemene
Ginir
Awasa
Mt. Batu
4307
Goba

**ERITREA**

Danakil
Desert

Uele
Ango
Titule
Poko
Buta
Isiro
Dungu
Watsa
Faradje
Yei
Kajo Kaji
3187
Torit

Banalia
Bafwasende
Wamba
Mungbere
Bunia
L. Albert
Murchison
Falls
Arua
Pakwach
2444
Gulu

**Kisangani**
Chutes
Boyoma
Butembo
Luberoo
L. Edward
Masindi
Kasese
Kampala
Entebbe
Jinja
Tororo
Mbale
Mt. Elgon
4321

Ubundu
Lubutu
Mbarara
Kabale
Kisumu
Kisii
Kericho
Kakamega
Nyahururu
Nakuru

Kalima
Goma
Gisenyi
**Kigali**
**RWANDA**
Butare
Bukavu
L.
Kivu
**BURUNDI**
Gitega
**Bujumbura**

Kampene
Uvira
Fizi

Lokitaung
L.
Turkana
378
Lodwar
South Horn
Mega
Moyale
El Wak
Marsabit
Wajir

3206
**KENYA**
Kitale
Eldoret
Meru
Nanyuki
Mt. Kenya
5199
Murang'a
Kitui
Thika
**NAIROBI**
Machakos
Kibwezi

Dif
Garissa

Kôndoa
Nzega
L.
Natron
Meru
4565
Kilimanjaro
5895
Moshi
Arusha
Vol

Tanga
Pemba I.
Wete
Pangani
Zanzibar
Zanzibar
Bagamoyo
**DAR ES
SALAAM**
Mafia I.

Lamu
Malindi
**Mombasa**

Kibombo
Kasongo
Kongolo
Kabalo
Kalemie
Nyunzu
Moba

Ujiji
Uvinza
Urambo
Tabora
Singida
3418

Mpanda
Mbeya
Mpwapwa
Kilosa
Dodoma
Iringa
Morogoro
Gt. Ruaha
Rufiji

**TANZANIA**

Kabongo
Manono
Mwanza
L.
Kamina
Mitwaba
Malimba
2460
Mts. Mitumba
tanga
(Shaba)
Lubudi
Likasi
Kolwezi

L.
Upemba
Kasenga
Chambeshi
Kasama
L. Mweru
Mbala
Karonga
Tukuyu
Mt. Rungwe
2961
Sumbawanga
L.
Rukwa
Chunya
Ifakara
Mahenge
Kilwa Kivinje

**ZAMBIA**
Mpika
Mzuzu
L. Nyasa
(L. Malawi)
Songea
Nachingwea
Masasi
Lindi
Mtwara-Mikindani
C. Delgado
Mocimboa
da Praia

Mansa
Bangweulu
Hambilima
Falls

**GO
EP.**
Kindu
Kibombo

Mwanza
Kamina

Kolwezi

Kapoeta
Jinja
**Kampala**
Mubende
Lake
Victoria
Bukoba
Mwanza
Musoma
Shinyanga
L. Eyasi

Mbarara
Masaka

 Entebbe

A
B
C
D
E
F

15
5
5
10

COPYRIGHT PHILIP'S

ANGOLA

Lobito
Benguela
Lubango
Namibe
Tombua
Chibia
Chibemba

Ovamboland
Oshikoti
Ondangwa
Etosha
Pan
Tsumeb
Grootfontein

Damaraland
Outjo
Otjiwarongo

NAMIBIA
Omaruru
Usakos
Swakopmund
Walvis Bay
Windhoek
Rehoboth
Gobabis

BOTSWANA

Kalahari

Maltahohe
Mariental
Gibeon

Namaland
Lüderitz
Keetmanshoop

SOUTH AFR

Port Nolloth
Nababeep
Bitterfontein

CAPE TOWN
Cape of Good Hope

ATLANTIC OCEAN

Tropic of Capricorn

**59**

Scale bars:
100 0 100 200 300 400 500 600 km
100 0 100 200 300 400 miles

**Zambia / Zimbabwe region**

Kipushi · Lubumbashi · Mpika · Lundazi · Lugenda · Quissanga
Solwezi · Chililabombwe · Mufulira · Lichinga · Marrupa · Pemba
Chingola · Kitwe · Ndola · Nchatokota · Chipata · Montepuez
Kasempa · Luanshya · Kapiri Mposhi · Petauke · Mangoche · Cuamba · Namapa · Nacala
Luhaka Swamp · Kabwe · Lilongwe · Salima · Malemo · Nampula · Moçambique
Mazabuka · Lusaka · Fingoe · Zomba · L. Chilwa · Alto Molocue · Angoche
Kafue · Monze · L. de Cuhora Bassa · Songo · Blantyre · Pte Manje 3000 · Mocuba · Moma
Choma · Kariba Dam · Mashonaland · Tete · Nsanje · Pebane
Livingstone · Kariba Gorge · Mazoe · Chemba · Quelimane
Victoria Falls · Lake Kariba · Chinhoyi · Bindura · Chinde
Hwange · Shangani · Chegutu · HARARE · Marondera · Chitungwiza
Matabeleland · Kadoma · Odzi · Monica · Mutare · Shimoia
Tuium · ZIMBABWE · Kwekwe · Gweru · Mvuma
Bulawayo · Shurugwi · Masvingo · Zvishavane · Beira
Plumtree · Gwanda · Chiredzi
Makgadikgadi Salt Pans · Francistown · Beitbridge · I. do Bazaruto · Bassas da India (Réunion)
Orapa · Selebi-Pikwe · Musina · Vilanculos
Serowe · Palapye · Makhado · Thohoyandou · Pta. da Barra Falsa · Île Europa (Réunion)
Mahalapye · Polokwane · Tzaneen · Massinga
Molepolole · Mochudi · Madimolle · Mokopane · Guijá · Inhambane
Gaborone · Thabazimbi · Marão · Inharrime
Lobatse · Rustenburg · Nelspruit
JOHANNESBURG · PRETORIA · Benoni · Witbank · Xai-Xai
Soweto · Germiston · Springs · MAPUTO
Potchefstroom · Vereeniging · Mbabane · SWAZILAND · Mayotte (Fr)
Klerksdorp · Kroonstad · Piet Retief · Bela Vista
Bloemhof · Bethlehem · Mdadeni · Vryheid
Welkom · Virginia · Ladysmith · Empangeni
Bloemfontein · Thaba Nchu 3483 · Richards Bay
Maseru · LESOTHO · Pietermaritzburg
Mafeteng · DURBAN · Kwa Mashu · Umlazi
Aliwal North · Kokstad · Maclear · Port Shepstone
Queenstown · Umzimvubu
Zwelitsha · Gcuwa · Umtata
East London · Mdantsane · Grahamstown

**INDIAN OCEAN**

**MADAGASCAR**
On same scale

Is. Glorieuses (Réunion)
T.'i Bobrsomby · Antsiranana
Andoany Nosy Be · Ambilobe · Iharana
Ambanja · Tsaratanana 2876 · Andapa
Antsohihy · Antalaha · Maroantsetra
Sofia · T.'i Masoala
Mahajanga · Mandritsara
Marovoay · Nosy Boraha
Besalampy · Maevatanana · Fenoarivo Atsinanana
Morafenobe · Ambatondrazaka · Toamasina
Nosy Barren · Antananarivo · Moramanga
Belo-Tsiribihina · Ankaratra 2643 · Ambatolampy
Miandrivazo · Antsirabe
Morondava · Mahabo · Ambositra · Nosy Varika
Ambohimahasoa · Mananjary
Morombe · Mangoky · Fianarantsoa · Ambalavao
T. Ankaboa · Pic Boby 2658 · Manakara
Ranohira · Ihosy · Farafangana
Toliara · Onilahy · Betroka · Vangaindrano
Ampanihy
Ambovombe · Taolanaro
T.'i Vohemar

**INDIAN OCEAN**
Tropic of Capricorn

COPYRIGHT PHILIP'S

Projection: Lambert's Equivalent Azimuthal

East from Greenwich

100 0 100 200 300 400 500 600 700 800 km
100 0 100 200 300 400 500 miles

**7** 145 **8** 150 **9** 155 **10** **11** 160

New
Guinea
Mount Hagen ○ 4508 ▲ Mt. Wilhelm Lae
**PAPUA NEW GUINEA**
Owen Stanley Range
Fly
Gulf of
Papua
Port ⊕
Moresby
D'Entrecasteaux
Islands
Louisiade
Archipelago

2743 ▲ Mt. Balbi Bougainville
9140 ▲
New Britain
Solomon
Sea
New
Georgia
Choiseul **SOLOMON
ISLANDS**
Santa Isabel
Honiara ○ ▲ 2439
Guadalcanal
Malaita
San
Cristóbal
Rennell

B

Torres Strait
C. York

10

Weipa ○ **Cape
York
Peninsula**
Cooktown ○

*Coral Sea*

C

Wellesley
Is.
Mitchell
Normanton ○
Forsayth ○
Cairns
1611 ▲

*P A C I F I C*

15

CORAL
SEA
ISLANDS
TERRITORY
Îles Chesterfield
Îles D'Entrecasteaux
Kajabbi ○
Flinders
Mount
Isa
Cloncurry
Dajarra ○
Townsville ○
Charters Towers ○
Hughenden ○

*O C E A N*

D

20

Winton ○
**QUEENSLAND**
Mackay
E

Emerald
Rockhampton ○
Gladstone
Tropic of Capricorn

**L I A**
Longreach ○
Yaraka ○
Diamantina
Bundaberg
Maryborough
Gympie

25

Creek
Charleville ○
Quilpie ○
Cooper
Lake Eyre
A
Marree ○
Roma
Toowoomba ○
**BRISBANE**
Ipswich
Gold
Coast

F

Thargomindah ○
Cunnamulla ○
Dirranbandi ○
Warrego
Moree ○
Lismore ○
Grafton ○

Bourke ○
Walgett ○
Round
Mt. ▲ 1615

30

Port
Augusta
Flinders Ranges
Broken Hill ○
Cobar ○
Tamworth ○
Port
Macquarie
Taree ○

**NEW SOUTH**
Darling
Dubbo ○
**Newcastle** ○
Bathurst ○

Lord Howe I.
(Austral.)
▼ 734

G

Port Pirie
St Vincent
**ADELAIDE**
Murray
Mildura ○
Griffith ○
Hay ○
Orange ○
**WALES**
Goulburn ○
**SYDNEY**
Wollongong

*T a s m a n   S e a*

35

Gulf
Encounter
Swan Hill ○
Wagga Wagga ○
Mt.
Kosciuszko
2230 ▲
Shepparton ○
Albury
Wodonga
**Canberra**
A.C.T.
Bombala ○

Murray
Snowy Mts.

Hersham ○
Bendigo ○
Ballarat ○
**VICTORIA**
**MELBOURNE**
Geelong
Sale ○
C. Howe

H

Mount Gambier ○
Warrnambool ○

*Bass Strait*

King I.
Furneaux Group
▼ 5267

40

**N**

Burnie ○
Launceston ○

J

**TASMANIA**
1617 ▲ Mt. Ossa
Hobart
S.E. Cape

**6** 140 **7** **8** 150 **9** **10** **11**

East from Greenwich

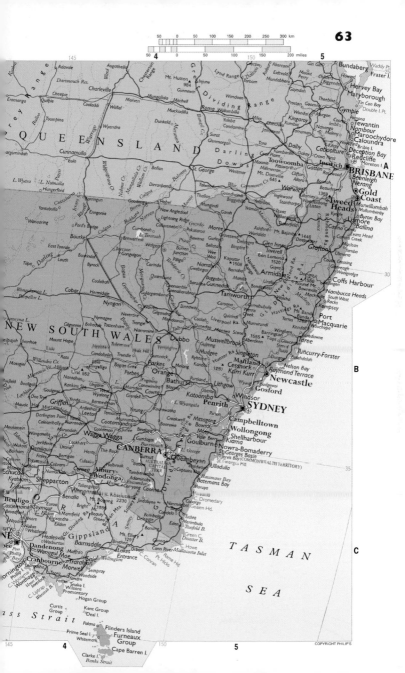

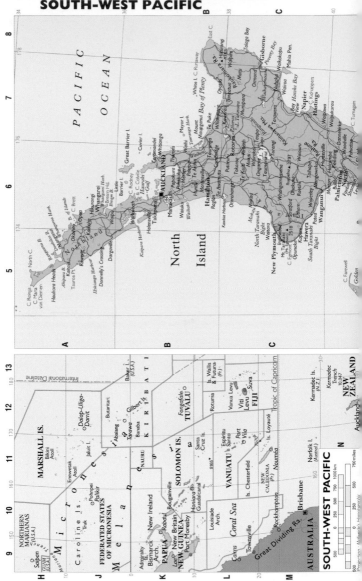

PACIFIC OCEAN

North Island

AUCKLAND

Hamilton

New Plymouth

Napier

Hastings

Wanganui

Palmerston North

SOUTH-WEST PACIFIC

NORTHERN MARIANAS (U.S.A.)

Saipan

GUAM (U.S.A.)

MARSHALL IS.

Bikini Atoll

Enewetak Atoll

Jaluit I.

Caroline Is.

Truk

FEDERATED STATES OF MICRONESIA

Pohnpei

Palikir

Micronesia

Melanesia

NAURU

Banaba

KIRIBATI

Tarawa

Abaiang

Gilbert Is.

Butaritari

Baker I. (U.S.A.)

International Dateline

Dalap-Uliga-Darrit

PAPUA NEW GUINEA

Port Moresby

Lae

New Britain

Rabaul

New Ireland

Bougainville

Admiralty Is.

Bismarck Arch.

SOLOMON IS.

Honiara

Guadalcanal

Santa Cruz Is.

TUVALU

Fongafale

Rotuma

Is. Wallis & Futuna (Fr.)

FIJI

Vanua Levu

Viti Levu

Suva

VANUATU

Espiritu Santo

Port Vila

Louisiade Arch.

Coral Sea

Is. Chesterfield

NEW CALEDONIA (Fr.)

Nouméa

Is. Loyauté

Tropic of Capricorn

Norfolk I. (Austral.)

Kermadec Is. (N.Z.)

Kermadec Trench 10,047

NEW ZEALAND

Auckland

AUSTRALIA

Brisbane

Rockhampton

Great Dividing Ra.

Townsville

Cairns

N

0   250   500   750   1000 km

0   250   500   750 miles

Projection: McBryde's Homolographic

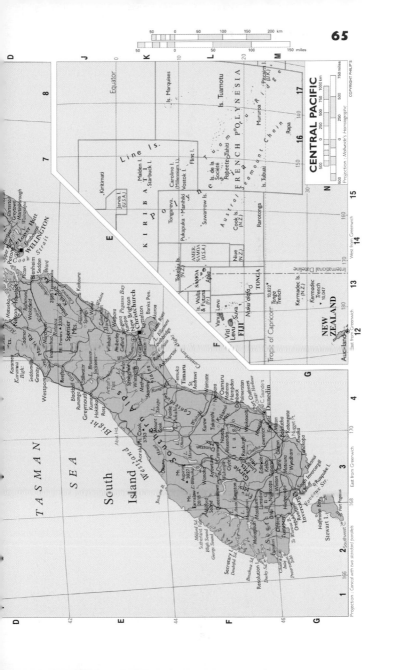

**65**

50   0   50   100   150   200 km
50   0   50   100   150 miles

TASMAN SEA

South Island

Southern Alps

Westland Bight

Stewart I.

Mt. Aspiring
2818 ▲
Mt. Cook 3753 ▲

Karamea Bight

WELLINGTON
Cook Strait
Lower Hutt
Petone
Porirua

Blenheim
Marlborough

Spenser Mts.
Mt. Travers ▲ 2338

Pegasus Bay
New Brighton
Christchurch
Lyttelton
Banks Pen.

Canterbury Plains

Timaru
St. Andrews
Oamaru

Dunedin

Invercargill
Foveaux Str.

Milford Sd.
Sutherland Falls
Bligh Sound
George Sound
Secretary I.
Doubtful Sd.
Dusky Sd.
Breaksea I.
Resolution I.
Dagg Sd.
Preservation Inlet

Fiordland

Half-moon Bay
Ruapuke I.

Port Pegasus

**NEW ZEALAND**

Auckland

Tropic of Capricorn

**FIJI**
Viti Levu
Suva
Vanua Levu

TONGA
Nuku'alofa
10,882 Tonga Trench

Kermadec Is. (N.Z.)
Kermadec Trench 10,047

Wallis & Futuna (Fr.)

SAMOA
AMER. SAMOA (U.S.A.)
Apia

Tokelau (N.Z.)

Niue (N.Z.)

Pukapuka · Manihiki
Suwarrow (N.Z.)
Cook Is. (N.Z.)
Rarotonga

Tongareva

Caroline I.
(Millennium I.)
Vostok I.
Flint I.

Malden I.
Starbuck I.

KIRIBATI
Jarvis I. (U.S.A.)

Line Is.

· Kiritimati

Is. Marquises

Is. Tuamotu

Is. de la Société
Papeete · Tahiti
FRENCH POLYNESIA

Tuamotu

Austral or Tubuai Is.
Is. Tubuai
Rapa

Tuamotu Chain

Mururoa I.
Pitcairn I. (U.K.)

Equator

International Dateline

**CENTRAL PACIFIC**
500   0   250   500   750   1000 km
500   0   250   500   750 miles
Projection: Molweide's Homolographic

COPYRIGHT PHILIP'S

Projection: Conical with two standard parallels

West from Greenwich
East from Greenwich

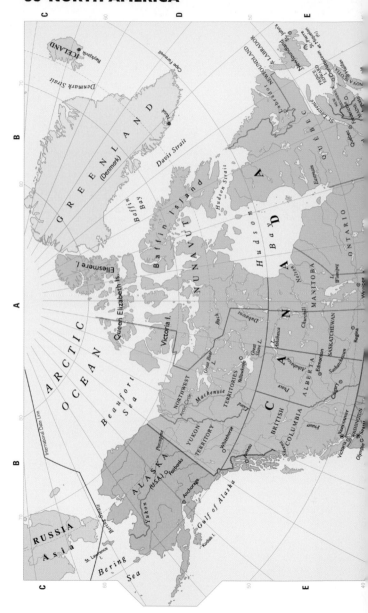

100   0   100   200   300   400   500   600 km
100   0   100   200   300   400 miles

**ALASKA**

100   0   100   200   300   400   500   600 km
100   0   100   200   300   400 miles

Projection : Bonne

COPYRIGHT PHILIP'S

PACIFIC OCEAN

ONTARIO

MANITOBA

SASKATCHEWAN

ALBERTA

BRITISH COLUMBIA

WASHINGTON

UNITED STATES

MINNESOTA

NORTH DAKOTA

SOUTH DAKOTA

NEBRASKA

IOWA

MONTANA

ST. PAUL

MINNEAPOLIS

WISCONSIN

Winnipeg

Lake Winnipeg

Regina

Saskatoon

Calgary

Edmonton

VANCOUVER

SEATTLE

Vancouver I.

Omaha

Duluth

Superior

Lake of the Woods

Rocky Mountains

Selkirk Mts.

Cascade Range

CHUKCHI SEA

BERING SEA

GULF OF ALASKA

ALASKA

R U S S I A

Brooks Range

Fairbanks

Anchorage

Nome

Kodiak I.

Aleutian Is.

Andreanof Is.

Near Is.

Rat Is.

St Lawrence I.

St Matthew I.

Pribilof Is.

Nunivak I.

Queen Charlotte Is.

Alexander Archipelago

Prudhoe Bay

Mt McKinley
6194

West from Greenwich

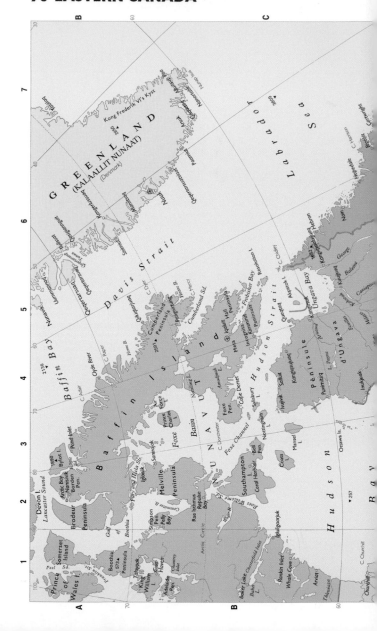

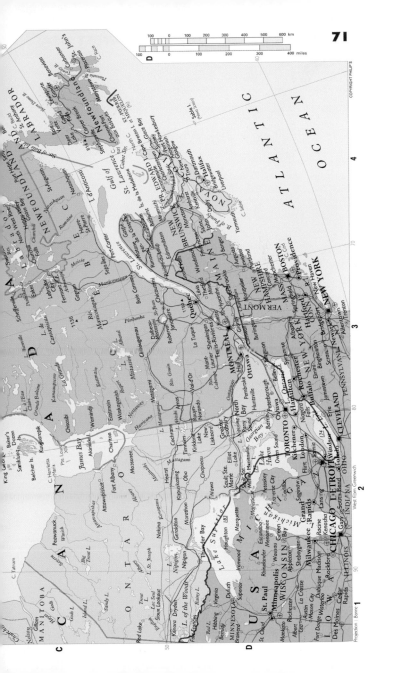

D

| 100 | 0 | 100 | 200 | 300 | 400 | 500 | 600 km |

| 100 | 0 | 100 | 200 | 300 | 400 miles |

50

40

COPYRIGHT PHILIP'S

King George I.
Baker's
Dozen
Sankikluaq
Kuujjuaraapik
Pte. Louis XIV

Belcher Is.
C. Henrietta
Maria

James Bay
Akimiski I.
Fort Albany
Attawapiskat

CANADA

Nelson
Gillam
Kettle
Split L.
Shamattawa
Hayes
God's L.
Island L.
God's River

C. Tatnam

MANITOBA

Churchill

Seal
Sandy L.
Deer L.
Big
Trout L.
L. St. Joseph
Ogoki
Nakina
Kwenagami

Red L.
L. of the Woods
Kenora
Rainy L.
Fort Frances

ONTARIO

Sachigo
Winisk
Peawanuck
Severn

Attawapiskat
Albany
Ogoki
Marathon
Geraldton
Longlac
L. Nipigon
Nipigon
Thunder Bay

Wawa

Fawn
Ekwan

Mesakamika
Lansdowne House

Moosonee
Moose
Moose Factory
Kapuskasing
Hearst
Obo
Mattagami
Chapleau

Missinaibi
Kesagami
L. Abitibi
Cochrane
Timmins
Kirkland
Lake
New
Liskeard

Charlton I.

Chisasibi
La Grande
Kanaaupscow
Eastmain

Wemindji

Nemiscau

QUÉBEC

La Grande Rivière

Mistassini
L. Mistassini
Waswanipi
Matagami
Rouyn-
Noranda
Val-d'Or
Senneterre
Amos

Chibougamau

LABRADOR

Schefferville
Fermont
Wabush

Kaniapiskau

Eskei
Gagnon
L. de
Caniapiscau

Gander

NEWFOUNDLAND

Péribonka
Chicoutimi
Dolbeau
Mistassini
St-Félicien
Roberval
Alma
L. St-Jean

Rés.
Manicouagan
Baie Comeau

Pte. des Monts
Hauterive

Sept-Îles
Port-Cartier

Havre-
St-Pierre
Natashquan
Romaine

Moisie

Labrador
City

LABRADOR

Harrington
Nain
Hopedale
Makkovik
Cartwright
North West River
Happy Valley-Goose Bay
Lake
Melville
Churchill
Falls

NEWFOUNDLAND

L'Anse au Loup
St-Augustin

Blanc
Sablon

1136

Nutshimit

La Tuque

Shawinigan
Trois-Rivières

Mont-
Laurier

Grand'Mère

MONTRÉAL
Hull
Ottawa
Cornwall

St-Hyacinte
Drummondville
Sherbrooke
Granby

QUÉBEC
Lévis

Montmagny

Matane

Rimouski
Mont-Joli
Rivière-du-Loup
Édmundston

NEW
BRUNSWICK

Campbellton
Bathurst

Gaspé
Chaleur Bay
Campbellton
Miramichi
Newcastle

Moncton

Î. d'Anticosti
Gulf of
St. Lawrence

PRINCE
EDWARD
ISLAND

Charlottetown
Summerside
Magdalen Is.
Îs. de la Madeleine

Cabot Str.
North Pt.
Cape Breton I.
Sydney
Glace Bay

NOVA
SCOTIA

New Glasgow
Truro
Amherst
Pictou
Antigonish
Port Hawkesbury

Dartmouth
Halifax

Bridgewater
Liverpool
C. Sable

St. Pierre
et Miquelon
(Fr.)
ST-PIERRE
et MIQUELON

Burgeo
Port aux
Basques

Corner Brook
Deer Lake
Stephenville

St-Barbe

NEWFOUNDLAND

Botwood
Grand Falls
Gander
Bonavista

Placentia

St. John's
C. Race

Sable I.
(Nova Scotia)

ATLANTIC
OCEAN

MAINE
Houlton
Presque Isle
Woodstock
Fredericton
Saint John
Bay of Fundy
Bangor
Augusta
Waterville
Lewiston
Portland

NEW
HAMPSHIRE
Concord
Manchester

VERMONT
Montpelier
Burlington

NEW
YORK

Montréal

Ogdensburg
Potsdam
Watertown

Lake
Ontario

Syracuse
Rochester
Buffalo
Niagara
Falls

L. Erie

Jamestown
Erie

Belleville
Kingston
Peterborough
Barrie
Orillia

Owen Sound
Georgian
Bay

Greater
Sudbury
North
Bay
Sturgeon
Falls

L. Nipissing
Pembroke
Huntsville
Parry
Sound

Sault Ste.
Marie

Espanola
Manitoulin
I.

Lake
Huron

Sarnia
London
Kitchener
Hamilton
TORONTO
Oshawa

Bridgeport
New Haven
Hartford

MASS.
BOSTON
Providence
C. Cod

CONN.

NEW YORK
Allentown
Trenton
Newark

PENNSYLVANIA
Scranton
Binghamton
Elmira

Albany
Schenectady

CLEVELAND
OHIO

DETROIT
Windsor
Flint
Lansing
Saginaw
Bay City
Pontiac

MICHIGAN

I-24
I-75

South Bend
INDIANA

Gary
CHICAGO

ILLINOIS

Rockford

Lake
Michigan

Milwaukee
Racine
Kenosha

WISCONSIN
Madison
Sheboygan
Green
Bay
Appleton
Oshkosh
Wausau
Rhinelander

Escanaba
Menominee

Marquette
Houghton

Lake
Superior

Duluth
Superior

Ironwood

MINNESOTA

St. Cloud
Minneapolis
St. Paul

Brainerd
Bemidji
Hibbing
Virginia

IOWA

Des Moines
Cedar
Rapids
Dubuque
Waterloo
Mason City
Fort Dodge
Austin
Albert Lea
La Crosse
Rochester
Mankato

USA

Projection : Bonne

West from Greenwich

C

1

2

3

4

90

80

70

VANCOUVER
Port Coquitlam
Nanaimo
Lodysmith
Vancouver Island
Duncan
Chillwack
BRITISH CO

C. Flattery
Neah Bay
La Push
Strait of Juan de Fuca
Victoria
Esquimalt
C. Alava
Port Angeles
Port Townsend
New Westminster
Bellingham
Baker Mt.
▲3285
Oliver
Grand Forks
Rossland
Republic
Metaline Falls

NORTH
CASCADES
NAT. PARK
Sedro Woolley
Mount Vernon
Concrete
Glacier Peak
▲3285
Winthrop
Okanogan
Omak
Franklin D.
Roosevelt L.
Kettle Falls
Colville
Chewelah
Newport
Sandpoint
Bonners
Priest

C. Alava
Mt. Olympus
▲2428
OLYMPIC
NAT. PARK
Moclips
Hoquiam
Aberdeen
Grays Harbor
Hoodsport
Shelton
Bremerton
SEATTLE
Tacoma
WASHINGTON
Renton
Everett
Edmonds
Leavenworth
Wenatchee
Coulee
Grand Coulee
Davenport
Spokane
Opportunity
Deer Park
Coeur
d'Alene
Post Falls
St. Maries

Ocean Park
Long Beach
C. Disappointment
Raymond
Willapa
B.
Olympia
Elma
Centralia
Chehalis
Puyallup
Ellensburg
MOUNT RAINIER
NAT. PARK
Mt. Rainier
▲4392
Naches
Ephrata
Moses Lake
Columbia
Basin
Cheney
Ritzville
Colfax
Pullman
Moscow
Bovill

46
Warrenton
Astoria
Seaside
Cannon Beach
Longview
Kelso
St. Helens
Columbia
Cathlamet
Mt. St.
Helens
▲2549
Centralia
Mt. Adams
▲3751
Yakima
Toppenish
Sunnyside
Grandview
Prosser
Othello
Connell
Kennewick
Pasco
Richland
Wallula
Waitsburg
Dayton
Lewiston
Orofino

Tillamook
C. Meares
PORTLAND
Beaverton
Milwaukie
Newberg
Oregon City
Vancouver
Camas
The Dalles
Klickitat
Goldendale
Columbia
Hood River
Mt. Hood
▲3427
Arlington
Hermiston
Milton-Freewater
Weston
Walla Walla
Winchester
Grangeville

Lincoln
City
Newport
McMinnville
Dallas
Salem
Keizer
Woodburn
Canby
Silverton
Stayton
Madras
Condon
Fossil
Pendleton
Pilot Rock
Elgin
Wallowa
Enterprise
White Bird
Riggins

44
Toledo
Waldport
Monmouth
Corvallis
Albany
Lebanon
Philomath
Sweet Home
Mt. Jefferson
▲3206
Prineville
John Day
Spray
Long
Creek
North Powder
La Grande
Haines
Baker City
Blue
Mountains
New
Meadows
McCall

Florence
Reedsport
North Bend
Coos Bay
Coquille
Junction City
Eugene
Springfield
Cottage Grove
McKenzie
Three Sisters
▲3166
Redmond
Bend
Mitchell
Dayville
Prairie City
Huntington
Brogan
Council
Cascade
Res.
Cascade

E
Myrtle Point
Bandon
Roseburg
Myrtle Creek
Canyonville
Oakridge
La Pine
Brothers
OREGON
Riley
Burns
Harney Basin
Crane
Weiser
Payette
Ontario
Nyssa
New Plymouth
Emmett
Caldwell
Nampa
Boise
S

C. Blanco
Port Orford
Gold Beach
Rogue
R.
Coos
Valley
Greens
Grants Pass
Sutherlin
White Mt.
McLoughlin
CRATER LAKE
NAT. PARK
Silver L.
Chemult
Summer L.
Paisley
Malheur
L.
Owyhee
Murphy
Jordan
Valley
Idaho City
Mountain
Home
Bru

Brookings
42
Crescent
City
Happy
Camp
Hornbrook
Central Point
Medford
Ashland
Klamath Falls
Altamont
Chiloquin
Upper
Klamath L.
Valley Falls
Lakeview
Alvord
Desert
Steens Mountain
▲2962
McDermitt
Owyhee
Mountain City
Contact

REDWOOD
NAT. PARK
Arcata
Eureka
Klamath
Weed
Mt. Shasta
▲4317
Mount Shasta
Dorris
Alturas
Clear Lake
Goose
L.
Warner
Mts.
Upper
Alkali L.
Middle
Alkali L.
Lower
Alkali L.
Cedarville
Paradise
Valley
Winnemucca
Golconda
Battle
Mountain
Carlin
Elko
Wells

F
Elkota
Fortuna
Scotia
Weott
Garberville
Redding
Anderson
Red Bluff
LASSEN
VOLCANIC
NAT. PARK
Lassen Peak
▲3187
Burney
Bieber
Eagle L.
Susanville
Greenville
Rye Patch
Res.
Imlay
Lovelock
Humboldt
R.
Independence Mts.
Dunphy
Ruby Mts.
Franklin
Ruby
Diamond Mts.

124
Pt. Brago
Medocino
Willits
Ukiah
Upper
Lake
Clearlake
Orland
Willows
Chico
Paradise
Oroville
Quincy
Portola
Truckee
Wadsworth
Fernley
Carson
Sink
Stillwater Ra.
Trinity
Ra.
Battle
Mountain
Austin
Eureka
McGill
Ely

G
Cloverdale
Santa Rosa
Petaluma
Napa
San Rafael
Vacaville
Fairfield
Vallejo
Berkeley
Richmond
Arbuckle
Woodland
Davis
Sacramento
Lodi
Yuba City
Marysville
Roseville
Auburn
Placerville
Camino
South Lake
Tahoe
Carson
City
Minden
Schurz
Walker L.
Mt. Grant
▲3408
Hawthorne
Luning
Toiyabe
Ra.
Shoshone Mountains
Round
Mountain
Currant
NEVADA
Range

38
San
Richmond
Golden Gate
Fairfield
Concord
Lodi
Jackson
Tone
Carson
Virginia City
Sparks
Reno
Fernley
Fallon
Hawthorne

50  0  50  100  150  200 km
50  0  50  100  150 miles

116  **6**  114  **7**  112  **8**  110  **9**  108  **10**

A

**C O L U M B I A**   **A**   **L   B   E   R   T   A**   **C   A   N   A   D   A**   **SASKATCHEWAN**

Crowsnest Pass
Fernie
Coalhurst
Picture Butte
Taber
Medicine
Maple Creek
Swift Current
Gull Lake
GravelBourg
Pontelx
50

Cranbrook
Crowsnest
Pass
Macleod
Lethbridge
Island
Hat
Eastend
Shaunavon

B

Mt Cleveland
3190
Babb
Cardston
Raymond
Magrath
Milk River
Sweetgrass
Sunburst
Turner
Opheim

Eureka
GLACIER
NAT PARK
Stryker
Whitefish
Browning
Shelby
Hingham
Chester
Fremo
Chinook
Harlem
Dodson

Kalispell
Columbia
Falls
Evergreen
Cut Bank
Valier
Conrad
Big Sandy
Bearpaw Mts.
Havre
Motta
Glasgow
Nashua

Somers
Flathead L.
Dupuyer
2708
Baldy Mt.
Fort Peck
Dam
Fort Peck

Thompson
Falls
Plains
Swan Range
2891
Choteau
Teton
Fort
Benton
Missouri
Fort Peck Lake

St Regis
Ronan
St Ignatius
Augusta
Cascade
Geraldine
Jordan

Superior
Missoula
Blackfoot
Wolf Creek
Belt
Geyser
Benton
Roy
Winnett
C
Helena
Stanford
Lewistown

Stevensville
Garrison
East Helena
White Sulphur
Springs
Judith Gap
Grass
Range
Rock Springs

Hamilton
Philipsburg
Deer Lodge
Townsend
Harlowton
Roundup
Melstone
Ingomar

Anaconda
Butte
Boulder
Crazy
Mts.
Ryegate
Musselshell

Trapper Pk.
3090
Whitehall
Three Forks
Wilsall
Big Timber
Billings
Forsyth

Wisdom
Divide
Belgrade
Bozeman
Livingston
Columbus
Laurel
Hardin
Crow Agency
Lame Deer
Ashland
46

Dillon
Twin Bridges
Ennis
Virginia City
Red Lodge
Belfry
Bridger
Bighorn
Lodge Grass

Lima
Gardiner
Granite Peak
4001
Clarks Fork
YELLOWSTONE
Powell
Lovell
Ranchester
Sheridan

D
Hebgen
L.
West
Yellowstone
Junction
NATIONAL PARK
Cody
Greybull
Dayton
Nevada

GRAND TETON
NAT PARK
Jackson
L.
Yellowstone
Basin
Meeteetse
Worland
Cloud Peak
4013
Bighorn
Buffalo

St
Anthony
Driggs
Grand Teton
4009
Moran
Junction
Franks Pk.
4009
Thermopolis
Kaycee
44

Idaho
Falls
Jackson
Green
Riverton
Shoshoni
Lander
Powder River
Midwest

Blackfoot
Gannett Peak
4202
Wind
Waltman
Casper
E

Pocatello
Daniel
Pinedale
Hudson
Lander
Alcova
Glenrock

Soda
Springs
Afton
Big Piney
Sweetwater
Jeffrey
City
Lamont
Pathfinder
Reservoir

Malad City
Montpelier
Paris
La Barge
Fontenelle
Res.
Farson
Seminoe
Res.

Preston
Cokeville
Green
River
Rock
Springs
Wamsutter
Rawlins
Hanna
Walcott
Medicine
Bow
42

Logan
Kemmerer
Granger
Bitter Creek
Sinclair
Saratoga
Baggs
Laramie

Great Salt
Lake
1282
Brigham City
Evanston
Fort Bridger
Flaming
Gorge Reservoir
Encampment

Ogden
Morgan
Lyman
Manila
Mountain
Steamboat
Springs
Walden
ROCKY
MOUNTAIN
NAT PARK

West Valley City
Salt Lake
City
King's Peak
4123
Uinta Mountains
DINOSAUR
NATIONAL MONUMENT
Craig
Hayden
Granby
F

Great
Salt Lake
Desert
Tooele
Jordan
Heber City
Vernal
Meeker
Kremmling
40

Provo
Orem
Springville
Duchesne
Roosevelt
C O L O R A D O
Central City
Georgetown

Sevier
Nephi
Spanish
Fork
Strawberry
White
Rangely
Glenwood
Springs
Breckenridge

Desert
Manti
Mt.
Pleasant
Helper
Price
Roan Plateau
Rifle
Eagle
G

Delta
Ephraim
Castle Dale
Huntington
Carbondale

**7**  West from Greenwich  **8**  **9**  **10**  COPYRIGHT PHILIP'S  **11**

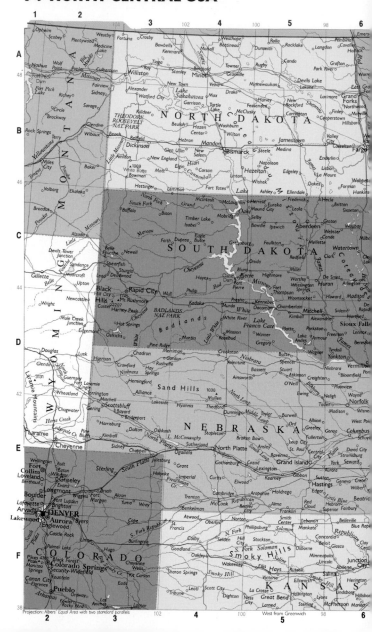

West from Greenwich

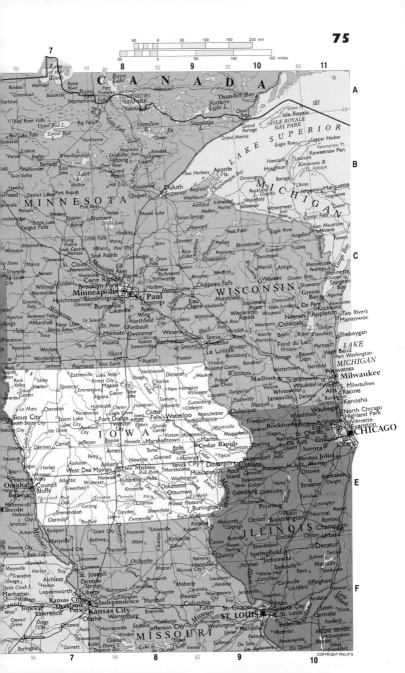

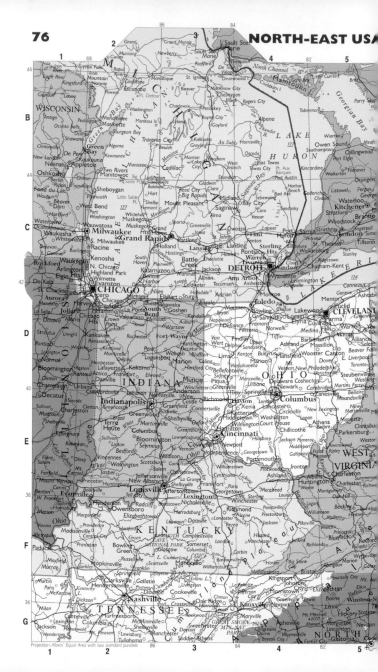

Projection: Albers' Equal Area with two standard parallels

**NEVADA**

San Francisco, Oakland, San Mateo, Redwood City, Sunnyvale, Hayward, Fremont, San Jose, Santa Cruz, Watsonville, Pacific Grove, Monterey, Seaside, Gonzales, Salinas, Gilroy, Hollister, Stockton, Manteca, Modesto, Turlock, Atwater, Merced, Los Banos, Gustine, Patterson, Mariposa, Madera, Fresno, Clovis, Mendota, Kingsburg, Reedley, Selma, Hanford, Lemoore, Tulare, Corcoran, Visalia, Delano, Wasco, Shafter, Earlimart, Porterville, Lindsay, Bakersfield, Taft, Buttonwillow, Maricopa, Lebec, Tehachapi, Ridgecrest, Searles L., Mojave, Lancaster, Palmdale, Barstow, Victorville, Hesperia, Ludlow, Los Angeles, Burbank, Glendale, Pasadena, Beverly Hills, Santa Monica, Inglewood, Long Beach, Huntington Beach, Newport Beach, Anaheim, Santa Ana, Mission Viejo, Ontario, San Bernardino, Riverside, Corona, Banning, Hemet, Palm Springs, Indio, Twentynine Palms, Coachella, San Clemente, Oceanside, Carlsbad, Escondido, Ramona, La Mesa, El Cajon, San Diego, Chula Vista, Tijuana, Tecate, Mexicali, El Centro, Calexico, Brawley, Westmorland, Calipatria, Holtville, San Luis Río Colorado, Somerton, San Luis, Wellton, Yuma

**SEQUOIA NAT. PARK**, **KINGS CANYON NAT. PARK**, **YOSEMITE NAT. PARK**, **DEATH VALLEY NAT. PARK**, **JOSHUA TREE NAT. PARK**, **CHANNEL IS. NAT. PARK**

Las Vegas, North Las Vegas, Henderson, Boulder City, Goldfield, Tonopah, Warm Springs, Pioche, Panaca, Caliente, Hiko, Alamo, Indian Springs, Mesquite, Overton, Kingman, Bullhead City, Needles, Topock, Yucca, Parker, Blythe, Quartzsite, Salome

**PACIFIC OCEAN**

Mojave Desert, New York Mts., Sonoran Desert, Desierto de Altar, Sierra de Juárez, Sierra de San Pedro Mártir, Ensenada, Pta. Santo Tomas, Santo Tomas, C. Colonet, San Telmo, San Quintín, C. San Quintín, El Rosario, Pta. Baja, Pta. San Antonio, San Felipe, Puerto Peñasco, B. San Jorge, Cerro de la Encantada 3078, **BAJA CALIFORNIA**, **Golfo de California**, I. San Luis, I. Ángel de la Guarda, Canal de Ballenas, Isla Cedros, Punta Prieta, B. Sebastián Vizcaíno, Sierra Vizcaíno

**HAWAII**

Kauai, Niihau, Kaula, Kapaa, Lihue, Oahu, Wahiawa, Pearl City, Honolulu, Kaneohe, Molokai, Lanai, Kaunakakai, Wailuku, Kihei, Kahoolawe, Maui, Hawaii, Kamuela, Kailua, Kona, Mauna Kea 4205, Mauna Loa 4169, Hilo, Kilauea, Pahala, Mountain View

Kauai Channel, Pailolo Channel, Alenuihaha Channel, **Hawaiian Islands**, **PACIFIC OCEAN**

Projection: Albers' Equal Area with two standard parallels

0 50 100 km
0 50 100 miles

**79**

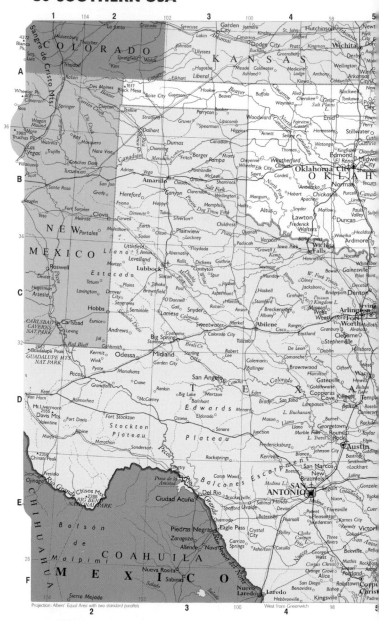

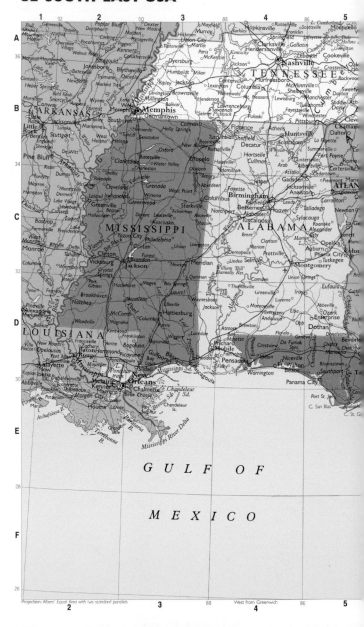

GULF OF

MEXICO

50 0 50 100 150 200 km
50 0 50 100 150 miles

**6** 82 **7** 80 **8** 78 **9** 76 **10**

A

Harlan Big Stone Gap
Middlesboro Abingdon Coeburn Marion
Kingsport Bristol Mountain City South Boston Danville Martinsville Mt. Airy Reidsville Eden Oxford Henderson Roanoke Rapids Emporia Murfreesboro Elizabeth City Edenton Albemarle Sd. Manteo Roanoke
La Follette Morristown Johnson City Elizabethton Elkin Greensboro Burlington Wake Forest High Durham Rocky Mount Tarboro Enfield Williamston Plymouth
Jefferson Greeneville Erwin Boone Winston-Salem Thomasville Point Rebel Hill Raleigh Wilson Greenville Bethel Washington
Maryville Asheville Mt. Mitchell Lenoir Hickory Statesville Lexington Cary Smithfield Goldsboro Kinston New Bern
NAT SMOKY MTS. NAT. PARK Waynesville Marion Newton Salisbury Kannapolis Asheboro Sanford Dunn Clinton Jacksonville Havelock Morehead City
Clingmans Dome Bryson City Brevard Hendersonville Shelby Gastonia Concord NORTH CAROLINA Southern Pines Fayetteville C. Lookout
2037 1458 Charlotte Kings Mtn. Monroe Rockingham Hamlet Clinton Wallace Onslow Bay

B

Toccoa Spartanburg Gaffney Cheraw Laurinburg
Greenville Union Rock Hill Chester Lancaster Bennettsville Dillon Lumberton Wilmington
Easley Clinton Winnsboro Darlington Mullins Conway
Anderson Clemson Laurens Newberry Camden Hartsville Florence Marion North Myrtle Beach C. Fear
Seneca Abbeville Manning Kingstree Myrtle Beach
Greenwood SOUTH CAROLINA Sumter Andrews Long Bay
Athens Elberton Columbia Orangeburg Santee Georgetown
Commerce Winder Washington Edgefield Aiken Bamberg St. George C. Romano
Lawrenceville Thomson Augusta North Augusta Barnwell Allendale Summerville North Charleston
Decatur Monroe Covington Greensboro Martinez Waynesboro Hampton Walterboro Goose Creek Moncks Corner Charleston
GEORGIA Eatonton Milledgeville Sandersville Millen Sylvania Ridgeland Beaufort Mount Pleasant
Griffin Macon Swainsboro Statesboro Burton Parris I.
Thomaston Warner Robins Dublin Garden City Hilton Head Island
Valley Perry Cochran Eastman Vidalia Hinesville Savannah
Americus Cordele Hazlehurst Ossabaw I.
Fitzgerald Baxley St. Catherines I.
Sylvester Ocilla Alma Jesup Sapelo I.
Tifton Douglas St. Simons Island
Camilla Nashville Adel Brunswick Jekyll I.
Moultrie Waycross Cumberland I.
Okefenokee Folkston St. Marys
Swamp Fernandina Beach
Monticello Valdosta Jasper
Madison Jacksonville St. Johns Jacksonville Beach
Lake Middleburg
Perry City Starke Green St. Augustine
Apalachee Cross City Cove Spr. Palm Coast
B. Alachua Palatka
Gainesville
Ocala Ormond Beach
Daytona Beach
Beverly Hills Holly Hill Port Orange
Crystal River De Land New Smyrna Beach
Inverness Eustis Deltona
Leesburg Mt. Dora Titusville
Brooksville Winter Garden Sanford C. Canaveral
Spring Hill Clermont Orlando Merritt Island
New Port Richey Dade City Kissimmee Cocoa
Tarpon Springs Lakeland Winter Haven St. Cloud Melbourne
Dunedin Plant Haines City
Clearwater TAMPA Sun City Bartow Ft. Meade Palm Bay
Largo Center Avon Park Vero Beach
St. Petersburg Bradenton Sebring Fort Pierce
Longboat Key Arcadia Lake Port St. Lucie
Sarasota Okeechobee Stuart
Venice Lake Hobe Sound
Port Charlotte Punta Gorda Okeechobee
Charlotte Harb. La Belle Pahokee Palm Beach
Cape Coral Fort Myers Lehigh Acres Glade West Palm Beach
Sanibel Immokalee Worth Boynton Beach
BIG Coral Springs Delray Beach
Naples CYPRESS Boca Raton
PRESERVE Pompano Beach
Fort Lauderdale
EVERGLADES Hollywood
Hialeah Miami Beach
NAT. PARK Kendall MIAMI
Coral Gables Biscayne B.

C

34

32

D

30

E

28

F

G

26

A T L A N T I C

O C E A N

Grand Cay
Great Sale Cay Little Abaco I.
Hope Town
Marsh Harbour
Freeport Grand Bahama Moore's Great Abaco I.

BAHAMAS

Southwest Pt.

COPYRIGHT PHILIP'S

84 **6** 82 Mexico **7** 80 **8** **9**

SAN DIEGO
Tijuana
Ensenada
Mexicali
PHOENIX
Punta
Casa Grande
Tucson
Deming
Las Cruces
Roswell
Lubbock
Wichita Falls
Fort Worth
3078
San Felipe
Sonoita
Nogales
Douglas
Agua Prieta
Ciudad Juárez
El Paso
Carlsbad
Abilene
Colorado
San Quintin
I. Angel de la Guarda
Caborca
Cananea
Nacozari
Ahumada
Pecos
Fort Stockton
Odessa
San Angelo
Wac
UNITE
30
Bahia Sebastián Vizcaíno
Sta. Rosalia
I. Tiburón
Hermosillo
Magdalena
Nuevo Casas Grandes
Madera
Chihuahua
Cuauhtémoc
Ojinaga
Rio Grande
Ciudad Acuña
Del Rio
SAN ANTONIO
Austin
Guaymas
Empalme
Ciudad Obregón
Navojoa
Sierra
Delicias
Ciudad Camargo
Piedras Negras
Eagle Pass
Victoria
B
Huatabampo
El Fuerte
Jiménez
Hidalgo del Parral
Nueva Rosita
Sabinas
Nuevo Laredo
Laredo
Falcon Res.
Cor
Chr
Los Mochis
Topolobampo
Fuerte
3150
San Pedro de las Colonias
Monclova
Sabinas Hidalgo
Brownsville
Loreto
Guamúchil
Guasave
Gómez Palacio
Tepehuanes
Torreón
Concepción del Oro
MONTERREY
Saltillo
Reynosa
Matamo
25
Villa Constitución
C. San Lázaro
B. de la Paz
La Paz
2408
Culiacán
Rosario
El Salto
Durango
Sombrerete
Matehuala
Charcas
4054
Montemorelos
Linares
San Ferna
C. San Lucas
Mazatlán
Rosario
Escuinapa
Acaponeta
Jerez
Fresnillo
Zacatecas
3353
San Luis Potosí
Ciudad Victoria
Ciudad Mante
Ciudad Ma
C
Tuxpan
Tepic
Aguascalientes
Ciudad de Valles
Tample
C. Ro
20
Is. de Revillagigedo
(Mex.)
Islas Marias
GUADALAJARA
Puerto Vallarta
C. Corrientes
Ameca
León
Irapuato
Guanajuato
Celaya
Querétaro
Pachuca
Tulancingo
Tuxt
Poza
Popo
Xa
D
Ciudad Guzmán
Nevado de Colima 4339
Zamora
Morelia
MEXICO
Popocatépetl 5465
Puebla
Oriz
Manzanillo
Colima
Uruapan
Toluca
Cuernavaca
Iguala
Tlaxcala
Tecomán
Balsas
Chilpancingo
Tlapa
Chilapa
Oaxaca
Tex
Lázaro Cárdenas
Balsas
Acapulco
Ometepec
15
E
PACIFIC
10
I. Clipperton
(Fr.)
OCEAN
F

100 0 100 200 300 400 500 600 km
100 0 100 200 300 400 miles

6      7      8      9

Little Rock
Huntsville
Sherman      Greenville      Columbia      Wilmington
Texarkana      Birmingham      ATLANTA      Long
DALLAS   Shreveport      Tuscaloosa   Macon   Augusta   Bay
Tyler   Monroe   Jackson   Meridian   Montgomery   Columbus   Savannah   Charleston   C. Roman
Nacogdoches      Natchez   Alexandria      Hattiesburg   Dothan   Albany   Almelha
Bryan
Beaumont   Lake Charles   Baton Rouge   Mobile   Pensacola   Tallahassee   Jacksonville   30
Port Arthur   Lafayette   NEW ORLEANS   C. San
HOUSTON      Blas      Daytona Beach
Galveston      Mississippi River      Orlando
Matagorda I.   Delta      C. Canaveral
TAMPA   Melbourne   B
St. Petersburg   West Palm   Grand
Sarasota   L. Okeechobee   Beach   Bahama
Fort   Freeport
G U L F   O F   M E X I C O   MIAMI   Lauderdale
Bimini Is.   25
C. Sable
Key West   Straits of Florida   Andros I.
Tropic of Cancer
Yucatan Channel   Matanzas   Sagua la Grande   C
LA HABANA   Cárdenas   Bahía
Pinar del Río   Güira   Clara   Placetas
C. San   Güines   Santo Domingo   C U B A   Morón
Antonio   G. de   Cienfuegos   Sancti Spíritus   Ciego de Ávila
C. Catoche   Batabanó
Progreso   Motul   Tizimín      Trinidad
Cancún
Mérida   Valladolid   I. de la
Ticul   Isla   Juventud
Valladolid
Peto   Cozumel   Cozumel   20
Golfo de   Campeche   Champotón   Yucatán   Felipe   Cayman Is.
Campeche   Carrillo Puerto   (U.K.)
Ciudad del Carmen   Escárcega   Grand
San Andrés Tuxtla   Chetumal   Cayman
Coatzacoalcos   Corozal   7680
Minatitlán   Villahermosa   Laguna de   Ambergris Cay   Is. Santanilla
Isthmus de   Términos   Belize City   Turneffe Is.   (Honduras)
Tehuantepec   Tuxtla   Escárcega   BELIZE   D
Gutiérrez   San Cristóbal   Dangriga   Gulf of Honduras
Juchitán   de las Casas   Puerto Barrios   Puerto Cortés
Salina   Comitán   GUATEMALA   San Pedro Sula   La Ceiba   Trujillo   L. de Caratasca
Cruz   Tonalá   Cobán
G. de   Huixtla   4063   3834   HONDURAS
Tehuantepec   Quezaltenango   GUATEMALA   Juticalpa   15
Escuintla   Guatemala   Tegucigalpa   Puerto Cabezas
Santa Ana   San   I. de Providencia
SAN SALVADOR   Vicente   Matagalpa   (Colombia)
Sonsonate   San Miguel   Choluteca   Río Grande   I. de San Andrés   E
EL SALVADOR   La Unión   NICARAGUA   (Colombia)
G. de Fonseca   Chinandega   Managua
León   Masaya   Granada   Bluefields
Lago de
Rivas   Nicaragua
Pen.   Volcán Irazú   COSTA RICA   G. de los Mosquitos
de Nicoya   3432   Puerto Limón   Panama   10
Puntarenas   Alajuela   Cartago   Colón   Panama   F
San José   PANAMA   La
Palmar Sur   Volcán   David   Chitré   Arch. de   Palma
3475   Santiago   las Perlas   El Real
Puerto   Pen. de   G. de
Armuelles   I. de Coiba   Azuero   Panamá   Jaqué

6      7      8      9

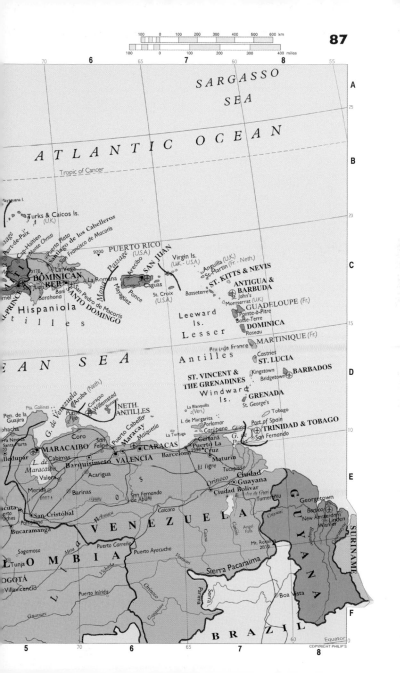

100 0 100 200 300 400 500 600 km
100 0 100 200 300 400 miles

70    **6**    65    **7**    60    **8**    55

**A**

SARGASSO
SEA

25

A T L A N T I C    O C E A N

**B**

Tropic of Cancer

Mayaguana I.

Turks & Caicos Is.
(U.K.)

20

age
Cap-Haïtien
Port-de-Paix       Puerto Plata  Santiago de los Cabelleros
Monte Christi
San Francisco de Macorís
9200    PUERTO RICO
(U.S.A.)
Virgin Is.    Anguilla (U.K.)
(U.K.-U.S.A.)    St-Martin (Fr.-Neth.)

**C**

La Vega
**DOMINICAN**
**REP.**
3175    La Romana
San Juan    San Pedro de Macorís
Bani    Barahona
P.PRINCE    SANTO DOMINGO
Hispaniola
Arecibo
Mayagüez    SAN JUAN
Ponce
Caguas
St. Croix
(U.S.A.)
Basseterre
Montserrat (U.K.)
**ST. KITTS & NEVIS**
**ANTIGUA &**
**BARBUDA**
St. John's
**GUADELOUPE** (Fr.)
Pointe-à-Pitre
Basse-Terre

Antilles    Leeward
Is.
Lesser    **DOMINICA**
Roseau

15

**EAN    SEA**    Antilles
Fort-de-France
Pte

Castries
**MARTINIQUE** (Fr.)
**ST. LUCIA**

**D**

Pen. de la
Guajira
Pta. Gallinas
Golfo de Venezuela
Aruba (Neth.)
Curaçao    Willemstad    **NETH.**
**ANTILLES**
Punta
Fijo
Maracaibo
Coro
San
Felipe
Puerto Cabello
Maracay
Maiquetía
**ST. VINCENT &**
**THE GRENADINES**
Kingstown
Bridgetown    **BARBADOS**
Windward
Is.    **GRENADA**
St. George's

La Blanquilla
(Ven.)
I. de Margarita
Porlamar
La Tortuga
Cumaná
Tobago
Port of Spain
Carúpano    Güiria
**TRINIDAD & TOBAGO**
G. de Paria    San Fernando

10

**E**

ohacha
ra Nevada
Santa Marta
lledupar
**MARACAIBO**
Cabimas
**VALENCIA**
Barquisimeto
**CARACAS**
Puerto La
Cruz
Barcelona
Maturín
Acarigua
L. de
Maracaibo
Valera
Merida
cuta
erto
ches
San Cristóbal
Bucaramanga
Barinas
San Fernando
de Apure
El Tigre
Tucupita
Ciudad
**Guayana**
Ciudad Bolívar
Orinoco

**G U Y A N A**
Georgetown
New Amsterdam
Linden
Wisma

**SURINAME**

Sogamoso
**C O L O M B I A**
Tunja
**BOGOTÁ**
Villavicencio
Arauca
Caicara
Puerto Carreño
Vichada
Puerto Ayacucho
Meta
Puerto Inírida
Guaviare

**V E N E Z U E L A**
Apure
Tumeremo
El Dorado
Caroní
Angel
Falls
Mt. Roraima
2810
Caura

**F**

Sierra    Pacaraima
Parima
Orinoco
Casiquiare

Boa Vista

**B R A Z I L**
Equator    0
60

COPYRIGHT PHILIP'S

5    70    **6**    65    **7**    60    **8**

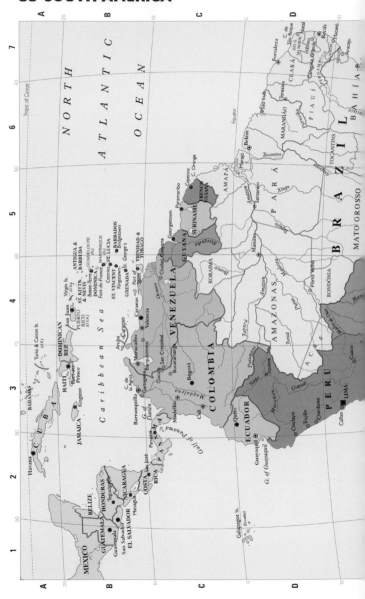

A B C D

7 6 5 4 3 2 1

Tropic of Cancer

Equator

NORTH

ATLANTIC

OCEAN

Caribbean Sea

MEXICO
GUATEMALA
Guatemala
San Salvador
EL SALVADOR
BELIZE
HONDURAS
Tegucigalpa
NICARAGUA
Managua
COSTA RICA
San José
PANAMA
Panamá

BAHAMAS
Havana
CUBA
JAMAICA
Kingston
HAITI
Port-au-Prince
DOMINICAN REP.
Turks & Caicos Is. (UK)
PUERTO RICO (USA)
San Juan
Virgin Is. (US & UK)
ST. KITTS & NEVIS
ANTIGUA & BARBUDA
GUADELOUPE (Fr)
Basse-Terre
DOMINICA
MARTINIQUE (Fr)
Fort-de-France
ST. LUCIA
Castries
ST. VINCENT
Kingstown
BARBADOS
Bridgetown
GRENADA
St. George's
TRINIDAD & TOBAGO
Port of Spain

Aruba
Curaçao
C. de la Vela
Barranquilla
Cartagena
Gulf of Darién
Gulf of Panama

Maracaibo
Valencia
Caracas
Barquisimeto
Cúcuta
San Cristóbal
Bucaramanga
Medellín
Bogotá
Cali
COLOMBIA

VENEZUELA
Ciudad Guayana
Orinoco
RORAIMA

GUYANA
Georgetown
SURINAME
Paramaribo
FRENCH GUIANA
Cayenne
C. Orange
AMAPÁ
Macapá

QUITO
ECUADOR
Guayaquil
G. of Guayaquil
Galápagos Is. (Ecuador)

Iquitos
Napo
Marañón
Chiclayo
Trujillo
Chimbote
Callao
LIMA
PERU
Cuzco
ACRE
Ucayali
Madre de Dios
Purús
Juruá
Javari
Jutaí
Putumayo

AMAZONAS
Manaus
Negro
Branco
Essequibo
Amazon
Japurá
Tapajós
Xingu
Tocantins
Santarém
Belém
PARÁ
MATO GROSSO
RONDÔNIA
Pôrto Velho
Mamoré

BRAZIL
Fortaleza
CEARÁ
Teresina
PIAUÍ
São Luís
MARANHÃO
PARAÍBA
Natal
RIO G. DO NORTE
Recife
João Pessoa
Campina Grande
Maceió
Aracaju
SERGIPE
Salvador
BAHIA
C. de São Roque
PERNAMBUCO

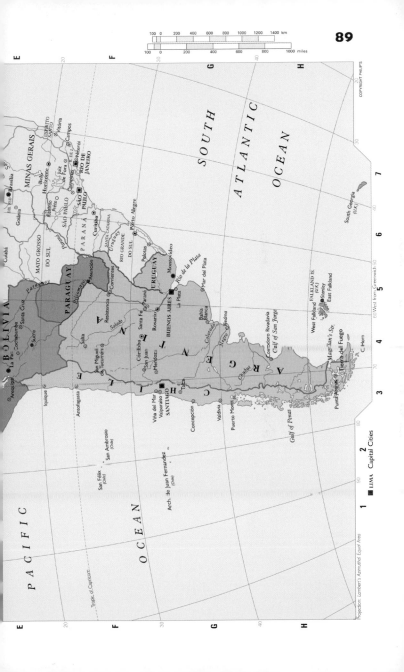

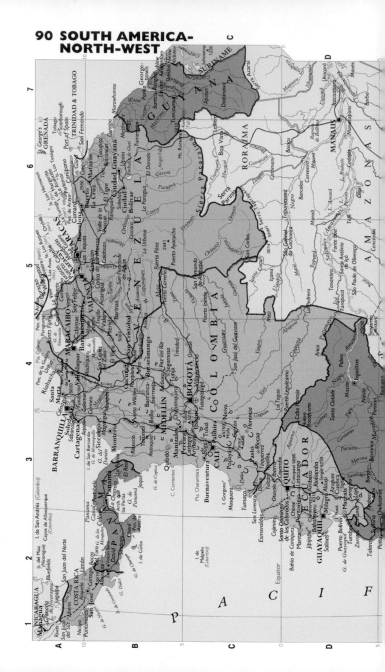

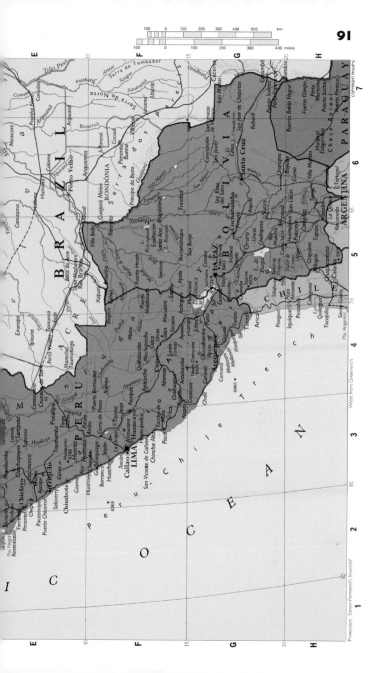

**91**

Projection: Sanson-Flamsteed's Sinusoidal

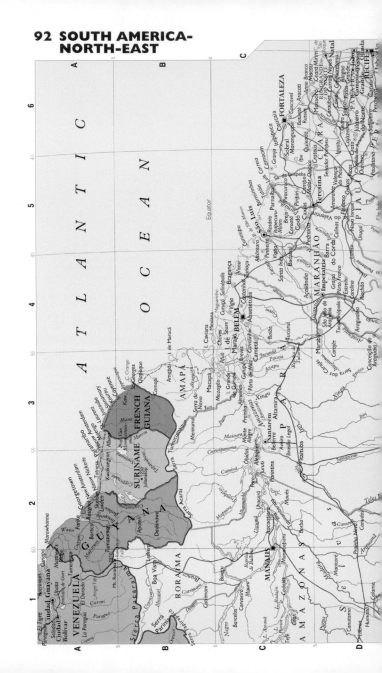

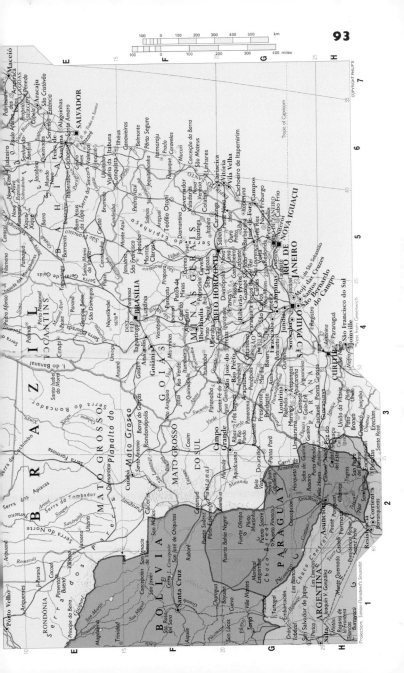

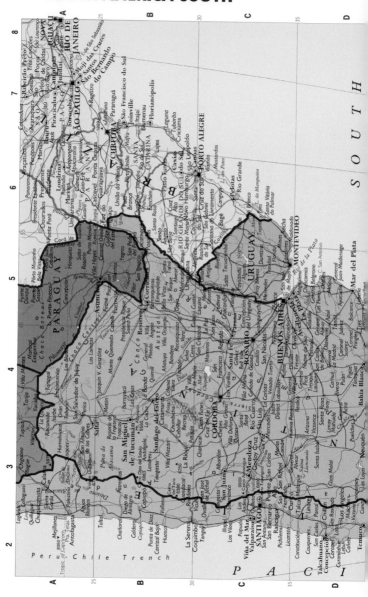

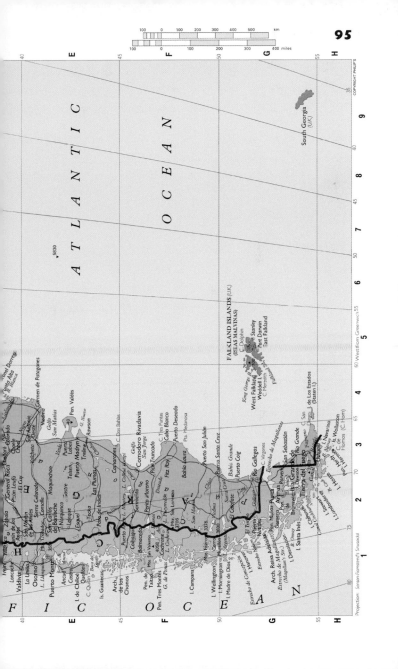

100  0  100  200  300  400  500  km

100  0  100  200  300  400 miles

E

F

G

H

A T L A N T I C

O C E A N

▲5830

E

F

G

H

South Georgia
(U.K.)

FALKLAND ISLANDS (U.K.)
(ISLAS MALVINAS)

C. Dolphin

West Falkland
Weddell I.  C. Meredith
                Falkland Sd
King George B.  Stanley
                Port Darwin
                East Falkland
                C. Pembroke

Chiloé Archipelago region (Argentina/Chile):

Frías  Valdivia
Loncoche
Valdivia
La Unión
Osorno
Puerto Montt
Ancud
I. de Chiloé
Castro  Quellón
C. Quilán
Arch. de los Chonos
Pen. de Taitao  C. Tres Montes
I. Campana
I. Wellington
I. Mornington
I. Madre de Dios

Nahuel Huapí  Neuquén
San Martín de los Andes
San Carlos de Bariloche
Esquel
Maquinchao
Ingeniero Jacobacci
Teka

Sierra de los Andes

Colorado
San Antonio Oeste
Golfo San Matías
Valdés  Viedma
Pen. Valdés  G. Nuevo
Puerto Madryn
Trelew  Rawson
Puerto Lobos
Gaiman
Telsen
Gastre

La Plumas
Camarones
Sarmiento
Perito Moreno
L. Colhué Huapí
L. Musters
Dolavon

Comodoro Rivadavia
Golfo San Jorge
Pico Truncado
Puerto Deseado
Cabo Blanco
Tres Puntas
Pta. Medanosa

Puerto San Julián
Bahía Grande
Puerto Coig
Puerto Santa Cruz
Río Gallegos
C. Vírgenes

Estrecho de Magallanes
Punta Arenas
Porvenir
San Sebastián
Río Grande
Tierra del Fuego
I. Grande de Tierra del Fuego
I. de Los Estados
(Staten I.)

C. San Diego

I. Navarino
I. Hoste
I. Wollaston
C. de Hornos (C. Horn)

Ushuaia
Canal Beagle

Pen. Muñoz Gamero
Isla Santa Inés
I. Desolación
I. Clarence
I. Dawson
Estrecho de Magallanes (Magellan's Str.)
Arch. Reina Adelaida
Estrecho de Concepción

Balmaceda
Coyhaique
Mte. San Lorenzo
Mte. San Valentín
Cochrane
L. Cochrane
L. Buenos Aires
Río Chico
L. Pueyrredón
Gob. Gregores
San Martín
L. Viedma
L. Argentino
Fitz Roy 3375
Cerro San Valentín 4058

N

Projection: Sanson-Flamsteed's Sinusoidal

80

75

70

65

60 West from Greenwich 55

50

45

40

35

COPYRIGHT PHILIP'S

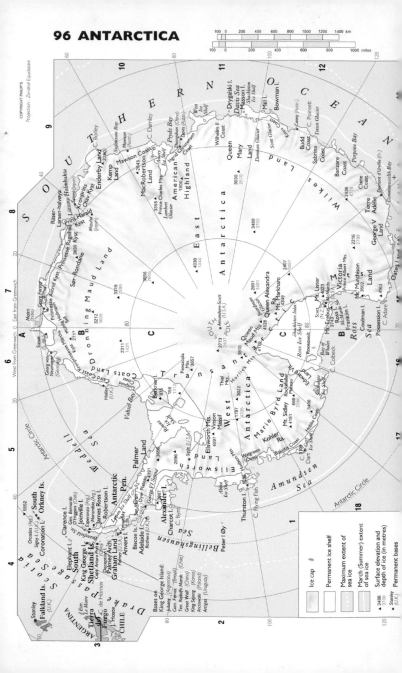

# Index to Map Pages

The index contains the names of all principal places and features shown on the maps. Physical features composed of a proper name (Erie) and a description (Lake) are positioned alphabetically by the proper name. The description is positioned after the proper name and is usually abbreviated:

Erie, L. . . . . . . . . **76 C5**

Where a description forms part of a settlement or administrative name, however, it is always written in full and put in its true alphabetical position:

Lake Charles . . . **81 D7**

Names beginning St. are alphabetized under Saint, but Sankt, Sant, Santa and San are all spelt in full and are alphabetized accordingly.

The number in bold type which follows each name in the index refers to the number of the map page where that feature or place will be found. This is usually the largest scale at which the place or feature appears.

The letter and figure which are in bold type immediately after the page number give the grid square on the map page, within which the feature is situated.

Rivers are indexed to their mouths or confluences, and carry the symbol → after their names. The following symbols are also used in the index: ■ country, ☑ overseas territory or dependency, □ first order administrative area, △ national park, ◠ nature park or reserve.

## A

A Coruña . . . . . 18 **A1**
Aachen . . . . . 14 **C4**
Aalborg =
   Ålborg . . . . 9 **D7**
Aarhus = Århus 9 **D8**
Aba . . . . . . 53 **G7**
Ābādān . . . . . 47 **E7**
Abakan . . . . . 30 **D7**
Abancay . . . . 91 **F4**
Abaya, L. . . . . 55 **G6**
Abbeville . . . . 12 **A4**
Abéché . . . . . 55 **F3**
Abeokuta . . . . 53 **G6**
Aberdeen,
   S. Dak., U.S.A. 74 **C5**
Aberdeen,
   Wash., U.S.A. 72 **C2**
Aberystwyth . . 11 **E4**
Abidjan . . . . 53 **G5**
Abilene . . . . 80 **C4**
Abitibi I. . . . . 71 **D2**
Abkhazia □ . . 25 **E5**
Åbo = Turku . . 9 **C10**
Abomey . . . . 53 **G6**
Absaroka Range 73 **D9**
Abu Dhabi =
   Abū Ẓaby . . 44 **E3**
Abu Hamed . . 55 **E5**
Abū Ẓaby . . . 44 **E3**
Abuja . . . . . 53 **G7**
Abunā . . . . . 91 **E5**
Abunã → . . . . 91 **E5**
Acaponeta . . . 84 **C3**
Acapulco . . . 84 **D5**
Accra . . . . . 53 **G5**
Aceh □ . . . . 38 **D1**
Achill I. . . . . 11 **E1**
Acklins I. . . . 86 **B5**

Aconcagua,
   Cerro . . . . 94 **C3**
Acre = 'Akko . 46 **D3**
Acre □ . . . . . 91 **E4**
Acre → . . . . . 91 **E5**
Ad Dammām . . 47 **F7**
Ad Dawḥah . . 44 **E2**
Ad Dīwānīyah . 47 **E6**
Adamaoua,
   Massif de l' . 55 **G1**
Adam's Bridge 43 **Q11**
Adana . . . . . 46 **C3**
Adapazarı =
   Sakarya . . . 46 **B2**
Adare, C. . . . 96 **B15**
Addis Ababa =
   Addis Abeba 49 **F2**
Addis Abeba . . 49 **F2**
Adelaide . . . . 62 **B2**
Adelaide I. . . . 96 **A3**
Adelaide Pen. . 68 **B10**
Adélie, Terre . . 96 **A14**
Aden = Al 'Adan 49 **E4**
Aden, G. of . . 49 **E4**
Adirondack Mts. 77 **C8**
Adour → . . . . 12 **E3**
Adrar des Iforas 52
Adriatic Sea . . 20 **C5**
Adzhar
   Republic =
   Ajaria □ . . . 25 **E5**
Ægean Sea . . 23 **E5**
Aerhtai Shan . . 34 **B4**
Afghanistan ■ . 45 **C6**
Afyon . . . . . 46 **C2**
Afyonkarahisar =
   Afyon . . . . 46 **C2**
Agadez . . . . 53 **E7**
Agadir . . . . . 52 **B4**
Agartala . . . . 41 **F8**
Agen . . . . . 12 **D4**
Agra . . . . . 42 **F10**

Ağrı . . . . . . 25 **F5**
Ağrı Dağı . . . 46 **C6**
Ağrı Karakose =
   Ağrı . . . . . 25 **F5**
Agrigento . . . 21 **F4**
Agua Prieta . . 84 **A3**
Aguascalientes 84 **C4**
Agulhas, C. . . 58 **E4**
Agulhas → . . . 52 **D7**
Ahmadabad . . 43 **H8**
Ahmadnagar . . 43 **K9**
Ahmadpur . . . 42 **E7**
Ahmedabad =
   Ahmadabad . 43 **H8**
Ahmednagar =
   Ahmadnagar 43 **K9**
Ahvāz . . . . . 47 **E7**
Ahvenanmaa =
   Åland . . . . 9 **C10**
Aihui . . . . . 35 **A7**
Aïn . . . . . . 25 **E7**
Aisne → . . . . 13 **B5**
Aix-en-Provence 13 **E6**
Aix-la-Chapelle =
   Aachen . . . 14 **C4**
Aix-les-Bains . 13 **D6**
Aizawl . . . . 41 **F9**
Aizuwakamatsu 33 **E6**
Ajaccio . . . . 13 **F8**
Ajaria □ . . . . 25 **E5**
Ajdābiyā . . . . 54 **B3**
'Ajman . . . . 44 **E3**
Ajmer . . . . . 42 **F9**
Akhisar . . . . 23 **E6**
Akimiski I. . . . 71 **C2**
Akita . . . . . 32 **D7**
'Akko . . . . . 46 **D3**
Aklavik . . . . 68 **B6**
Akmolinsk =
   Astana . . . 29 **D8**
Akola . . . . . 43 **J10**
Akpatok I. . . . 70 **B4**
Akron . . . . . 76 **D5**

Aksai Chin . . 42 **B11**
Aksaray . . . . 46 **C3**
Aksu . . . . . 34 **B3**
Aktyubinsk =
   Aqtöbe . . . 29 **D6**
Akure . . . . . 53 **G7**
Akureyri . . . . 8 **B2**
Akyab = Sittwe 41 **G9**
Al 'Adan . . . . 49 **E4**
Al Bāsā =
   Hasa □ . . . 47 **F7**
Al 'Aqabah . . 47 **E3**
Al 'Aramah . . 47 **F6**
Al Baḥral
   Mayyit = Dead
   Sea . . . . . 47 **E3**
Al Baṣrah . . . 47 **E6**
Al Bayḍā . . . 54 **B3**
Al Fāw . . . . 47 **E7**
Al Ḥillah, Iraq . 47 **D6**
Al Ḥillah,
   Si. Arabia . . 47 **G6**
Al Hoceima . . 52 **A5**
Al Ḥudaydah . 49 **E3**
Al Ḥufūf . . . . 47 **F7**
Al Jawf, Libya . 54 **D3**
Al Jawf,
   Si. Arabia . . 47 **E4**
Al Jazirah . . . 46 **D5**
Al Khalīl . . . . 47 **E3**
Al Kufrah . . . 54 **D3**
Al Kūt . . . . . 47 **D6**
Al Kuwayt . . . 47 **E7**
Al Lādhiqiyah . 46 **D3**
Al Madīnah . . 47 **F4**
Al Manāmah . . 44 **E2**
Al Mawṣil . . . 46 **C5**
Al Mubarraz . . 47 **F7**
Al Mukallā . . . 49 **E4**
Al Musayyib . . 47 **D6**
Al Qāmishlī . . 46 **C5**
Al Qaṭīf . . . . 47 **F7**

Al Quds =
   Jerusalem . . 47 **E3**
Alabama □ . . . 82 **C4**
Alabama → . . . 82 **D4**
Alagoas □ . . . 93 **D6**
Alagoinhas . . 93 **E6**
Åland . . . . . 9 **C10**
Åland . . . . . 9 **C10**
Alamosa . . . . 79 **B10**
Åland . . . . . 9 **C10**
Alania = North
   Ossetia □ . . 25 **E5**
Alanya . . . . . 46 **C2**
Alappuzha =
   Alleppey . . . 43 **Q10**
Alaşehir . . . . 23 **E7**
Alaska □ . . . . 69 **B4**
Alaska, G. of . . 69 **C5**
Alaska Peninsula 69 **C4**
Alaska Range . 69 **B4**
Albacete . . . . 19 **C5**
Albania ■ . . . 23 **D3**
Albany,
   Australia . . 60 **H2**
Albany, Ga.,
   U.S.A. . . . . 83 **D5**
Albany, N.Y.,
   U.S.A. . . . . 77 **C9**
Albany, Oreg.,
   U.S.A. . . . . 72 **D2**
Albany → . . . 71 **C2**
Albert, L. . . . 57 **D6**
Albert Nile → . 57 **D6**
Albertville . . . 13 **D7**
Albi . . . . . . 12 **E5**
Ålborg . . . . . 9 **D7**
Alborz, Reshteh-
   ye Kūhhā-ye . 44 **B3**
Albuquerque . 79 **C9**
Albury-
   Wodonga . . 63 **C4**
Alcalá de
   Henares . . . 18 **B4**
Alchevsk . . . 25 **D4**
Aldabra Is. . . 51 **G8**

Aldan → ..... 31 C10
Alderney ..... 11 G5
Alegrete ..... 94 B5
Alençon ..... 12 B4
Aleppo = Ḥalab 46 C4
Alès ..... 13 D6
Alessándria ..... 20 B2
Ålesund ..... 8 C7
Aleutian Is. ..... 69 C2
Alexander Arch. 69 C6
Alexander I. ..... 96 A3
Alexandria = El
 Iskandarîya ..... 54 B4
Alexandria, La.,
 U.S.A. ..... 81 D7
Alexandria, Va.,
 U.S.A. ..... 77 E7
Algarve ..... 18 D1
Algeciras ..... 18 D3
Alger ..... 52 A6
Algeria ■ ..... 52 C6
Algiers = Alger 52 A6
Alhucemas = Al
 Hoceïma ..... 52 A5
Alicante ..... 19 C5
Alice Springs ..... 60 E5
Aligarh ..... 42 F11
Alipur Duar ..... 41 D7
Alkmaar ..... 14 B3
Allahabad ..... 40 E3
Allegheny → ..... 77 D7
Allegheny Mts. 77 F5
Allentown ..... 77 D8
Alleppey ..... 43 Q10
Allier → ..... 13 C5
Alma Ata =
 Almaty ..... 29 E8
Almaty ..... 29 E8
Almelo ..... 14 B4
Almería ..... 19 D4
Alnwick ..... 10 D6
Alor ..... 37 F2
Alor Setar ..... 38 C2
Alps ..... 14 E5
Alsace ..... 13 B7
Alsask ..... 69 C9
Altai = Aerhtai
 Shan ..... 34 B4
Altanbulag ..... 35 A5
Altay ..... 34 B3
Alton ..... 75 F9
Altoona ..... 77 D6
Altun Shan ..... 34 C3
Alwar ..... 42 F10
Alxa Zuoqi ..... 35 C5
Amadjuak L. ..... 70 B3
Amagasaki ..... 33 F4
Amapá ..... 92 B3
Amapá □ ..... 92 B3
Amarillo ..... 80 B3
Amazon =
 Amazonas → 92 C3
Amazonas □ ..... 90 D6
Amazonas → ..... 92 C3
Ambala ..... 42 D10
Ambato ..... 90 D3
Ambergris Cay 85 D7
Ambikapur ..... 40 F4
Ambilobé ..... 59 G9
Ambon ..... 37 E3
Amchitka I. ..... 69 C1
Ameca ..... 84 C4
American
 Highland ..... 96 B10
American
 Samoa ☑ ..... 65 L13
Ames ..... 75 D8
Amherst ..... 71 D4
Amiens ..... 12 B5
Amirante Is. ..... 26 K9
ʻAmmãn ..... 47 E3
Ammochostos =
 Famagusta . 46 D3
Amoy = Xiamen 35 D6
Amravati ..... 43 J10
Amreli ..... 43 J7
Amritsar ..... 42 D9

Amroha ..... 42 E11
Amsterdam ..... 14 B3
Amudarya → ..... 29 E6
Amundsen Gulf 68 A7
Amundsen Sea 96 B1
Amur → ..... 31 D12
An Nafûd ..... 47 E5
An Najaf ..... 47 D6
Anaconda ..... 73 C7
Anadolu ..... 46 C2
Anaheim ..... 78 D4
Anambas,
 Kepulauan ..... 39 D3
Anamur ..... 46 C3
Anápolis ..... 93 F4
Anár ..... 44 D3
Anatolia =
 Anadolu ..... 46 C2
Añatuya ..... 94 B4
Anchorage ..... 69 B5
Ancohuma,
 Nevada ..... 91 G5
Ancona ..... 20 C4
Ancud ..... 95 E2
Ancud, G. de ..... 95 E2
Andalgalá ..... 94 B3
Andalucía □ ..... 18 D3
Andalusia ..... 82 D4
Andaman Is. ..... 27 H13
Andaman Sea . 38 B1
Anderson ..... 76 D3
Anderson → ..... 68 B7
Andes, Cord. de
 los ..... 91 G4
Andhra
 Pradesh □ ..... 43 L11
Andijon ..... 29 E8
Andorra ■ ..... 19 A6
Andreanof Is. ..... 69 C2
Ándria ..... 20 D6
Andropov =
 Rybinsk ..... 24 B4
Andros I. ..... 86 B4
Ángara → ..... 30 D7
Angarsk ..... 30 D8
Ånge ..... 8 C9
Angeles ..... 36 A2
Ångermanälven →
 ..... 8 C9
Angers ..... 12 C3
Angola ■ ..... 58 A3
Angoulême ..... 12 D4
Angoumois ..... 12 D4
Angren ..... 29 E8
Anguilla ☑ ..... 87 C7
Anhui □ ..... 35 C6
Anjou ..... 12 C3
Ankang ..... 35 C5
Ankara ..... 46 C3
Ann Arbor ..... 76 C4
Annaba ..... 52 A7
Annan ..... 11 D5
Annapolis ..... 77 E7
Annecy ..... 13 D7
Anning ..... 34 D5
Anniston ..... 82 C5
Annobón ..... 51 G4
Anqing ..... 35 C6
Anshan ..... 35 B7
Anshun ..... 35 D5
Antakya ..... 46 C4
Antalya ..... 46 C2
Antananarivo ..... 59 H9
Antarctic Pen. ..... 96 A4
Antarctica ..... 96 C
Anti Atlas ..... 52 C4
Antibes ..... 13 E7
Anticostí, Î. d' . 71 D4
Antigua &
 Barbuda ■ ..... 87 C7
Antioquia ..... 90 B3
Antofagasta ..... 94 A2
Antrim ..... 11 D3
Antsirabe ..... 59 H9
Antsiranana ..... 59 G9
Antwerpen ..... 14 C3

Anvers =
 Antwerpen ..... 14 C3
Anxi ..... 34 B4
Anyang ..... 35 C6
Aomen = Macau 35 D6
Aomori ..... 32 C7
Aoraki Mount
 Cook ..... 65 E4
Apaporis → ..... 90 D5
Apeldoorn ..... 14 B3
Apennines =
 Appennini ..... 20 B3
Apia ..... 65 L13
Appalachian
 Mts. ..... 77 F5
Appennini ..... 20 B3
Appleton ..... 76 B1
Apure → ..... 90 B5
Apurímac → ..... 91 F4
Aqaba = Al
 ʻAqabah ..... 47 E3
Aqaba, G. of ..... 47 E3
Aqmola =
 Astana ..... 29 D8
Aqtöbe ..... 29 D6
Ar Rachidiya =
 Er Rachidia . 52 B5
Ar Ramādī ..... 46 D5
Ar Riyāḍ ..... 47 F6
Ara ..... 40 E5
Arab, Shatt al → 47 E7
Arabian Desert =
 Es Saḥrâʾ Esh
 Sharqîya ..... 54 C5
Arabian Gulf =
 Gulf, The ..... 44 E2
Arabian Sea ..... 26 H10
Aracaju ..... 93 E6
Aracati ..... 92 C6
Araçatuba ..... 93 G3
Aracuaí ..... 93 F5
Arad ..... 16 E5
Arafura Sea ..... 37 F4
Aragón □ ..... 19 B5
Araguacema ..... 92 D4
Araguaia → ..... 92 D4
Araguari ..... 93 F4
Arakan Coast ..... 41 H9
Arakan Yoma ..... 41 H10
Araks = Aras,
 Rüd-e → ..... 46 B7
Aral ..... 29 E7
Aral Sea ..... 29 E7
Aralsk = Aral ..... 29 E7
Aralskoye
 More = Aral
 Sea ..... 29 E6
Aran I. ..... 10 D2
Aran Is. ..... 11 E2
Araripe,
 Chapada do . 92 D6
Aras, Rüd-e → 46 B7
Arauca → ..... 90 B5
Araxá ..... 93 F4
Arbil ..... 46 C6
Arbroath ..... 10 C5
Arcachon ..... 12 D3
Archangel =
 Arkhangelsk . 28 C5
Arctic Bay ..... 70 A2
Arctic Red
 River =
 Tsiigehtchic . 68 B6
Ardabīl ..... 46 C7
Ardenne ..... 14 D3
Ardmore ..... 80 B5
Arecibo ..... 87 C6
Arendal ..... 9 D7
Arequipa ..... 91 G4
Ararat, Mt. =
 Ağrı Dağı ..... 46 C6
Araripe,
 Chapada do . 92 D6
Argentan ..... 12 B3
Argentina ■ ..... 94 D3
Argentino, L. ..... 95 G2
Århus ..... 9 D8

Arica ..... 91 G4
Arinos → ..... 91 F7
Aripuanã → ..... 90 E6
Arizona □ ..... 79 C7
Arkansas □ ..... 81 B7
Arkansas → ..... 81 C8
Arkansas City . 80 A5
Arkhangelsk ..... 28 C5
Arklow ..... 11 E3
Arles ..... 13 E6
Arlington ..... 77 E7
Arlon ..... 14 D3
Armagh ..... 11 D3
Armavir ..... 25 D5
Armenia ■ ..... 25 E5
Arnaud → ..... 70 B3
Arnhem ..... 14 C3
Arnhem, C. ..... 60 C6
Arnhem Land . 60 C5
Arrah = Ara ..... 40 E5
Arran ..... 10 D4
Arras ..... 13 A5
Arrecife ..... 52 C3
Artigas ..... 94 C5
Artois ..... 12 A5
Artvin ..... 46 B5
Aru, Kepulauan 37 F4
Arua ..... 57 D6
Aruanã ..... 93 E3
Aruba ☑ ..... 87 D6
Arunachal
 Pradesh □ ..... 41 C10
Arusha ..... 57 E7
Arviat ..... 68 B10
Arxan ..... 35 B6
Arzamas ..... 24 B5
As Sohar =
 Şuḥār ..... 44 E4
As
 Sulaymānīyah 46 D6
As Şuwayrah ..... 47 D6
Asahigawa ..... 32 B8
Asansol ..... 40 F6
Ascension I. ..... 51 G2
Aseb ..... 49 E3
Ash Shāriqah ..... 44 E3
Asheville ..... 83 B6
Ashford ..... 11 F7
Ashgabat ..... 29 F6
Ashkhabad =
 Ashgabat ..... 29 F6
Ashqelon ..... 47 E3
Ashtabula ..... 76 D5
Ashuanipi, L. ..... 71 C4
ʻAsīr □ ..... 48 D3
Asir, Ras ..... 49 E5
Asmera ..... 55 E6
Assab = Aseb . 49 E3
Assam □ ..... 41 D9
Assen ..... 14 B4
Assiniboia ..... 69 D9
Assiniboine → . 69 D10
Assisi ..... 20 C4
Astana ..... 29 D8
Asti ..... 20 B2
Astoria ..... 72 C2
Astrakhan ..... 25 D6
Asturias □ ..... 18 A3
Asunción ..... 94 B5
Aswân ..... 54 D5
Aswan Dam =
 Sadd el Aali . 54 D5
Asyût ..... 54 C5
Aţ Ţāʾif ..... 48 C3
Atacama,
 Desierto de . 94 A3
ʻAtbara ..... 55 E5
ʻAtbara, Nahr → 55 E5
Athabasca ..... 69 C8
Athabasca → . 68 C8
Athabasca, L. ..... 68 C8
Athens = Athínai 23 F4
Athens ..... 83 C6
Athínai ..... 23 F4
Athlone ..... 11 E3
Áthos ..... 23 D5
Athy ..... 11 E3

Atlanta ..... 83 C5
Atlantic City ..... 77 E8
Atlas Mts. =
 Haut Atlas ..... 52 B4
Attawapiskat → 71 C2
Atyraü ..... 29 E6
Aube → ..... 13 B5
Aubusson ..... 12 D5
Auch ..... 12 E4
Auckland ..... 64 B6
Aude → ..... 13 E5
Augsburg ..... 14 D6
Augusta, Ga.,
 U.S.A. ..... 83 C7
Augusta, Maine,
 U.S.A. ..... 77 B11
Aunis ..... 12 C3
Aurangabad,
 Bihar, India ..... 40 E5
Aurangabad,
 Maharashtra,
 India ..... 43 K9
Aurillac ..... 12 D5
Aurora, Colo.,
 U.S.A. ..... 74 F2
Aurora, Ill.,
 U.S.A. ..... 76 D1
Austin ..... 80 D5
Austral Is. =
 Tubuai Is. ..... 65 M16
Austral
 Seamount
 Chain ..... 65 M16
Australia ■ ..... 60 E6
Australian
 Capital
 Territory □ ..... 63 C4
Austria ■ ..... 15 E8
Autun ..... 13 C6
Auvergne ..... 13 D5
Auvergne, Mts.
 d' ..... 13 D5
Auxerre ..... 13 C5
Avallon ..... 13 C5
Avellaneda ..... 94 C5
Avellino ..... 21 D5
Aviemore ..... 10 C5
Avignon ..... 13 E6
Ávila ..... 18 B3
Avranches ..... 12 B3
Awash ..... 49 F3
Axiós → ..... 23 D4
Ayacucho,
 Argentina ..... 94 D5
Ayacucho, Peru 91 F4
Aydın ..... 23 F6
Ayers Rock ..... 60 F5
Aylmer, L. ..... 68 B8
Ayr ..... 10 D4
Ayvalık ..... 23 E6
Az Zahrãn ..... 47 F7
Az Zarqã ..... 46 D4
Azamgarh ..... 40 D4
Azärbayjan =
 Azerbaijan ■ 25 E6
Azbine = Aïr ..... 53 E7
Azerbaijan ■ . 25 E6
Azores ..... 50 C2
Azov ..... 25 D5
Azov, Sea of ..... 25 D5
Azul ..... 94 D5

## B

Bab el Mandeb 49 E3
Bābā, Koh-i- ..... 42 B5
Bābol ..... 44 B3
Babruysk ..... 17 B9
Babuyan Chan. 36 A2
Babylon ..... 47 D6
Bacău ..... 17 E8
Back → ..... 68 B9
Bacolod ..... 36 B2
Bad Lands ..... 74 D3

Badagara ..... 43  P9
Badajoz ...... 18  C2
Badalona ..... 19  B7
Baden-Baden .. 14  D5
Baden-
  Württemberg □
  ........... 14  D5
Bâdghis □ .... 42  B3
Baffin B. ..... 70  A4
Baffin I. ..... 70  B3
Bafoulabé .... 53  F3
Bagé ........ 94  C6
Baghdād ..... 46  D6
Baghlān ...... 42  A6
Bago = Pegu .. 41  J11
Baguio ....... 36  A2
Bahamas ■ ... 86  A4
Baharampur .. 40  E7
Bahawalpur .. 42  E7
Bahía = Salvador 93  E6
Bahía □ ...... 93  E5
Bahía Blanca .. 94  D4
Bahraich ..... 40  D3
Bahrain ■ .... 44  E2
Baia Mare .... 17  E6
Baidoa ....... 49  G3
Baie-Comeau .. 71  D4
Ba'iji ........ 46  D5
Baikal, L. =
  Baykal, Oz. .. 30  D8
Baile Atha
  Cliath = Dublin 11  E3
Baiyin ....... 35  C5
Baja, Pta. .... 84  B1
Baja California . 84  A1
Baker, L. ..... 68  B10
Baker I. ...... 64  J13
Baker Lake ... 68  B10
Bakers Dozen Is. 71  C3
Bakersfield ... 78  C3
Bākhtarān .... 46  D6
Bakı ........ 25  E6
Bakony ...... 16  E3
Baku = Bakı .. 25  E6
Baky = Bakı .. 25  E6
Balabac Str. ... 38  C5
Balaklava .... 25  E4
Balakovo ..... 24  C6
Balashov ..... 24  C5
Balasore =
  Baleshwar ... 40  G6
Balaton ...... 16  E3
Baleares, Is. .. 19  C7
Balearic Is. =
  Baleares, Is. . 19  C7
Baleine =
  Whale → .... 70  C4
Baleshwar .... 40  G6
Bali ......... 39  F5
Balıkeşir ..... 23  E6
Balıkpapan ... 39  E5
Balkan Mts. =
  Stara Planina 22  C4
Balkhash,
  Ozero =
  Balqash Köl .. 29  E8
Ballarat ...... 62  C3
Ballater ...... 10  C5
Ballina ....... 11  D2
Ballinasloe ... 11  E2
Ballymena .... 11  D3
Balochistan =
  Baluchistan □ 42  F4
Balqash Köl ... 29  E8
Balrampur .... 40  D4
Balsas → ..... 84  D4
Bălţi ........ 17  E8
Baltic Sea .... 9  D9
Baltimore .... 77  E7
Baluchistan □ . 42  F4
Bamako ...... 53  F4
Bambari ..... 56  C4
Bamberg ..... 14  D6
Bamenda ..... 53  G8
Bāmīān □ ..... 42  B5
Ban Mê Thuôt =
  Buon Ma
  Thuot ...... 38  B3

Bananal, I. do . 93  E3
Banaras =
  Varanasi .... 40  E4
Banda,
  Kepulauan .. 37  E3
Banda Aceh ... 38  C1
Banda Sea .... 37  F3
Bandar =
  Machilipatnam 40  J3
Bandar-e Abbās 44  E4
Bandar-e Anzali 46  C7
Bandar-e
  Bushehr =
  Büshehr .... 44  D2
Bandar-e
  Torkeman ... 44  B3
Bandar
  Maharani =
  Muar ...... 39  D2
Bandar
  Penggaram =
  Batu Pahat .. 39  D2
Bandar Seri
  Begawan ... 38  D5
Bandirma .... 23  D7
Bandon ...... 11  F2
Bandundu .... 56  E3
Bandung ..... 39  F3
Banff, Canada . 69  C8
Banff, U.K. ... 10  C5
Bangalore .... 43  N10
Banggai,
  Kepulauan .. 37  E2
Banghāzī ..... 54  B3
Bangka ...... 39  E3
Bangkok ..... 38  B2
Bangladesh ■ . 41  E7
Bangor, Down,
  U.K. ...... 11  D4
Bangor,
  Gwynedd,
  U.K. ...... 11  E4
Bangor, U.S.A. 77  B11
Bangui ...... 56  D3
Bangweulu, L. . 57  G6
Bani ........ 87  C5
Banja Luka ... 20  B6
Banjarmasin .. 39  E4
Banjul ....... 53  F2
Banks I. ..... 68  A7
Bannu ....... 42  C7
Bantry ....... 11  F2
Banyak,
  Kepulauan .. 39  D1
Baoding ..... 35  C5
Baoji ....... 35  C5
Baoshan ..... 34  D4
Baotou ...... 35  B6
Ba'qūbah .... 46  D6
Bar-le-Duc ... 13  B6
Baracoa ..... 86  B5
Barahona ..... 87  C5
Barakaldo .... 19  A4
Baranavichy .. 17  B8
Baranof I. .... 69  C6
Barbacena .... 93  G5
Barbados ■ ... 87  D8
Barcelona, Spain 19  B7
Barcelona,
  Venezuela ... 90  A6
Barddhaman .. 40  F6
Bardīyah ..... 54  B4
Bareilly ...... 42  E11
Barhi ........ 40  E5
Bari ......... 20  D6
Baring, C. .... 68  B8
Barisal ...... 41  F8
Barkly Tableland 60  D6
Barlee, L. .... 60  F2
Barletta ..... 20  D6
Barmer ...... 42  G7
Barnaul ..... 29  D9
Barnsley ..... 11  E6
Barnstaple ... 11  F4
Baroda =
  Vadodara ... 43  H8
Barquísimeto . 90  A5

Barra, Brazil .. 93  E5
Barra, U.K. ... 10  C3
Barraigh = Barra 10  C3
Barrancabermeja
  .......... 90  B4
Barranquilla .. 90  A4
Barreiras .... 93  E5
Barretos ..... 93  G4
Barrow ...... 69  A4
Barrow-in-
  Furness .... 11  D5
Barry ....... 11  F5
Barstow ..... 78  C4
Bartlesville ... 81  A6
Barysaw ..... 17  A9
Basarabia =
  Bessarabiya . 17  E9
Basel ....... 14  E4
Bashkortostan □ 29  D6
Basilan I. ..... 36  C2
Basildon ..... 11  F7
Basingstoke .. 11  F6
Basle = Basel . 14  E4
Basque
  Provinces =
  País Vasco □ 19  A4
Basra = Al
  Başrah ..... 47  E6
Bass Str. ..... 61  H8
Bassas da India 59  C7
Bassein ...... 41  J10
Basseterre .... 87  C7
Basti ........ 40  D4
Bastia ....... 13  E8
Bata ........ 56  D1
Batabanó, G. de 86  B3
Batangas ..... 36  B2
Batdambang .. 38  B2
Bath ........ 11  F5
Bathurst,
  Australia ... 63  B4
Bathurst,
  Canada .... 71  D4
Bathurst, C. .. 68  A7
Bathurst Inlet . 68  B9
Batman ..... 46  C5
Ratna ....... 53  A7
Baton Rouge .. 81  D8
Battambang =
  Batdambang 38  B2
Battle Creek .. 76  C3
Batu, Kepulauan 39  E1
Batu Pahat ... 39  D2
Batumi ...... 25  E5
Baturité ..... 92  C6
Bauru ....... 93  G4
Bavaria =
  Bayern □ ... 15  D6
Bay City ..... 76  C4
Bayamo ..... 86  B4
Bayan Har Shan 34  C4
Bayan Hot =
  Alxa Zuoqi .. 35  C5
Bayanhongor .. 35  B5
Bayḑhabo = ...
Baydoa ..... 49  G3
Bayern □ ..... 15  D6
Bayeux ...... 12  B3
Baykal, Oz. ... 30  D8
Bayonne ..... 12  E3
Bayrūt ...... 46  D3
Beagle, Canal . 95  G3
Beardmore
  Glacier .... 96  C14
Béarn ....... 12  E3
Beauce, Plaine
  de la ...... 12  B4
Beaufort Sea .. 66  B6
Beaufort West . 58  E4
Beaumont .... 81  D6
Beaune ...... 13  C6
Beauvais .... 12  B5
Beaver → .... 69  C9
Beawar ...... 42  F9
Béchar ...... 52  B5
Bedford ..... 11  E6
Be'er Sheva .. 47  E3

Beersheba =
  Be'er Sheva . 47  E3
Bei Jiang → .. 35  D6
Bei'an ....... 35  B7
Beihai ....... 35  D5
Beijing ...... 35  C6
Beinn na
  Faoghla =
  Benbecula .. 10  C3
Beira ........ 59  B6
Beirut = Bayrūt 46  D3
Beitbridge .... 59  C6
Béja ........ 54  A1
Bejaia ....... 52  A7
Békéscsaba .. 16  E5
Bela ........ 42  F5
Belarus ■ .... 24  C2
Belau = Palau ■ 36  C4
Belaya Tserkov =
  Bila Tserkva . 17  D10
Belcher Is. ... 71  C3
Beled Weyne =
  Belet Uen ... 49  G4
Belém ....... 92  C4
Belet Uen .... 49  G4
Belfast ...... 11  D4
Belfort ...... 13  C7
Belgaum ..... 43  M9
Belgium ■ ... 14  C3
Belgorod .... 24  C4
Belgorod-
  Dnestrovskiy =
  Bilhorod-
  Dnistrovskyy 25  D3
Belgrade =
  Beograd .... 22  B3
Belitung ..... 39  E3
Belize ■ ..... 85  D7
Belize City ... 85  D7
Bell Peninsula . 70  B2
Bell Ville .... 94  C4
Bellary ...... 43  M10
Belle-Île ..... 12  C2
Belle Isle .... 71  C5
Belle Isle, Str. of 71  C5
Belleville .... 71  D3
Bellin =
  Kangirsuk ... 70  C4
Bellingham ... 72  B2
Bellingshausen
  Sea ....... 96  A2
Bellinzona ... 13  C8
Belmonte .... 93  F6
Belmopan .... 85  D7
Belo Horizonte . 93  F5
Belomorsk ... 28  C4
Belorussia =
  Belarus ■ ... 24  C2
Beloye, Ozero . 24  A4
Beloye More . . 8  B13
Beltsy = Bălţi . 17  E8
Bemidji ...... 75  B7
Ben Nevis .... 10  C4
Benares =
  Varanasi ... 40  E4
Benbecula .... 10  C3
Bend ........ 72  D3
Bendery =
  Tighina .... 17  E9
Bendigo ..... 63  C3
Benevento ... 20  D5
Bengal, Bay of . 41  J7
Bengbu ...... 35  C6
Benghazi =
  Banghāzī ... 54  B3
Bengkulu .... 39  E2
Benguela .... 58  A2
Beni ........ 91  F5
Beni Mellal ... 52  B4
Beni Suef .... 54  C5
Benidorm .... 19  C5
Benin ■ ...... 53  G6
Benin, Bight of 53  H5
Benin City ... 53  G7
Benjamin
  Constant ... 90  D4
Benoni ...... 59  D5
Benton Harbor . 76  C2

Benue → ..... 53  G7
Benxi ....... 35  B7
Beograd ..... 22  B3
Beppu ....... 33  G2
Berber ...... 49  C4
Berberati .... 56  D3
Berbice → .... 90  B7
Berdichev =
  Berdychiv ... 17  D9
Berdyansk ... 25  D4
Berdychiv ... 17  D9
Berezina =
  Byarezina → 17  B10
Berezniki .... 28  D6
Bérgamo .... 20  B2
Bergen ...... 8  C7
Bergerac .... 12  D4
Bergisch
  Gladbach .... 14  C4
Berhampore =
  Baharampur . 40  E7
Berhampur =
  Brahmapur .. 40  H5
Bering Sea ... 69  C1
Bering Strait .. 69  B3
Berkeley ..... 72  H2
Berkner I. .... 96  B4
Berlin ....... 15  B7
Bermejo → ... 94  B5
Bermuda ☑ .. 67  F13
Bern ........ 14  E4
Berne = Bern . 14  E4
Berry ....... 12  C5
Berwick-upon-
  Tweed ..... 10  D6
Besançon .... 13  C7
Bessarabiya .. 17  E9
Bethel ...... 69  B3
Bethlehem,
  S. Africa ... 59  D5
Bethlehem,
  U.S.A. ..... 77  D8
Béthune ..... 13  A5
Bettiah ...... 40  D5
Betul ....... 43  J10
Beverley ..... 11  E6
Beyneu ...... 29  E6
Beypazarı ... 46  B2
Devachii □□□ .. 40  U2
Béziers ...... 13  E5
Bezwada =
  Vijayawada . 40  J3
Bhagalpur ... 40  E6
Bharat = India ■ 43  J10
Bharatpur ... 42  F10
Bhatpara ... 41  F7
Bhavnagar ... 43  J8
Bhilwara .... 43  G9
Bhima → .... 43  L10
Bhiwandi .... 43  K8
Bhiwani ..... 42  E10
Bhopal ...... 43  H10
Bhubaneshwar 40  G5
Bhuj ........ 43  H6
Bhusawal .... 43  J9
Bhutan ■ .... 41  D8
Biafra, B. of =
  Bonny, Bight
  of ........ 56  D1
Biała Podlaska 17  B6
Białystok .... 17  B6
Biarritz ...... 12  E3
Biddeford .... 77  C10
Bié, Planalto de 58  A3
Bielefeld .... 14  B5
Bielsko-Biała .. 16  D4
Bien Hoa .... 38  B3
Bienville, L. ... 71  C3
Big Horn Mts. =
  Bighorn Mts. 73  D10
Big Spring .... 80  C3
Big Trout L. .. 71  C2
Biggar ...... 69  C9
Bighorn → ... 73  C10
Bighorn Mts. . 73  D10
Bihar ....... 40  E5
Bihar □ ...... 40  E5
Bijagós,
  Arquipélago
  dos ....... 53  F2

Bikaner ....... 42　E8
Bikini Atoll .... 64　H11
Bila Tserkva ... 17　D10
Bilaspur ....... 42　F1
Bilbao ........ 19　A4
Bilbo = Bilbao . 19　A4
Bilecik ........ 25　E3
Bilhorod-
　Dnistrovskyy 25　D3
Billings ....... 73　D9
Billiton Is. =
　Belitung ... 39　E3
Bilma ......... 55　E1
Biloxi ........ 81　D9
Binghamton ... 77　C8
Binzert = Bizerte 54　A1
Bioko ......... 56　D1
Birmingham,
　U.K. ....... 11　E6
Birmingham,
　U.S.A. ...... 82　C4
Birr .......... 11　E3
Biscay, B. of .. 12　D2
Bishkek ....... 29　E8
Biskra ........ 52　B7
Bismarck ...... 74　B4
Bismarck Arch. . 64　K9
Bissagos =
　Bijagós,
　Arquipélago
　dos ........ 53　F2
Bissau ........ 53　F2
Bitola ........ 22　D3
Bitolj = Bitola .. 22　D3
Bitterfontein ... 58　E3
Bitterroot Range 73　D6
Biwa-Ko ...... 33　F5
Bizerte ....... 54　A1
Black Forest =
　Schwarzwald 14　D5
Black Hills .... 74　D3
Black Sea ..... 25　E3
Blackburn ..... 11　E5
Blackpool ..... 11　E5
Blackwater → .. 11　E2
Blagoveshchensk
　............ 31　D10
Blanc, Mont ... 13　D7
Blanca, B. .... 95　D4
Blanca Peak ... 79　B10
Blantyre ...... 59　B6
Blenheim ...... 65　D5
Blida ......... 52　A6
Bloemfontein .. 59　D5
Blois ......... 12　C4
Bloomington,
　Ill., U.S.A. .. 75　E10
Bloomington,
　Ind., U.S.A. .. 76　E2
Blue Mts. ..... 72　D4
Blue Nile = Nîl el
　Azraq → .... 55　E5
Blue Ridge Mts. 83　A7
Bluefields ..... 86　D3
Blumenau ..... 94　B7
Bo Hai ........ 35　C6
Boa Vista ..... 90　C6
Bobo-Dioulasso 53　F5
Bóbr → ....... 16　B2
Bobruysk =
　Babruysk ... 17　B9
Bochum ....... 14　C4
Boden ........ 8　B10
Bodensee ..... 13　C8
Bodø ......... 8　B8
Bodrog → ..... 16　D5
Bodrum ....... 23　F6
Bogalusa ..... 81　D9
Bogor ........ 39　F3
Bogotá ....... 90　C4
Bogra ........ 41　E7
Bohemian
　Forest =
　Böhmerwald 15　D7
Böhmerwald .. 15　D7
Bohol Sea .... 36　C2
Boise ......... 72　E5

Bole ......... 34　B3
Bolivia ■ ..... 91　G6
Bologna ...... 20　B3
Bologoye ..... 24　B3
Bolshoy
　Kavkas =
　Caucasus
　Mountains .. 25　E5
Bolton ........ 11　E5
Bolu ......... 25　E3
Bolvadin ...... 46　C2
Bolzano ...... 20　A3
Bom Jesus da
　Lapa ...... 93　E5
Boma ......... 56　F2
Bombala ...... 63　C4
Bombay =
　Mumbai ... 43　K8
Bon, C. ...... 21　F3
Bonaire ...... 87　D6
Bonavista .... 71　D5
Bongor ....... 55　F2
Bonifacio ..... 13　F8
Bonin Is. ..... 27　G18
Bonn ......... 14　C4
Bonny, Bight of 56　D1
Boosaaso =
　Bosaso ..... 49　E4
Boothia, Gulf of 70　A2
Boothia Pen. .. 68　A10
Borås ........ 9　D8
Bordeaux ..... 12　D3
Borger ........ 80　B3
Borhoyn Tal ... 35　B6
Borisoglebsk .. 24　C5
Borisov =
　Barysaw ... 17　A9
Borkou ....... 55　E2
Borneo ....... 39　D4
Bornholm ..... 9　D9
Borovichi ..... 24　B3
Borüjerd ..... 46　D7
Bosaso ....... 49　E4
Bosnia-
　Herzegovina ■ 20　B6
Bosporus =
　İstanbul
　Boğazı .... 22　D7
Bossangoa ... 56　C3
Boston Hu .... 34　B3
Boston, U.K. .. 11　E6
Boston, U.S.A. . 77　C10
Bothnia, G. of . 8　C10
Botletle → .... 58　C4
Botoşani ..... 17　E8
Botswana ■ .. 58　C4
Botucatu ..... 93　G4
Bouaké ....... 53　G4
Bouar ........ 56　C3
Bouârfa ...... 52　B5
Bougie = Bejaïa 52　A7
Boulder ...... 74　E2
Boulder Dam =
　Hoover Dam . 78　B5
Boulogne-sur-
　Mer ....... 12　A4
Bourbonnais .. 13　C5
Bourg-en-Bresse 13　C6
Bourges ...... 12　C5
Bourgogne ... 13　C6
Bourke ....... 63　B4
Bournemouth . 11　F6
Boyne → ..... 11　E3
Boyoma, Chutes 57　D5
Bozeman ..... 73　D8
Bozen = Bolzano 20　A3
Bozoum ...... 56　C3
Bräcke ....... 8　C9
Bradenton .... 83　F6
Bradford ..... 11　E6
Braga ........ 18　B1
Bragança ..... 92　C4
Brahmanbaria . 41　F8
Brahmani → .. 40　G6
Brahmapur ... 40　H5
Brahmaputra → 41　F7
Brăila ........ 17　F8

Branco → ..... 90　D6
Brandenburg . 15　B7
Brandenburg □ 15　B7
Brandon ...... 69　D10
Brantford ..... 76　C5
Brasília ....... 93　F4
Braşov ....... 17　F7
Bratislava .... 16　D3
Bratsk ....... 30　D8
Braunschweig . 14　B6
Bravo del Norte,
　Rio = Grande,
　Rio → ..... 81　F5
Bray ......... 11　E3
Brazil ■ ...... 93　E4
Brazos → ..... 81　E6
Brazzaville ... 56　E3
Brecon ....... 11　F5
Breda ........ 14　C3
Bregenz ...... 14　E5
Bremen ...... 14　B5
Bremerhaven .. 14　B5
Bremerton .... 72　C2
Brennerpass .. 15　E6
Bréscia ...... 20　B3
Breslau =
　Wrocław ... 16　C3
Brest, Belarus . 17　B6
Brest, France .. 12　B1
Brest-Litovsk =
　Brest ...... 17　B6
Bretagne ..... 12　B2
Brezhnev =
　Naberezhnyye
　Chelny .... 29　D6
Briançon ..... 13　D7
Bridgeport ... 77　D9
Bridgetown ... 87　D8
Bridgewater .. 71　D4
Bridlington ... 11　D6
Brigham City .. 73　F7
Brighton ..... 11　F6
Brindisi ...... 21　D6
Brisbane ..... 63　A5
Bristol ....... 11　F5
Bristol B. .... 69　C3
Bristol Channel 11　F4
British Indian
　Ocean Terr. =
　Chagos Arch. 27　K11
British Isles ... 11　D4
Brittany =
　Bretagne ... 12　B2
Brive-la-
　Gaillarde ... 12　D4
Brno ......... 16　D3
Brocken ...... 14　C6
Brodeur Pen. .. 70　A2
Broken Hill ... 62　B3
Brooks Range . 69　B5
Broome ...... 60　D3
Broughton
　Island =
　Qikiqtarjuaq 70　B4
Brownsville ... 80　F5
Brownwood ... 80　D4
Bruay-la-
　Buissière ... 13　A5
Bruce, Mt. ... 60　E2
Bruges = Brugge 14　C2
Brugge ....... 14　C2
Brumado ..... 93　E5
Brunei = Bandar
　Seri Begawan 38　D5
Brunei ■ ..... 38　D4
Brunswick =
　Braunschweig 14　B6
Brunswick .... 83　D7
Brussel ...... 14　C3
Brussels =
　Brussel .... 14　C3
Bruxelles =
　Brussel .... 14　C3
Bryan ........ 81　D5
Bryansk ...... 24　C3
Bucaramanga . 90　B4
Bucharest =
　Bucureşti .. 22　B6

Buckie ....... 10　C5
Bucureşti .... 22　B6
Budapest ..... 16　E4
Bude ......... 11　F4
Buenaventura . 90　C3
Buenos Aires .. 94　C5
Buenos Aires, L. 95　F2
Buffalo ....... 77　C6
Bug = Buh → .. 25　D3
Bug → ........ 16　B5
Bugun Shara .. 35　B5
Buguruslan ... 29　D6
Buh → ....... 25　D3
Buir Nur ...... 35　B6
Bujumbura ... 57　E5
Bukavu ...... 57　E5
Bukhara =
　Bukhoro ... 29　F7
Bukhoro ..... 29　F7
Bukittinggi ... 39　E2
Bulawayo .... 59　C5
Bulgaria ■ .... 22　C5
Bunbury ...... 60　G2
Buncrana .... 11　D3
Bundaberg ... 63　A5
Bundi ........ 43　G9
Bundoran .... 11　D2
Buon Ma Thuot 38　B3
Bûr Safâga ... 54　C5
Bûr Sa'îd ..... 54　B5
Bûr Sûdân ... 55　E6
Burao ........ 49　F4
Buraydah .... 47　F6
Burdur ....... 46　C2
Burdwan =
　Barddhaman 40　F6
Burgas ....... 22　C6
Burgos ....... 18　A4
Burgundy =
　Bourgogne .. 13　C6
Burhanpur ... 43　J10
Burkina Faso ■ 53　F5
Burlington,
　Iowa, U.S.A. 75　E9
Burlington, Vt.,
　U.S.A. ..... 77　B9
Burma ■ ..... 41　G11
Burnie ....... 62　D4
Burnley ...... 11　E5
Burnside → ... 68　B9
Bursa ........ 23　D7
Buru ......... 37　E3
Burundi ■ .... 57　E6
Bury St.
　Edmunds .. 11　E7
Busan = Pusan 35　C7
Büshehr ..... 44　D2
Bushire =
　Büshehr ... 44　D2
Butaritari .... 64　J12
Butha Qi ..... 35　B7
Buton ........ 37　E2
Butte ........ 73　C7
Butterworth .. 38　C2
Butuan ....... 36　C3
Butung = Buton 37　E2
Buzău ........ 17　F8
Buzuluk ...... 29　D6
Byarezina → .. 17　B10
Bydgoszcz ... 16　B3
Byelorussia =
　Belarus ■ .. 24　C2
Bylot I. ....... 70　A3
Bytom ....... 16　C4

C

Ca Mau ...... 38　C3
Cabanatuan .. 36　A2
Cabedelo .... 92　D7
Cabimas ..... 90　A4
Cabinda □ ... 56　F2
Cabo Frio .... 93　G5
Cabonga,
　Réservoir ... 71　D3

Cabora Bassa
　Dam = Cahora
　Bassa,
　Reprêsa de . 59　B6
Cabot Str. .... 71　D5
Čačak ........ 22　C3
Cáceres ...... 18　C2
Cachimbo, Serra
　do ......... 93　D2
Cachoeira .... 93　E6
Cachoeira do Sul 94　C6
Cachoeiro de
　Itapemirim .. 93　G5
Cádiz ........ 18　D2
Caen ......... 12　B3
Caetité ...... 93　E5
Cagayan de Oro 36　C2
Cágliari ...... 21　E2
Caguas ....... 87　C6
Cahora Bassa,
　Reprêsa de .. 59　B6
Cahors ....... 12　D4
Cairns ....... 61　D8
Cairo = El Qâhira 54　B5
Cajamarca ... 91　E3
Calabar ...... 53　H7
Calábria □ ... 21　E6
Calais ....... 12　A4
Calama ...... 94　A3
Calamar ..... 90　A4
Calamian Group 36　B1
Calapan ..... 36　B2
Calbayog .... 36　B2
Calcutta =
　Kolkata .... 41　F7
Caldera ...... 94　B2
Caldwell ..... 72　E5
Calgary ...... 69　C8
Cali ......... 90　C3
Calicut ...... 43　P9
California □ ... 78　B3
California, G. de 84　B2
Callao ....... 91　F3
Caltanissetta .. 21　F5
Calvi ........ 13　E8
Calvinia ...... 58　E3
Camagüey .... 86　B4
Camargue .... 13　E6
Cambay =
　Khambhat .. 43　H8
Cambay, G. of =
　Khambhat, G.
　of ......... 43　J8
Cambodia ■ .. 38　B3
Cambrai ..... 13　A5
Cambrian Mts. . 11　E5
Cambridge, U.K. 11　E7
Cambridge,
　U.S.A. ..... 77　C10
Camden, Ark.,
　U.S.A. ..... 81　C7
Camden, N.J.,
　U.S.A. ..... 77　E8
Cameroon ■ .. 56　C2
Cameroun, Mt. 56　D1
Camocim ..... 92　C5
Campana, I. .. 95　F1
Campánia □ .. 21　D5
Campbellton .. 71　D4
Campbeltown . 10　D4
Campeche .... 85　D6
Campeche,
　Golfo de .. 85　D6
Campina Grande 92　D6
Campinas .... 94　A7
Campo Grande 93　G3
Campos ...... 93　G5
Campos Belos . 93　E4
Camrose ..... 69　C8
Can Tho ..... 38　B3
Canada ■ .... 68　C8
Çanakkale ... 23　D6
Çanakkale
　Boğazı .... 23　D6

Cananea ...... 84 A2
Canarias, Is. .. 52 C2
Canary Is. =
  Canarias, Is. . 52 C2
Canavieiras .. 93 F6
Canberra ..... 63 C4
Candia = Iráklion 23 G5
Canea = Khaniá 23 G5
Caniapiscau → 70 C4
Caniapiscau, L.
  de ...... 71 C4
Çankırı ...... 46 B3
Cannanore .... 43 P9
Cannes ...... 13 E7
Canoas ...... 94 B6
Canora ...... 69 C9
Cantabria □ .. 18 A4
Cantabrian
  Mts. =
  Cantábrica,
  Cordillera .. 18 A3
Cantábrica,
  Cordillera .. 18 A3
Canterbury .... 11 F7
Canterbury Bight 65 F4
Canterbury
  Plains ... 65 E4
Canton =
  Guangzhou . 35 D6
Canton ...... 76 D5
Cap-Haïtien .. 87 C5
Cape Breton I. . 71 D4
Cape Coast .. 53 G5
Cape Dorset .. 70 B3
Cape Town ... 58 E3
Cape Verde Is. ■ 50 E1
Cape York
  Peninsula .. 61 C7
Capela ...... 93 E6
Capri ...... 21 D5
Caprivi Strip .. 58 B4
Caquetá → ... 90 D5
Caracas ...... 90 A5
Caracol ...... 93 D5
Caratasca, L. .. 86 C3
Caratinga .... 93 F5
Caravelas .... 93 F6
Carbonear ... 71 D5
Carcassonne .. 12 E5
Carcross ...... 68 B6
Cárdenas .... 86 B3
Cardiff ...... 11 F5
Cardigan B. ... 11 E4
Cardston ..... 69 D8
Cariacica .... 93 G5
Caribbean Sea . 86 D5
Cariboo Mts. .. 69 C7
Carinhanha ... 93 E5
Carinthia =
  Kärnten □ .. 15 E7
Carlisle ...... 11 D5
Carlow ...... 11 E3
Carlsbad ..... 80 C1
Carmacks .... 68 B6
Carmarthen ... 11 F4
Carmaux ..... 12 D5
Carnarvon,
  Australia ... 60 E1
Carnarvon,
  S. Africa ... 58 E4
Carnegie, L. .. 60 F3
Caroline I. ... 65 K15
Caroline Is. ... 64 J10
Caroní → ..... 90 B6
Carpathians .. 16 D5
Carpaţii
  Meridionali .. 17 F7
Carpentaria, G.
  of ...... 60 C6
Carpentras ... 13 D6
Carrauntoohill . 11 E2
Carrick-on-Suir 11 E3
Carson City .. 72 G4
Cartagena,
  Colombia .. 90 A3
Cartagena,
  Spain ...... 19 D5

Cartago ...... 90 C3
Carthage ..... 81 A6
Cartwright ... 70 C5
Caruaru ...... 92 D6
Carúpano .... 90 A6
Casablanca .. 52 B4
Cascade Ra. ... 72 C3
Cascavel ..... 94 A6
Caseyr, Raas =
  Asir, Ras ... 49 E5
Casiquiare → . 90 C5
Casper ...... 73 E10
Caspian Sea .. 29 E6
Castelló de la
  Plana ...... 19 C5
Castelsarrasin . 12 D4
Castilla-La
  Mancha □ .. 18 C4
Castilla y Leon □ 18 A3
Castlebar .... 11 E2
Castleblaney .. 11 D3
Castres ...... 12 E5
Castries ...... 87 D7
Castro ...... 95 E2
Castro Alves .. 93 E6
Cat I. ...... 86 B4
Catalão ...... 93 F4
Catalonia =
  Cataluña □ .. 19 B6
Cataluña □ ... 19 B6
Catamarca ... 94 B3
Catanduanes □ 36 B2
Catanduva ... 93 G4
Catánia ...... 21 F5
Catanzaro .... 21 E6
Catoche, C. ... 85 C7
Catskill Mts. ... 77 C8
Cauca → ..... 90 B4
Caucasus
  Mountains .. 25 E5
Caura → ..... 90 B6
Cauvery → ... 43 P11
Cavan ...... 11 D3
Caviana, I. ... 92 B3
Cawnpore =
  Kanpur ... 40 D3
Caxias ...... 92 C5
Caxias do Sul .. 94 B6
Cayenne ..... 92 A3
Cayman Is. ☑ .. 86 C3
Ceanannus Mor 11 E3
Ceará =
  Fortaleza .. 92 C6
Ceará □ ...... 92 D6
Cebu ...... 36 B2
Cedar L. ..... 69 C10
Cedar Rapids .. 75 E9
Cegléd ...... 16 E4
Celaya ...... 84 C4
Celebes =
  Sulawesi □ . 37 E2
Celebes Sea .. 37 D2
Celtic Sea .... 11 F2
Central,
  Cordillera .. 90 C3
Central African
  Rep. ■ ..... 56 C4
Central Makran
  Range ...... 42 F4
Cephalonia =
  Kefallinía ... 23 E3
Ceram = Seram 37 E3
Ceram Sea =
  Seram Sea .. 37 E3
Cerignola .... 20 D5
Cerigo = Kíthira 23 F4
České
  Budějovice .. 16 D2
Českomoravská
  Vrchovina ... 16 D2
Çeşme ...... 23 E6
Ceuta ...... 18 E3
Cévennes .... 13 D5
Ceylon = Sri
  Lanka ■ .... 43 R12
Chachapoyas .. 91 E3
Chad ■ ...... 55 E2

Chad, L. =
  Tchad, L. .... 55 F1
Chagai Hills =
  Chãh Gay Hills 42 E3
Chagos Arch. .. 27 K11
Chãh Gay Hills . 42 E3
Chakradharpur 40 F5
Chalisgaon .... 43 J9
Chalon-sur-
  Saône ...... 13 C6
Châlons-en-
  Champagne . 13 B6
Chambal → ... 42 F11
Chambéry .... 13 D6
Chamonix-Mont
  Blanc ...... 13 D7
Champagne .. 13 B6
Champaign ... 76 D1
Champlain, L. . 77 B9
Chañaral ..... 94 B2
Chandigarh ... 42 D10
Chandpur .... 41 F8
Chandrapur ... 43 K11
Chang Jiang → 35 C7
Changchun ... 35 B7
Changde ..... 35 D6
Changhua .... 35 D7
Changhua ... 35 D6
Changsha .... 35 D6
Changzhi .... 35 C6
Changzhou ... 35 C6
Chania = Khaniá 23 G5
Channel Is. ... 11 G5
Chantrey Inlet . 68 B10
Chaozhou .... 35 D6
Chapala, L. de . 84 C4
Chapayevsk .. 24 C6
Chapra =
  Chhapra ... 40 E5
Charaña ..... 91 G5
Chardzhou =
  Chärjew .... 29 F7
Chari → ..... 55 F1
Chärikär ..... 42 B6
Chärjew ..... 29 F7
Charleroi .... 14 C3
Charles, C. ... 77 F8
Charleston, S.C.,
  U.S.A. ..... 83 C8
Charleston,
  W. Va., U.S.A. 76 E5
Charleville .... 63 A4
Charleville-
  Mézières ... 13 B6
Charlotte .... 83 B7
Charlottesville . 77 E6
Charlottetown . 71 D4
Charolles .... 13 C6
Charters Towers 61 E8
Chartres ..... 12 B4
Chascomús ... 94 D5
Châteaubriant . 12 C3
Châteaulin ... 12 B1
Châteauroux .. 12 C4
Châtellerault .. 12 C4
Chatham =
  Chatham-Kent 71 D2
Chatham =
  Miramichi .. 71 D4
Chatham ..... 11 F7
Chatham-Kent . 71 D2
Chattanooga .. 82 B5
Chaumont ... 13 B6
Cheb ...... 16 C1
Cheboksary .. 24 B6
Chech, Erg ... 52 D5
Chechenia □ .. 25 E6
Chechnya =
  Chechenia □ 25 E6
Cheduba I. ... 41 H9
Chegutu ..... 59 B6
Cheju do ..... 35 C7
Chekiang =
  Zhejiang □ .. 35 D7
Chełm ...... 17 C6
Chelmsford ... 11 F7

Chelyabinsk ... 29 D7
Chelyuskin, Mys 30 B8
Chemnitz .... 15 C7
Chenab → .... 42 D7
Chengchou =
  Zhengzhou .. 35 C6
Chengde ..... 35 B6
Chengdu ..... 35 C5
Chengjiang ... 34 D5
Ch'engtu =
  Chengdu ... 35 C5
Chennai ..... 43 N12
Cher → ...... 12 C4
Cherbourg ... 12 B3
Cherepovets .. 24 B4
Cherkasy .... 24 D3
Chernigov =
  Chernihiv ... 24 C3
Chernihiv .... 24 C3
Chernivtsi .... 17 D7
Chernobyl =
  Chornobyl .. 17 C10
Chernovtsy =
  Chernivtsi ... 17 D7
Cherrapunji ... 41 E8
Chervonohrad . 17 C7
Chesapeake B. . 77 E7
Cheshskaya
  Guba ...... 28 C5
Chester, U.K. .. 11 E5
Chester, U.S.A. 77 E8
Chesterfield ... 11 E6
Chesterfield, Is. 64 L10
Chesterfield Inlet 68 B10
Chetumal .... 85 D7
Cheviot Hills .. 10 D5
Chew Bahir ... 55 H6
Cheyenne .... 74 E2
Cheyenne → .. 74 C4
Chhapra ..... 40 E5
Chi → ...... 38 A2
Chiai ...... 35 D7
Chiamussu =
  Jiamusi .... 35 B8
Chiba ...... 33 F7
Chibougamau . 71 D3
Chicago ..... 76 D2
Chichagof I. ... 69 C6
Chichihar =
  Qiqihar ... 35 B7
Chiclana ..... 18 D2
Chiclayo ..... 91 E3
Chico ...... 72 G3
Chico →,
  Chubut,
  Argentina ... 95 E3
Chico →,
  Santa Cruz,
  Argentina ... 95 F3
Chicoutimi ... 71 D3
Chidley, C. ... 70 B4
Chieti ...... 20 C5
Chihli, G. of = Bo
  Hai ...... 35 C6
Chihuahua ... 84 B3
Chilapa ...... 84 D5
Chilaw ...... 43 R11
Chile ■ ...... 94 D2
Chililabombwe 59 A5
Chilin = Jilin .. 35 B7
Chilka L. ..... 40 H5
Chillán ...... 94 D2
Chiloé, I. de ... 95 E2
Chilpancingo .. 84 D5
Chilung ..... 35 D7
Chilwa, L. .... 59 B7
Chimborazo .. 90 D3
Chimbote .... 91 E3
Chimkent =
  Shymkent .. 29 E7
Chin □ ...... 41 F9
China ■ ..... 35 C5
Chinandega .. 85 E7
Chincha Alta .. 91 F3
Chindwin → .. 41 G10
Chingola ..... 59 A5
Clermont-

Chiniot ...... 42 D8
Chinnampo =
  Namp'o ... 35 C7
Chinon ...... 12 C4
Chíos = Khíos . 23 E6
Chipata ..... 59 A6
Chişinău ..... 17 E9
Chistopol .... 24 B7
Chita ...... 30 D9
Chitral ...... 42 B7
Chittagong ... 41 F8
Chittagong □ . 41 E8
Chkalov =
  Orenburg .. 29 D6
Cholet ...... 12 C3
Choluteca .... 85 E7
Chon Buri .... 38 B2
Chŏngjin ..... 35 B7
Chongqing ... 35 D5
Chŏnju ...... 35 C7
Chonos, Arch.
  de los ...... 95 F2
Chornobyl ... 17 C10
Chorzów ..... 16 C4
Choybalsan ... 35 B6
Christchurch .. 65 E5
Christmas I. =
  Kiritimati ... 65 J15
Ch'unchou =
  Quanzhou .. 35 D6
Chubut → .... 95 E3
Chudskoye,
  Ozero ...... 24 B2
Ch'unch'ŏn ... 35 C7
Chungking =
  Chongqing .. 35 D5
Chuquicamata . 94 A3
Chur ...... 13 C8
Churchill .... 68 C10
Churchill →,
  Man., Canada 68 C10
Churchill →,
  Nfld. & L.,
  Canada ... 71 C4
Churchill, C. .. 68 C10
Churchill L. ... 69 C9
Churu ...... 42 E9
Chusovoy .... 28 D6
Chuvashia □ .. 24 B6
Cicero ...... 76 D2
Ciechanów ... 16 B5
Ciego de Avila . 86 B4
Cienfuegos ... 86 B3
Cill Chainnigh =
  Kilkenny ... 11 E3
Cincinnati ... 76 E3
Cinto, Mte. ... 13 E8
Circle ...... 69 B5
Cirebon ..... 39 F3
Citlaltépetl =
  Orizaba, Pico
  de ...... 84 D5
Ciudad Bolívar . 90 B6
Ciudad del
  Carmen .... 85 D6
Ciudad
  Delicias =
  Delicias ... 84 B3
Ciudad Guayana 90 B6
Ciudad Juárez . 84 A3
Ciudad Madero 84 C5
Ciudad Obregón 84 B3
Ciudad Real .. 18 C4
Ciudad Trujillo =
  Santo
  Domingo ... 87 C6
Ciudad Victoria 84 C5
Cizre ...... 46 C5
Clarksdale ... 81 B8
Clarksville ... 82 A4
Clear, C. ..... 11 F2
Clearwater ... 83 F6
Clearwater Mts. 73 C6
Clermont-
  Ferrand ..... 13 D5

# Cleveland

Cleveland ...... 76 D5
Clinton ....... 75 E9
Clinton Colden
  L. ...... 68 B9
Clones ...... 11 D3
Clonmel ...... 11 E3
Clovis ...... 80 B2
Cluj-Napoca ... 17 E6
Clyde → ...... 10 D4
Clyde, Firth of . 10 D4
Clyde River ... 70 A4
Coast Mts. .... 68 C7
Coast Ranges . 72 F2
Coats I. ...... 70 B2
Coats Land ... 96 B5
Coatzacoalcos . 85 D6
Cobar ...... 63 B4
Cóbh ...... 11 F2
Cobija ...... 91 F5
Cocanada =
  Kakinada ... 40 J4
Cochabamba .. 91 G5
Cochin ...... 43 Q10
Cochin China =
  Nam-Phan .. 38 B3
Cochrane .... 71 D2
Cockburn, Canal 95 G2
Coco → ...... 86 D3
Cod, C. ...... 77 C10
Codó ...... 92 C5
Cœur d'Alene . 72 C5
Cognac ...... 12 D3
Coimbatore ... 43 P10
Coimbra ...... 18 B1
Colatina ...... 93 F5
Colchester ... 11 F7
Coleraine .... 11 D3
Colima ...... 84 D4
Coll ...... 10 C3
Colmar ...... 13 B7
Cologne = Köln 14 C4
Colomb-
  Béchar =
  Béchar = ... 52 B5
Colombia ■ ... 90 C4
Colombo .... 43 R11
Colonsay .... 10 C3
Colorado □ .. 79 A10
Colorado →,
  Argentina ... 95 D4
Colorado →,
  N. Amer. ... 78 E5
Colorado
  Plateau .... 79 B7
Colorado
  Springs .... 74 F2
Columbia, Mo.,
  U.S.A. .... 75 F8
Columbia, S.C.,
  U.S.A. .... 83 B7
Columbia, Tenn.,
  U.S.A. .... 82 B4
Columbia → .. 72 C1
Columbia,
  District of □ . 77 E7
Columbus, Ga.,
  U.S.A. .... 82 C5
Columbus,
  Miss., U.S.A. 82 C3
Columbus, Ohio,
  U.S.A. .... 76 E4
Colville → .... 69 A4
Colwyn Bay .. 11 E5
Comilla ...... 41 F8
Committee B. . 70 B2
Communism
  Pk. =
  Kommunizma,
  Pik ...... 29 F8
Como ...... 20 B2
Como, Lago di . 20 B2
Comodoro
  Rivadavia .. 95 F3
Comorin, C. .. 43 Q10
Comoros ■ ... 51 H8
Compiègne ... 13 B5

Conakry ...... 53 G3
Conceição da
  Barra ...... 93 F6
Concepción,
  Chile ...... 94 D2
Concepción,
  Paraguay ... 94 A5
Concepción del
  Oro ...... 84 C4
Concepción del
  Uruguay ... 94 C5
Conchos → .. 84 B3
Concord .... 77 C10
Concordia .... 94 C5
Condeúba .... 93 E5
Congo
  (Brazzaville) =
  Congo ■ ... 56 E3
Congo
  (Kinshasa) =
  Congo, Dem.
  Rep. of the ■ 56 E4
Congo ■ ..... 56 E3
Congo → ..... 56 F2
Congo, Dem.
  Rep. of the ■ 56 E4
Conjeeveram =
  Kanchipuram 43 N11
Conn, L. ...... 11 D2
Connacht □ .. 11 E2
Connecticut □ . 77 D9
Connecticut → . 77 D9
Connemara ... 11 E2
Conselheiro
  Lafaiete .... 93 G5
Constance =
  Konstanz ... 14 E5
Constance, L. =
  Bodensee .. 13 C8
Constanța .... 22 B7
Constantine .. 52 A7
Constitución .. 94 D2
Contas → .... 93 E6
Coober Pedy .. 62 A1
Cooch Behar =
  Koch Bihar . 41 D7
Cook, Mt. =
  Aoraki Mount
  Cook ...... 65 E4
Cook Inlet ... 69 C4
Cook Is. .... 65 L14
Cook Strait ... 65 D6
Cooktown .... 61 D8
Coondapoor .. 43 N9
Copenhagen =
  København .. 9 D8
Copiapó .... 94 B2
Coppermine =
  Kugluktuk .. 68 B8
Coppermine → 68 B8
Coquimbo .... 94 C2
Coracora .... 91 G4
Coral Harbour . 70 B2
Coral Sea .... 64 L10
Corby ...... 11 E6
Corcaigh = Cork 11 F2
Córdoba,
  Argentina ... 94 C4
Córdoba, Spain 18 D3
Córdoba, Sierra
  de ...... 94 C4
Cordova .... 69 B5
Corfu = Kérkira 23 E2
Corinth =
  Kórinthos .. 23 F4
Corinth, G. of =
  Korinthiakós
  Kólpos .... 23 E4
Corinto .... 23 E4
Cork ...... 11 F2
Corner Brook . 71 D5
Cornwall .... 71 D3
Coro ...... 90 A5
Corocoro .... 91 G5
Coronation Gulf 68 B8
Coronel Suárez 94 D4
Corpus Christi . 80 F5

Corrib, L. ..... 11 E2
Corrientes .... 94 B5
Corrientes, C.,
  Colombia ... 90 B3
Corrientes, C.,
  Mexico .... 84 C3
Corse ...... 13 E8
Corse, C. .... 13 E8
Corsica = Corse 13 E8
Corsicana .... 81 C5
Corte ...... 13 E8
Çorum ...... 46 B3
Corumbá .... 91 G7
Corunna = A
  Coruña .... 18 A1
Corvallis .... 72 D2
Cosenza .... 21 E6
Costa Blanca .. 19 C5
Costa Brava .. 19 B7
Costa del Sol .. 18 D3
Costa Dorada .. 19 B6
Costa Rica ■ .. 86 E3
Cotabato .... 36 C2
Côte d'Azur .. 13 E7
Côte-d'Ivoire =
  Ivory Coast ■ 53 G4
Cotentin .... 12 B3
Cotonou .... 53 G6
Cotopaxi .... 90 D3
Cotswold Hills . 11 F5
Cottbus .... 15 C8
Council Bluffs . 75 E7
Courantyne → . 90 B7
Courtrai =
  Kortrijk .... 14 C2
Coventry .... 11 E6
Covington → .. 76 E3
Cox's Bazar .. 41 G8
Cozumel, Isla . 85 C7
Cracow =
  Kraków .... 16 C4
Cradock .... 59 E5
Craigavon .... 11 D3
Craiova .... 22 B5
Cranbrook .... 69 D8
Crateús .... 92 D5
Crato ...... 92 D6
Crawley .... 11 F6
Cremona .... 20 B3
Crete = Kríti .. 23 G5
Creuse → .... 12 C4
Crewe ...... 11 E5
Crimean Pen. =
  Krymskyy
  Pivostriv .. 25 D3
Crişul Negru → 16 E5
Crna Gora =
  Montenegro □ 22 C2
Croatia ■ .... 20 B6
Croker, C. .... 60 C5
Cromer ...... 11 E7
Cross Sound .. 69 C6
Crowsnest Pass 69 D8
Cruzeiro do Sul 91 E4
Cuando → .... 58 B4
Cuango =
  Kwango → .. 56 E3
Cuanza → .... 56 F2
Cuba ■ ...... 86 B4
Cubango → .. 58 B4
Cúcuta ...... 90 B4
Cuddalore ... 43 P11
Cuenca, Ecuador 90 D3
Cuenca, Spain . 19 B4
Cuernavaca .. 84 D5
Cuiabá ...... 93 F2
Cuito → ...... 58 B4
Culiacán .... 84 C3
Cumaná .... 90 A6
Cumberland .. 77 E6
Cumberland
  Pen. ...... 70 B4
Cumberland
  Plateau .... 76 B4
Cumberland Sd. 70 B4
Cunene → .... 58 B2
Cúneo ...... 20 B1

Cunnamulla ... 63 A4
Curaçao .... 87 D6
Curicó ...... 94 C2
Curitiba .... 94 B7
Cuttack .... 40 G5
Cuxhaven .... 14 B5
Cuzco ...... 91 F4
Cwmbran .... 11 F5
Cyclades =
  Kikládhes .. 23 F5
Cyprus ■ .... 46 D3
Cyrenaica .... 54 C3
Czech Rep. ■ . 16 D2
Częstochowa .. 16 C4

# D

Da Hinggan Ling 35 B7
Da Lat ...... 38 B3
Da Nang .... 38 A3
Da Qaidam ... 34 C4
Daba Shan ... 35 C5
Dacca = Dhaka . 41 F8
Dadra & Nagar
  Haveli □ ... 43 J8
Dadu ...... 42 F5
Dagestan □ .. 25 E6
Dagö = Hiiumaa 24 B1
Dagupan .... 36 A2
Dahod ...... 43 H9
Dahomey =
  Benin ■ .... 53 G6
Dakar ...... 53 F2
Dakhla ...... 52 D2
Dalandzadgad . 35 B5
Dali ...... 34 D5
Dalian ...... 35 C7
Daliang Shan .. 34 D5
Dallas ...... 81 C5
Dalmacija ... 20 C6
Dalmatia =
  Dalmacija .. 20 C6
Dalua ...... 53 G4
Daly Waters .. 60 D5
Daman ...... 43 J8
Damaraland .. 58 C3
Damascus =
  Dimashq ... 46 D4
Damāvand,
  Qolleh-ye .. 44 C3
Dâmbovița → . 22 B6
Damietta =
  Dumyât .... 54 B5
Dammam = Ad
  Dammām ... 47 F7
Dampier .... 60 E2
Danbury .... 77 D9
Dandong .... 35 B7
Danger Is. =
  Pukapuka .. 65 L14
Dangla Shan =
  Tanggula
  Shan ...... 34 C4
Danube =
  Dunărea → . 17 F9
Danville .... 83 A8
Danzig = Gdańsk 16 A4
Dar el Beida =
  Casablanca . 52 B4
Dar es Salaam . 57 F7
Darbhanga ... 40 D5
Dardanelles =
  Çanakkale
  Boğazı .... 23 D6
Dârfûr ...... 55 F3
Darién, G. del . 90 B3
Darjeeling =
  Darjiling ... 40 D7
Darjiling .... 40 D7
Darling → .... 62 B3
Darling Ra. .. 60 G2
Darlington ... 11 D6
Darmstadt ... 14 D5
Darnah ...... 54 B3

Darnley, C. ... 96 A10
Darnley B. .... 68 B7
Dartmoor .... 11 F5
Dartmouth ... 71 D4
Darwin ...... 60 C5
Daryoi Amu =
  Amudarya → 29 E6
Dashen, Ras ... 57 B7
Dashhowuz ... 29 E6
Dasht → .... 42 G2
Datong ...... 35 B6
Daugava → .. 24 B1
Daugavpils ... 24 B2
Dauphin .... 69 C9
Dauphiné .... 13 D6
Davangere ... 43 M9
Davao ...... 36 C3
Davenport ... 75 E9
Davis Str. .... 70 B5
Dawna Ra. ... 41 J12
Dawson .... 68 B6
Dax ...... 12 E3
Daxian ...... 35 C5
Daxue Shan .. 34 C5
Dayr az Zawr .. 46 D5
Dayton ...... 76 E3
Daytona Beach 83 E7
Dead Sea .... 47 E3
Death Valley .. 78 B4
Debre Markos . 55 F6
Debrecen .... 16 E5
Decatur, Ala.,
  U.S.A. .... 82 B4
Decatur, Ill.,
  U.S.A. .... 75 F10
Deccan ...... 43 L11
Dee → ...... 10 C5
Dehra Dun ... 42 D11
Delaware □ .. 77 E8
Delgado, C. .. 57 G8
Delhi ...... 42 E10
Delicias .... 84 B3
Déline ...... 68 B7
Demanda, Sierra
  de la ...... 18 A4
Demavend =
  Damāvand,
  Qolleh-ye .. 44 C3
Den Haag =
  's-Gravenhage 14 B3
Den Helder ... 14 B3
Denmark ■ .. 9 D7
Denmark Str. .. 66 C17
Denpasar .... 39 F5
Denton ...... 80 C5
D'Entrecasteaux
  Is. ...... 61 B9
Denver ...... 74 F2
Deoghar .... 40 E6
Deolali ...... 43 K8
Dera Ghazi Khan 42 D7
Dera Ismail Khan 42 D7
Derbent .... 25 E6
Derby, Australia 60 D3
Derby, U.K. ... 11 E6
Derg, L. .... 11 E2
Derry =
  Londonderry 11 D3
Des Moines ■ . 75 E8
Des Moines → 75 E9
Dese ...... 49 E2
Desolación, I. .. 95 G2
Dessau .... 15 C7
Dessye = Dese . 49 E2
Detroit ...... 76 C4
Deutsche Bucht 14 A5
Deventer .... 14 B4
Dezfūl ...... 47 D7
Dezhneva, Mys 31 C16
Dhahran = Az
  Zahrān .... 47 F7
Dhaka ...... 41 F8
Dhaka □ .... 41 E8
Dhamtari .... 40 G3
Dhanbad .... 40 F6
Dhaulagiri ... 40 C4
Dhenkanal ... 40 G5

Dhodhekánisos 23 F6
Dhuburi ...... 41 D7
Dhule ....... 43 J9
Diamantina .. 93 F5
Diamantina → . 62 A2
Diamantino ... 93 E2
Dibrugarh .... 41 D10
Diefenbaker, L. 69 C9
Dieppe ....... 12 B4
Digby ....... 71 D4
Digne-les-Bains 13 D7
Dihang =
  Brahmaputra →
  .......... 41 F7
Dijlah, Nahr → 47 E6
Dijon ....... 13 C6
Dili ......... 37 F3
Dillingham ... 69 C4
Dimashq ..... 46 D4
Dîmbovița =
  Dâmbovița → 22 B6
Dimitrovgrad .. 24 C6
Dinajpur .... 41 E7
Dinan ....... 12 B2
Dinant ...... 14 C3
Dinara Planina . 20 B6
Dinaric Alps =
  Dinara Planina 20 B6
Dingle ...... 11 E1
Dingwall .... 10 C4
Dire Dawa ... 49 F3
Dirranbandi .. 63 A4
Disappointment,
  L. ......... 60 D3
Disko =
  Qeqertarsuaq 70 B5
Distrito
  Federal □ ... 93 F4
Diu ......... 43 J7
Divinópolis .. 93 G5
Diyarbakır ... 46 C5
Djakarta =
  Jakarta .... 39 F3
Djawa = Jawa . 39 F3
Djerba, I. de ... 54 B1
Djerid, Chott .. 52 B7
Djibouti ..... 49 E3
Djibouti ■ ... 49 E3
Dnepr =
  Dnipro → ... 25 D3
Dneprodzerzhinsk =
  Dniprodzerzhynsk
  .......... 25 D3
Dnepropetrovsk –
  Dnipropetrovsk
  .......... 25 D4
Dnestr =
  Dnister → ... 17 E10
Dnestrovski =
  Belgorod .... 24 C4
Dnieper =
  Dnipro → ... 25 D3
Dniester =
  Dnister → ... 17 E10
Dnipro → ..... 25 D3
Dniprodzerzhynsk
  .......... 25 D3
Dnipropetrovsk 25 D4
Dnister → .... 17 E10
Dnyapro =
  Dnipro → .... 25 D3
Doba ........ 55 G2
Doberai, Jazirah 37 E4
Dobrich ..... 22 C6
Dodecanese =
  Dhodhekánisos
  .......... 23 F6
Dodge City .. 80 A3
Dodoma ..... 57 F7
Doha = Ad
  Dawḩah .... 44 E2
Dolbeau-
  Mistassini .. 71 D3
Dole ........ 13 C6
Dolomites =
  Dolomiti ... 20 A3
Dolomiti ...... 20 A3

Dolores ...... 94 D5
Dolphin and
  Union Str. ... 68 B8
Dominica ■ .. 87 C7
Dominican
  Rep. ■ ..... 87 C5
Don →, Russia 25 D4
Don →, U.K. .. 10 C5
Donau =
  Dunărea → . 17 F9
Doncaster .... 11 E6
Donegal ..... 11 D2
Donets → .... 25 D5
Donetsk ..... 25 D4
Dongola ..... 55 E5
Dongting Hu .. 35 D6
Donostia-San
  Sebastián .. 19 A5
Dorchester, C. . 70 B3
Dordogne → .. 12 D3
Dordrecht .... 14 C3
Döröö Nuur .. 34 B4
Dortmund .... 14 C4
Dos Bahias, C. . 95 E3
Dothan ...... 82 D5
Douai ....... 13 A5
Douala ...... 56 D1
Doubs → ..... 13 C6
Douglas, U.K. . 11 D4
Douglas, U.S.A. 79 E8
Dourados .... 94 A6
Douro → ..... 18 B1
Dover ....... 11 F7
Dover, Str. of .. 11 F7
Dovrefjell .... 8 C7
Draguignan .. 13 E7
Drakensberg .. 59 E5
Drammen .... 9 D8
Drau = Drava → 20 B7
Drava → ..... 20 B7
Dresden ..... 15 C7
Dreux ....... 12 B4
Drina → ..... 20 B7
Drobeta-Turnu
  Severin .... 22 B4
Drogheda .... 11 E3
Drogobych =
  Drohobych .. 17 D6
Drohobych ... 17 D6
Droichead
  Atha =
  Drogheda .. 11 E3
Dronning Maud
  Land ...... 96 B7
Drumheller .. 69 C8
Drygalski I. .. 96 A11
Dubai = Dubayy 44 E3
Dubawnt → ... 68 B9
Dubawnt L. ... 68 B9
Dubayy ..... 44 E3
Dubbo ....... 63 B4
Dublin, Ireland . 11 E3
Dublin, U.S.A. . 83 C6
Dubrovnik ... 20 C7
Dudinka ..... 30 C6
Duero =
  Douro → ... 18 B1
Duisburg .... 14 C4
Dulce → ..... 94 C4
Duluth ...... 75 B8
Dumfries .... 11 D5
Dumyât ...... 54 B5
Dún Dealgan =
  Dundalk ... 11 D3
Dún Laoghaire . 11 E3
Duna =
  Dunărea → . 17 F9
Dunaj =
  Dunărea → . 17 F9
Dunărea → ... 17 F9
Dunav =
  Dunărea → . 17 F9
Dunbar ...... 10 C5
Duncan ...... 80 B5
Dundalk ..... 11 D3
Dundee ...... 10 C5

Dunedin ..... 65 F4
Dunfermline .. 10 C5
Dungarvan ... 11 E3
Dunhuang ... 34 B4
Dunkerque .. 12 A5
Dunkirk =
  Dunkerque .. 12 A5
Dúnleary = Dún
  Laoghaire .. 11 E3
Durance → ... 13 E6
Durango ..... 84 C4
Durazno ..... 94 C5
Durazzo =
  Durrës ..... 22 D2
Durban ...... 59 D6
Düren ....... 14 C4
Durg ........ 40 G3
Durgapur .... 40 F6
Durham, U.K. . 11 D6
Durham, U.S.A. 83 B8
Durrës ....... 22 D2
Dushanbe ... 29 F7
Düsseldorf ... 14 C4
Dutch Harbor .. 69 C3
Duyun ....... 35 D5
Duzdab =
  Zāhedān ... 45 D5
Dvina,
  Severnaya → 28 C5
Dvinsk =
  Daugavpils .. 24 B2
Dwarka ...... 43 H6
Dyer, C. ..... 70 B4
Dyersburg ... 81 A9
Dzamīn Üüd =
  Borhoyn Tal . 35 B6
Dzerzhinsk ... 24 B5
Dzhambul =
  Taraz ...... 29 E8
Dzhankoy ... 25 D3
Dzhezkazgan =
  Zhezqazghan 29 E7
Dzhizak =
  Jizzakh .... 29 E7
Dzungaria =
  Junggar Pendi 34 B3
Dzuumod .... 35 B5

# E

East Bengal ... 41 E7
East Beskids =
  Vychodné
  Beskydy ... 17 D5
East China Sea 35 C7
East Falkland . 95 G5
East Kilbride .. 10 D4
East London .. 59 E5
East Main =
  Eastmain ... 71 C3
East Sea =
  Japan, Sea of 32 D4
Eastbourne .. 11 F7
Eastern Ghats . 43 N11
Eastmain ... 71 C3
Eastmain → .. 71 C3
Eau Claire ... 75 C9
Ebetsu ...... 32 B7
Ebro → ...... 19 B6
Ech Chéliff .. 52 A6
Echo Bay .... 68 B8
Ecuador ■ ... 90 D3
Edinburgh ... 10 D5
Édirne ...... 22 D6
Edmonton ... 69 C8
Edmundston .. 71 D4
Edremit ..... 23 E6
Edson ....... 69 C8
Edward VII Land 96 C17
Edward, L. ... 57 E5
Edwards Plateau 80 D3
Eger = Cheb ... 16 C1
Eger ........ 16 E5
Egmont, Mt. =
  Taranaki, Mt. 64 C6

Eğridir ...... 46 C2
Eğridir Gölü .. 46 C2
Egypt ■ ..... 54 C5
Eifel ........ 14 C4
Eigg ........ 10 C3
Eindhoven ... 14 C3
Eire = Ireland ■ 11 E3
Eivissa ...... 19 C6
El Aaiún ..... 52 C3
El 'Alamein ... 54 B4
El Asnam = Ech
  Chéliff ..... 52 A6
El Centro .... 78 D5
El Djouf ..... 53 D4
El Dorado .... 81 C7
El Faiyûm ... 54 C5
El Fâsher .... 55 F4
El Ferrol = Ferrol 18 A1
El Fuerte .... 84 B3
El Gîza ...... 54 C5
El Iskandarîya . 54 B4
El Jadida .... 52 B4
El Khârga .... 54 C5
El Khartûm ... 55 E5
El Mahalla el
  Kubra ..... 54 B5
El Mansûra ... 54 B5
El Minyâ .... 54 C5
El Obeid ..... 55 F5
El Oued ..... 52 B7
El Paso ...... 79 E9
El Qâhira .... 54 B5
El Reno ..... 80 B5
El Salvador ■ . 85 E7
El Suweis .... 54 C5
El Tigre ..... 90 B6
El Uqsur ..... 54 C5
Elat ........ 47 E3
Elâziğ ....... 46 C4
Elba ........ 20 C3
Elbasan ..... 22 D3
Elbe → ...... 14 B5
Elbert, Mt. ... 79 A9
Elbeuf ...... 12 B4
Elbing = Elbląg 16 A4
Elbląg ....... 16 A4
Elburz Mts. =
  Alborz,
  Reshteh-ye
  Kühhā-ye .. 44 B3
Elche ....... 19 C5
Eldoret ..... 57 D7
Elefantes → .. 59 C6
Elektrostal ... 24 B4
Elephant I. ... 96 A4
Eleuthera .... 86 A4
Elgin, U.K. ... 10 C5
Elgin, U.S.A. .. 76 C1
Elgon, Mt. ... 57 D6
Elista ....... 25 D5
Elizabeth .... 77 D8
Elizabeth City . 83 A9
Elkhart ...... 76 D3
Elko ........ 72 F6
Ellice Is. =
  Tuvalu ■ ... 64 K12
Ellore = Eluru 40 J3
Ellsworth Land 96 B2
Eluru ....... 40 J3
Elx = Elche ... 19 C5
Ely ......... 11 E7
Emāmrūd ... 44 B3
Embarcación .. 94 A4
Emden ...... 14 B4
Emmen ..... 14 B4
Empalme .... 84 B2
Empangeni .. 59 D6
Empedrado .. 94 B5
Empty Quarter =
  Rub' al Khālī . 48 D4
Ems → ...... 14 B4
Enare = Inarijärvi 8 B13
Encarnación .. 94 B5
Encounter B. .. 62 C2
Ende ........ 37 F2

Enderby Land . 96 A9
Enewetak Atoll 64 H11
Enez ........ 23 D6
Engels ...... 24 C6
Enggano .... 39 F2
England □ ... 11 E6
English Bazar =
  Ingraj Bazar . 40 E7
English Channel 11 F5
Enid ........ 80 A5
Ennedi ...... 55 E3
Ennis ....... 11 E2
Enniskillen ... 11 D3
Enns → ..... 15 D8
Enschede ... 14 B4
Ensenada ... 84 A1
Entebbe ..... 57 D6
Entre Ríos □ .. 94 C5
Enugu ...... 53 G7
Épernay ..... 13 B5
Épinal ...... 13 B7
Equatorial
  Guinea ■ ... 56 D1
Er Rachidia .. 52 B5
Erāwadī Myit =
  Irrawaddy → 41 K10
Erbil = Arbīl .. 46 C6
Erciyaş Dağı .. 46 C3
Erebus, Mt. .. 96 B15
Ereğli, Konya,
  Turkey .... 46 C3
Ereğli,
  Zonguldak,
  Turkey .... 46 B2
Erfurt ...... 15 C6
Erie ........ 77 C5
Erie, L. ..... 76 C5
Eritrea ■ .... 49 E2
Erlangen .... 15 D6
Erne, Lower L. . 11 D3
Erode ....... 43 P10
Ertis = Irtysh → 28 C7
Erzgebirge ... 15 C7
Erzincan .... 46 C4
Erzurum .... 46 C5
Es Sahrâ' el
  Sharqîya ... 54 C5
Es Sînâ' ..... 54 C5
Esbjerg ..... 9 D7
Esch-sur-Alzette 13 B6
Escuinapa ... 84 C3
Eşfahan ..... 44 C2
Esh Sham =
  Dimashq ... 46 D4
Eskilstuna ... 9 D9
Eskimo Point =
  Arviat ..... 68 B10
Eskişehir .... 46 C2
Eslāmābād-e
  Gharb ..... 46 D6
Esperance ... 60 G3
Espinazo, Sierra
  del = ......
  Espinhaço,
  Serra do ... 93 F5
Espinhaço, Serra
  do ........ 93 F5
Espírito Santo □ 93 G5
Essaouira ... 52 B4
Essen ...... 14 C4
Essequibo → .. 90 B7
Estados, I. de
  Los ....... 95 G4
Estância .... 93 E6
Estevan ..... 69 D9
Estonia ■ ... 24 B2
Estrondo, Serra
  do ........ 93 E4
Etawah ..... 42 F11
Ethiopia ■ ... 49 F2
Etna ........ 21 F5
Etosha Pan ... 58 B3
Euboea = Évvoia 23 E5
Eugene ..... 72 E2
Euphrates =
  Furāt, Nahr
  al → ...... 47 E6

# Eureka

Eureka ... 72 F1
Europa, Île ... 59 J8
Europa, Picos de 18 A3
Evanston ... 76 C2
Evansville ... 76 F2
Everest, Mt. ... 40 C6
Everett ... 72 C2
Everglades △ .. 83 G7
Évora ... 18 C2
Évreux ... 12 B4
Évros → ... 22 D6
Évvoia ... 23 E6
Exeter ... 11 F5
Exmoor ... 11 F5
Exmouth ... 11 F5
Extremadura □ 18 C2
Eyasi, L. ... 57 E6
Eyre, L. ... 60 F6
Eyre Pen. ... 62 B2

## F

F.Y.R.O.M. =
  Macedonia ■ 22 D3
Føroe Is. =
  Føroyar ... 6 C4
Fair Isle ... 10 B6
Fairbanks ... 69 B5
Fairweather, Mt. 69 C6
Faisalabad ... 42 D8
Faizabad ... 40 D4
Falkland Is. ∅ .. 95 G5
Fall River ... 77 D10
Falmouth ... 11 F4
Falun ... 9 C9
Famagusta ... 46 D3
Fao = Al Fāw .. 47 E7
Farāh ... 42 C3
Farasān, Jazā'ir 49 D3
Farasan Is. =
  Farasān,
  Jazā'ir ... 49 D3
Fareham ... 11 F6
Farewell C. =
  Nunap Isua . 70 C6
Fargo ... 74 B6
Fārs □ ... 44 D3
Farvel, Kap =
  Nunap Isua . 70 C6
Fāryāb □ ... 45 B6
Fatehgarh ... 42 F11
Fatehpur, Raj.,
  India ... 42 F9
Fatehpur, Ut. P.,
  India ... 40 E3
Fayetteville,
  Ark., U.S.A. . 81 A6
Fayetteville,
  N.C., U.S.A. . 83 B8
Fazilka ... 42 D9
Fdérik ... 52 D3
Fécamp ... 12 B4
Fehmarn ... 15 A6
Feira de Santana 93 E6
Felipe Carrillo
  Puerto ... 85 D7
Felixstowe ... 11 F7
Fenyang ... 35 C6
Feodosiya ... 25 D4
Fernando Póo =
  Bioko ... 56 D1
Ferozepore =
  Firozpur ... 42 D9
Ferrara ... 20 B3
Ferret, C. ... 12 D3
Ferrol ... 18 A1
Fès ... 52 B5
Fetlar ... 10 A6
Feuilles → ... 70 C3
Fez = Fès ... 52 B5
Fezzan ... 54 C2
Fianarantsoa .. 59 J9
Figeac ... 12 D5

Fiji ■ ... 64 L12
Finike ... 46 C2
Finisterre, C. =
  Fisterra, C. . 18 A1
Finland ■ ... 8 C11
Finland, G. of . 9 D11
Finlay → ... 68 C7
Firat = Furāt,
  Nahr al → . 47 E6
Firenze ... 20 C3
Firozabad ... 42 F11
Firozpur ... 42 D9
Fish → ... 58 D3
Fishguard ... 11 E4
Fisterra, C. ... 18 A1
Fiume = Rijeka . 20 B5
Flagstaff ... 79 C7
Flanders =
  Flandre ... 14 C2
Flandre ... 14 C2
Flathead L. ... 73 C7
Flattery, C. ... 72 B1
Flensburg ... 14 A5
Flers ... 12 B3
Flin Flon ... 69 C9
Flinders → ... 61 D7
Flinders Ranges 62 B2
Flint ... 76 C4
Flint I. ... 65 L15
Florence =
  Firenze ... 20 C3
Florence ... 83 B8
Flores ... 37 F2
Flores Sea ... 37 F2
Florianópolis .. 94 B7
Florida ... 94 C5
Florida □ ... 83 F6
Florida, Straits
  of ... 86 B3
Florø ... 8 C7
Flushing =
  Vlissingen .. 14 C2
Fly → ... 61 B7
Focşani ... 17 F8
Fóggia ... 20 D5
Foix ... 12 E4
Folkestone ... 11 F7
Fongafale ... 64 K12
Fontainebleau . 13 B5
Fontenay-le-
  Comte ... 12 C3
Foochow =
  Fuzhou ... 35 D6
Forfar ... 10 C5
Forlì ... 20 B4
Formosa =
  Taiwan ■ ... 35 D7
Formosa ... 94 B5
Føroyar ... 6 C4
Forsayth ... 61 D7
Fort Albany ... 71 C2
Fort Collins ... 74 E2
Fort-de-France . 87 D7
Fort Dodge ... 75 D7
Fort Franklin =
  Déline ... 68 B7
Fort Good Hope 68 B7
Fort Lauderdale 83 F7
Fort Liard ... 68 B7
Fort Macleod .. 69 D8
Fort McPherson 68 B6
Fort Myers ... 83 F7
Fort Norman =
  Tulita ... 68 B7
Fort Peck L. ... 73 C10
Fort Providence 68 B8
Fort Resolution 68 B8
Fort Rupert =
  Waskaganish 71 C3
Fort Scott ... 81 A6
Fort Shevchenko 29 E6
Fort Simpson .. 68 B7
Fort Smith,
  Canada ... 68 B8
Fort Smith,
  U.S.A. ... 81 B6

Fort Wayne ... 76 D3
Fort William .. 10 C4
Fort Worth ... 80 C5
Fort Yukon ... 69 B5
Fortaleza ... 92 C6
Foshan ... 35 D6
Fougères ... 12 B3
Foula ... 10 A5
Fouta Djalon .. 53 F3
Foxe Basin ... 70 B3
Foxe Chan. ... 70 B2
Foxe Pen. ... 70 B3
Foz do Iguaçu . 94 B6
Franca ... 93 G4
France ■ ... 13 C5
Franceville ... 56 E2
Franche-Comté 13 C6
Francistown ... 59 C5
Frankfurt,
  Brandenburg,
  Germany ... 15 B8
Frankfurt,
  Hessen,
  Germany ... 14 C5
Franklin B. ... 68 B7
Franklin Mts. .. 68 B7
Franklin Str. ... 68 A10
Frantsa Iosifa,
  Zemlya ... 28 A6
Fraser → ... 69 D7
Fraserburgh ... 10 C5
Fredericksburg 77 E7
Fredericton ... 71 D4
Frederikshavn . 9 D8
Fredrikstad ... 9 D8
Freeport ... 86 A4
Freetown ... 53 G3
Freiburg ... 14 E4
French Guiana ∅ 92 B3
French
  Polynesia ∅ 65 M16
Fresnillo ... 84 C4
Fresno ... 78 B3
Fria, C. ... 58 B2
Friendly Is. =
  Tonga ■ ... 65 L13
Frobisher B. ... 70 B4
Frobisher Bay =
  Iqaluit ... 70 B4
Frunze = Bishkek 29 E8
Frutal ... 93 F4
Frýdek-Místek . 16 D4
Fuchou =
  Fuzhou ... 35 D6
Fuchū ... 33 F3
Fuerte → ... 84 B3
Fuerteventura . 52 C3
Fuhai ... 34 B3
Fuji ... 33 F6
Fuji-San ... 33 F6
Fujian □ ... 35 D6
Fujiyama, Mt. =
  Fuji-San ... 33 F6
Fukien =
  Fujian □ ... 35 D6
Fukui ... 33 E5
Fukuoka ... 33 G2
Fukushima ... 33 E7
Fukuyama ... 33 F3
Fulda ... 14 C5
Fulda → ... 14 C5
Funabashi ... 33 F7
Funafuti =
  Fongafale ... 64 K12
Funchal ... 52 B2
Fundy, B. of ... 71 D4
Furāt, Nahr al → 47 E6
Furneaux Group 62 D4
Fürth ... 14 D6
Fury and Hecla
  Str. ... 70 B2
Fushun ... 35 B7
Futuna ... 64 L12
Fuxin ... 35 B7
Fuzhou ... 35 D6
Fyn ... 9 D8

## G

Gabès ... 54 B1
Gabès, G. de .. 54 B1
Gabon ■ ... 56 E2
Gaborone ... 59 C5
Gabrovo ... 22 C5
Gachsārān ... 44 D2
Gadarwara ... 43 H11
Gadsden ... 82 B4
Gafsa ... 52 B7
Gagnoa ... 53 G4
Gagnon ... 71 C4
Gaillimh =
  Galway ... 11 E2
Gainesville, Fla.,
  U.S.A. ... 83 E6
Gainesville, Ga.,
  U.S.A. ... 83 B6
Gairdner, L. ... 62 B2
Galashiels ... 10 D5
Galaţi ... 17 F9
Galdhøpiggen . 8 C7
Galesburg ... 75 E9
Galicia □ ... 18 A2
Galilee, Sea of =
  Yam Kinneret 46 D3
Gallinas, Pta. .. 90 A4
Gallipoli =
  Gelibolu ... 23 D6
Gällivare ... 8 B10
Galloway, Mull
  of ... 11 D4
Galveston ... 81 E6
Galway ... 11 E2
Galway B. ... 11 E2
Gambia ■ ... 53 F2
Gambia → ... 53 F2
Gäncä ... 25 E6
Gand = Gent .. 14 C2
Gandak → ... 40 E5
Gander ... 71 D5
Gandhi Sagar . 43 G9
Ganga → ... 41 F8
Ganganagar ... 42 E8
Ganges =
  Ganga → ... 41 F8
Gangtok ... 41 D7
Gansu □ ... 34 C5
Ganzhou ... 35 D6
Gaoxiong =
  Kaohsiung .. 35 D7
Gap ... 13 D7
Gar ... 34 C2
Garabogazköl
  Aylagy ... 29 E6
Garanhuns ... 92 D6
Garda, L. di ... 20 B3
Garden City ... 80 A3
Gardez ... 42 C6
Garmisch-
  Partenkirchen 14 E6
Garmo, Qullai =
  Kommunizma,
  Pik ... 29 F8
Garoe ... 49 F4
Garonne → ... 12 D3
Garoowe =
  Garoe ... 49 F4
Garoua ... 55 G1
Garrison Res. =
  Sakakawea, L. 74 B4
Garry, L. ... 68 B9
Garwa = Garoua 55 G1
Gary ... 76 D2
Garzê ... 34 C5
Gascogne ... 12 E4
Gascogne, G. de 12 D2
Gascony =
  Gascogne ... 12 D4
Gaspé ... 71 D4
Gaspé, C. ... 71 D4
Gaspésie, Pén.
  de la ... 71 D4

Gasteiz = Vitoria-
  Gasteiz ... 19 A4
Gateshead ... 11 D6
Gauhati =
  Guwahati ... 41 D8
Gävle ... 9 C9
Gaxun Nur ... 34 B5
Gaya ... 40 E5
Gaza ... 47 E3
Gaziantep ... 46 C4
Gazimağosa =
  Famagusta .. 46 D3
Gdańsk ... 16 A4
Gdańska, Zatoka 16 A4
Gdynia ... 16 A4
Gebze ... 22 D7
Gedaref ... 55 F6
Gedser ... 9 E8
Geelong ... 63 C3
Gejiu ... 34 D5
Gelibolu ... 23 D6
Gelsenkirchen . 14 C4
General Acha .. 94 D4
General Alvear 94 D3
General Pico .. 94 D4
General Santos 36 C3
Geneva =
  Genève ... 14 E4
Geneva, L. =
  Léman, L. ... 13 C7
Genève ... 14 E4
Gennargentu,
  Mti. del ... 21 D2
Genoa = Génova 20 B2
Génova ... 20 B2
Génova, G. di . 20 C2
Gent ... 14 C2
George ... 58 E4
George → ... 70 C4
George River =
  Kangiqsualujjuaq
  ... 70 C4
George Town . 38 C2
George V Land 96 A14
Georgetown ... 90 B7
Georgia □ ... 83 C6
Georgia ■ ... 25 E5
Georgian B. ... 71 D2
Georgiu-Dezh =
  Liski ... 24 C4
Georgiyevsk ... 25 E5
Gera ... 15 C7
Geraldton ... 60 F1
Germany ■ ... 14 C6
Germiston ... 59 D5
Gerona = Girona 19 B7
Getafe ... 18 B4
Gettysburg ... 77 E7
Ghaghara → ... 40 E5
Ghana ■ ... 53 G5
Ghardaïa ... 52 B6
Gharyān ... 54 B1
Ghawdex =
  Gozo ... 21 F5
Ghazāl, Bahr
  el → , Chad . 55 F2
Ghazāl, Bahr
  el → , Sudan . 57 C6
Ghaziabad ... 42 E10
Ghazipur ... 40 E4
Ghazni ... 42 C6
Ghent = Gent .. 14 C2
Ghowr □ ... 42 C4
Gibraltar ∅ ... 18 D3
Gibraltar, Str. of 18 E3
Gibson Desert . 60 E4
Giebnegáisi =
  Kebnekaise .. 8 B9
Gifu ... 33 F5
Gijón ... 18 A3
Gila → ... 78 D5
Gilän □ ... 46 C7
Gilbert Is. ... 64 J12
Gilgit ... 42 B9
Giresun ... 46 B4
Girne = Kyrenia 46 D3
Girona ... 19 B7

Gironde → ..... 12 D3
Girvan ....... 10 D4
Gisborne .... 64 C8
Gitega ....... 57 E5
Giuba → ..... 49 G3
Gīza = El Gîza . 54 C5
Gjoa Haven ... 68 B10
Glace Bay .... 71 D5
Gladstone ... 61 E9
Glâma =
    Glomma → . 9 C8
Glasgow ..... 10 D4
Glazov ....... 28 D6
Gleiwitz =
    Gliwice ... 16 C4
Glendale .... 78 C3
Glenrothes .. 10 C5
Glens Falls .. 77 C9
Gliwice ...... 16 C4
Głogów ...... 16 C3
Glomma → .. 9 C8
Gloucester ... 11 F5
Gniezno ..... 16 B3
Goa ......... 43 M8
Goa □ ....... 43 M8
Gobi ........ 35 B6
Godavari → .. 40 J4
Godhra ..... 43 H8
Gods → ..... 69 C10
Gods L. ..... 69 C10
Godthåb = Nuuk 70 B5
Godwin
    Austen = K2 . 42 B10
Goeie Hoop,
    Kaap die =
    Good Hope, C.
    of ....... 58 E3
Gogra =
    Ghaghara → 40 E5
Goiânia ..... 93 F4
Goiás ....... 93 F3
Goiás □ ..... 93 E4
Goio-Erê .... 94 A6
Gold Coast .. 63 H6
Golden Gate . 72 H2
Goldsboro ... 83 B9
Golspie ..... 10 D5
Goma ....... 57 E5
Gomel = Homyel 17 B10
Gomera ..... 52 C2
Gómez Palacio 84 B4
Gonābād ..... 44 C4
Gonaïves .... 87 C5
Gonbad-e Kāvūs 44 B3
Gonda ....... 40 D3
Gonder ...... 55 F6
Gonghe ..... 34 C5
Good Hope, C.
    of ....... 58 E3
Gorakhpur ... 40 D4
Gore ........ 55 G6
Gorgān ...... 44 B3
Gorkiy = Nizhniy
    Novgorod .. 24 B5
Görlitz ...... 15 C8
Gorlovka =
    Horlivka ... 25 D4
Gorno-Altay □ 29 D9
Gorontalo ... 37 D2
Górzów
    Wielkopolski 16 B2
Göta kanal .. 9 D9
Göteborg ... 9 D8
Gotha ....... 14 C6
Gothenburg =
    Göteborg .. 9 D8
Gotland ..... 9 D9
Gotō-Rettō .. 33 G1
Göttingen ... 14 C5
Gottwaldov =
    Zlín ...... 16 D3
Gouda ...... 14 B3
Gouin, Rés. .. 71 D3
Goulburn ... 63 B4
Governador
    Valadares . 93 F5
Goya ....... 94 B5

Gozo ........ 21 F5
Graaff-Reinet . 58 E4
Gracias a Dios,
    C. ....... 86 D3
Grafton ..... 63 A5
Graham Land . 96 A3
Grahamstown . 59 E5
Grampian Mts. . 10 C4
Gran Canaria . 52 C2
Gran Chaco .. 94 B4
Gran Sasso
    d'Itália ... 20 C4
Granada, Nic. . 85 E7
Granada, Spain 18 D4
Granby ...... 71 D3
Grand Bahama . 86 A4
Grand Canyon . 79 B6
Grand Cayman 86 C3
Grand Coulee
    Dam ..... 72 C4
Grand Forks .. 74 B6
Grand Island . 74 E5
Grand Rapids,
    Canada ... 69 C10
Grand Rapids,
    U.S.A. .... 76 C3
Grand St-
    Bernard, Col
    du ....... 13 D7
Grand Teton . 73 E8
Grande →,
    Bolivia ... 91 G6
Grande →,
    Brazil .... 93 E5
Grande, B. .. 95 G3
Grande, Rio → 81 F5
Grande Baleine,
    R. de la → . 71 C3
Grantham ... 11 E6
Grasse ...... 13 E7
Graulhet .... 12 E4
's-Gravenhage . 14 B3
Graz ........ 15 E8
Great Abaco I. . 86 A4
Great Australian
    Bight ..... 60 G4
Great Barrier
    Reef ..... 61 D8
Great Basin .. 72 G5
Great Bear → 68 B7
Great Bear L. . 68 B7
Great Belt =
    Store Bælt . 9 D8
Great Dividing
    Ra. ...... 61 E8
Great Falls .. 73 C8
Great Inagua I. 86 B5
Great Indian
    Desert = Thar
    Desert .... 42 F7
Great Karoo . 58 E4
Great Ouse → . 11 E7
Great Saint
    Bernard
    Pass = Grand
    St-Bernard,
    Col du ... 13 D7
Great Salt L. . 73 F7
Great Salt Lake
    Desert .... 73 F7
Great Sandy
    Desert .... 60 E3
Great Sangi =
    Sangihe,
    Pulau .... 37 D3
Great Slave L. . 68 B8
Great Smoky
    Mts. △ .... 83 B6
Great Victoria
    Desert .... 60 F4
Great Wall .. 35 C5
Great Yarmouth 11 E7
Greater Antilles 86 C5
Greater
    Sudbury = 
    Sudbury ... 71 D2

Greater Sunda
    Is. ■ ..... 39 F4
Greece ■ .... 23 E4
Greeley ..... 74 E2
Green → .... 79 A8
Green Bay ... 76 B2
Greenland ☒ .. 66 C9
Greenock ... 10 D4
Greensboro .. 83 A8
Greenville, Ala.,
    U.S.A. .... 82 D4
Greenville,
    Miss., U.S.A. 81 C8
Greenville, S.C.,
    U.S.A. .... 83 B6
Greenwood .. 81 C8
Gremikha ... 28 C4
Grenada ■ ... 87 D7
Grenoble .... 13 D6
Grey Ra. .... 63 A3
Greymouth .. 65 E4
Griffith ..... 63 B4
Grimsby .... 11 E6
Gris-Nez, C. .. 12 A4
Grodno =
    Hrodna ... 17 B6
Groningen ... 14 B4
Grossglockner . 15 E7
Groznyy .... 25 E6
Grudziądz ... 16 B4
Guadalajara,
    Mexico ... 84 C4
Guadalajara,
    Spain .... 18 B4
Guadalcanal . 64 K11
Guadalete → . 18 D2
Guadalquivir → 18 D2
Guadalupe =
    Guadeloupe ☒ 87 C7
Guadalupe,
    Sierra de .. 18 C3
Guadarrama,
    Sierra de .. 18 B4
Guadeloupe ☒ . 87 C7
Guadiana → .. 18 D2
Guadix ..... 18 D4
Guafo, Boca del 95 E2
Guajará-Mirim . 91 F5
Guajira, Pen. de
    la ....... 90 A4
Gualeguaychú . 94 C5
Guam ☒ ..... 64 H9
Guamúchil ... 84 B3
Guanahani =
    San Salvador
    I. ....... 86 B5
Guanajuato .. 84 C4
Guane ...... 86 B3
Guangdong □ . 35 D6
Guangxi
    Zhuangzu
    Zizhiqu □ . 35 D5
Guangzhou ... 35 D6
Guantánamo . 86 B4
Guaporé → .. 91 F5
Guaqui ..... 91 G5
Guarapuava .. 94 B6
Guardafui, C. =
    Asir, Ras .. 49 E5
Guatemala .. 85 E6
Guatemala ■ . 85 D6
Guaviare → .. 90 C5
Guaxupé .... 93 G4
Guayaquil ... 90 D3
Guayaquil, G. de 90 D2
Guaymas .... 84 B2
Guelph ...... 76 C5
Guéret ...... 12 C4
Guernsey ... 11 G5
Guildford ... 11 F6
Guilin ...... 35 D6
Guinea ■ .... 53 F3
Guinea, Gulf of 51 F3
Guinea-Bissau ■ 53 F3
Guingamp ... 12 B2
Guiyang .... 35 D5
Guizhou □ ... 35 D5

Gujarat □ .... 43 H7
Gujranwala .. 42 C9
Gujrat ...... 42 C9
Gulbarga .... 43 L10
Gulf, The .... 44 E2
Guna ....... 43 G10
Guntur ..... 40 J3
Gurkha ..... 40 C5
Gurupi → ... 92 C4
Guryev = Atyraū 29 E6
Gusau ...... 53 F7
Guwahati ... 41 D8
Guyana ■ ... 90 B7
Guyane
    française =
    French
    Guiana ☒ . 92 B3
Guyenne .... 12 D4
Güzelyurt =
    Morphou .. 46 D3
Gwädar ..... 42 G3
Gwalior ..... 42 F11
Gwanda ..... 59 C5
Gweru ...... 59 B5
Gyandzha =
    Gäncä .... 25 E6
Gyaring Hu .. 34 C4
Gympie ..... 63 A5
Győr ....... 16 E3
Gyumri ..... 25 E5
Gyzylarbat ... 29 F6

## H

Haarlem .... 14 B3
Hachinohe .. 32 C7
Ḥadd, Ra's al . 45 F4
Ḥaḍramawt .. 49 D4
Haeju ...... 35 C7
Haerhpin =
    Harbin .... 35 B7
Hafizabad ... 42 C8
Hagen ...... 14 C4
Hague, C. de la 12 B3
Hague, The =
    's-Gravenhage 14 B3
Haguenau ... 13 B7
Haifa = Ḥefa . 46 D3
Haikou ...... 35 D6
Ḥāʼil ....... 47 F5
Hailar ...... 35 B6
Hainan □ .... 35 E5
Haiphong .... 35 D5
Haiti ■ ...... 87 C5
Hakodate ... 32 C7
Halab ...... 46 C4
Halberstadt .. 15 C6
Halden ..... 9 D8
Haldia ...... 40 F7
Haldwani ... 42 E11
Halifax, Canada 71 D4
Halifax, U.K. . 11 E6
Hall Beach =
    Sanirajak .. 70 B2
Halle ....... 15 C6
Halmahera .. 37 D3
Halmstad ... 9 D8
Hälsingborg =
    Helsingborg 9 D8
Hamadān ... 46 D4
Hamamatsu . 33 F5
Hamar ...... 8 C6
Hamburg ... 14 B5
Hämeenlinna . 8 C10
Hameln ..... 14 B5
Hamersley Ra. . 60 E2
Hamhung ... 35 C7
Hami ....... 34 B4
Hamilton,
    Canada ... 71 D3
Hamilton, N.Z. 64 B6
Hamilton, U.K. 10 D4

Hamlin =
    Hameln .... 14 B5
Hamm ..... 14 C4
Hammerfest .. 8 A10
Hammond ... 76 D2
Hampton ... 77 F7
Handan ..... 35 C6
Hangayn Nuruu 34 B4
Hangzhou =
    Hangzhou .. 35 C7
Hangzhou .. 35 C7
Hangzhou Wan 35 C7
Hanna ...... 69 C8
Hannibal ... 75 F9
Hannover ... 14 B5
Hanoi ...... 35 D5
Hanover =
    Hannover .. 14 B5
Hanover, I. .. 95 G2
Hanzhong ... 35 C5
Haora ...... 40 F7
Haparanda .. 8 B10
Happy Valley-
    Goose Bay . 71 C4
Har Hu ..... 34 C4
Har Us Nuur . 34 B4
Harad ...... 47 F7
Harare ..... 59 B6
Harbin ..... 35 B7
Hardangerfjorden
    ......... 8 C7
Hardwar =
    Haridwar .. 42 E11
Harer ...... 49 F3
Hargeisa ... 49 F3
Haridwar ... 42 E11
Haringhata → . 41 G7
Harlingen ... 80 F5
Harlow ..... 11 F7
Härnösand .. 8 C9
Harris ...... 10 C3
Harrisburg .. 77 D7
Harrison, C. .. 70 C5
Harrogate ... 11 D6
Hart → ..... 68 B6
Hartford .... 77 D9
Hartlepool ... 11 D6
Hartwell L. .. 83 B6
Harwich .... 11 F7
Haryana □ ... 42 E10
Harz ....... 14 C6
Hasa □ ..... 47 F7
Hastings, N.Z. . 64 C7
Hastings, U.K. 11 F7
Hastings, U.S.A. 74 E5
Hatay = Antalya 46 C2
Hatgal ..... 34 A5
Hathras .... 42 F11
Hatteras, C. .. 83 B10
Hattiesburg .. 81 D9
Haugesund .. 9 D7
Hauraki G. .. 64 B6
Haut Atlas .. 52 B4
Havana = La
    Habana ... 86 B3
Havant ..... 11 F6
Havel → .... 15 B7
Havre ...... 73 B9
Haverfordwest 11 F4
Havre ...... 73 B9
Hawaii □ ... 78 J12
Hawaiian Is. .. 78 H12
Hawick ..... 10 D5
Hawke B. ... 64 C7
Hay River ... 68 B8
Hayes → .... 69 C10
Hearst ..... 71 D2
Hebei □ .... 35 C6
Hebron = Al
    Khalīl .... 47 E3
Hebron ..... 70 C4
Hechi ...... 35 D5
Hechuan ... 35 C5
Heerlen .... 13 A6
Hefa ....... 46 D3
Hefei ...... 35 C6
Hegang .... 35 B8

Heidelberg .... 14 D5
Heilbronn ..... 14 D5
Heilongjiang □ 35 B7
Heimaey ...... 8 C1
Hejaz = Ḥijāz □ 47 F4
Hekou ........ 34 D5
Helena ....... 73 C7
Helgoland .... 14 A4
Heligoland B. =
    Deutsche
    Bucht ..... 14 A5
Hellespont =
    Çanakkale
    Boğazı .... 23 D6
Helmand → .. 42 D2
Helmsdale ... 10 B5
Helsingborg .. 9 D8
Helsinki ..... 9 C11
Helwân ...... 54 C5
Hemel
    Hempstead .. 11 F6
Henan □ ..... 35 C6
Hengyang .... 35 D6
Henrietta Maria,
    C. ........ 71 C2
Hentiyn Nuruu . 35 B5
Heraklion =
    Iráklion .... 23 G5
Herāt ........ 42 B3
Hereford ..... 11 E5
Herford ...... 14 B5
Hermosillo ... 84 B2
Hernád → .... 16 E5
Heroica
    Nogales =
    Nogales .... 84 A2
's-Hertogenbosch
    ........... 14 C3
Hessen □ ..... 14 C5
Hexham ...... 11 D5
Hialeah ...... 83 G7
Hibbing ...... 75 B8
Hidalgo del
    Parral ..... 84 B3
Higashiōsaka .. 33 F4
High River .... 69 C8
High Tatra =
    Tatry ..... 16 D4
High Wycombe 11 F6
Hiiumaa ..... 24 B1
Ḥijāz □ ...... 47 F4
Hildesheim .. 14 B5
Hilo ......... 78 J13
Hilversum ... 14 B3
Himachal
    Pradesh □ .. 42 D10
Himalaya .... 40 C5
Himeji ....... 33 F4
Ḥimş ........ 46 D4
Hindu Kush ... 42 B7
Hingoli ...... 43 K10
Hirosaki ..... 32 C7
Hiroshima ... 33 F3
Hisar ........ 42 E9
Hispaniola ... 87 C5
Hitachi ...... 33 E7
Hjälmaren ... 9 D9
Hkakabo Razi . 41 C11
Ho Chi Minh
    City = Thanh
    Pho Ho Chi
    Minh ...... 38 B3
Hoare B. ..... 70 B4
Hobart ....... 62 D4
Hodeida = Al
    Ḥudaydah ... 49 E3
Hodgson ..... 69 C10
Hódmezővásárhely
    ........... 16 E5
Höfu ......... 33 F2
Hoggar =
    Ahaggar ... 52 D7
Hoher Rhön =
    Rhön ...... 14 C5
Hohhot ...... 35 B6
Hokkaidō □ ... 32 B8

Holguín ...... 86 B4
Hollywood ... 83 G7
Holman ...... 68 A8
Holyhead .... 11 E4
Home B. ..... 70 B4
Homer ....... 69 C4
Homs = Ḥimş .. 46 D4
Homyel ...... 17 B10
Honan =
    Henan □ ... 35 C6
Honduras ■ .. 85 E7
Honduras, G. de 85 D7
Hong Kong □ . 35 D6
Hongjiang ... 35 D5
Hongshui He → 35 D5
Hongze Hu ... 35 C6
Honiara ...... 64 K10
Honolulu .... 78 H12
Honshū ...... 33 F4
Hood, Mt. ... 72 D3
Hooghly →
    Hugli → ... 40 G7
Hoorn ....... 14 B3
Hoover Dam .. 78 B5
Hopedale .... 70 B5
Hopei = Hebei □ 35 C6
Hopetown .... 58 D4
Horlivka ..... 25 D4
Hormozgān □ .. 44 E3
Hormuz, Str. of 44 E4
Horn, Cape =
    Hornos, C. de 95 H3
Hornavan .... 8 B9
Hornos, C. de .. 95 H3
Horqin Youyi
    Qianqi .... 35 B7
Horsham ..... 62 C3
Horton → .... 68 B7
Hoste, I. ..... 95 H3
Hot Springs .. 81 B7
Hotan ....... 34 C2
Houlton ..... 77 A12
Houma ...... 81 E8
Houston ..... 81 E6
Hovd ........ 34 B4
Hövsgöl Nuur .. 34 A5
Howe, C. .... 63 C5
Howrah = Haora 40 F7
Hoy ......... 10 B5
Høyanger .... 8 C7
Hradec Králové 16 C2
Hrodna ...... 17 B6
Hrvatska =
    Croatia ■ .. 20 B6
Hsiamen =
    Xiamen ... 35 D6
Hsian = Xi'an .. 35 C5
Huacho ...... 91 F3
Huai He → ... 35 C6
Huainan ..... 35 C6
Huallaga → ... 90 E3
Huambo ...... 58 A3
Huancavelica .. 91 F3
Huancayo ... 91 F3
Huang Hai =
    Yellow Sea .. 35 C7
Huang He → ... 35 C6
Huangshan ... 35 D6
Huangshi .... 35 C6
Huánuco .... 91 E3
Huaraz ...... 91 E3
Huascarán ... 91 E3
Huasco ...... 94 B2
Huatabampo .. 84 B3
Hubei □ ..... 35 C6
Huddersfield .. 11 E6
Hudiksvall ... 8 C9
Hudson → ... 77 D8
Hudson Bay .. 70 B2
Hudson Str. .. 70 B4
Hue ......... 38 A3
Huelva ...... 18 D2
Huesca ...... 19 A5
Hughenden ... 61 E7
Hugli → ..... 40 G7
Huila, Nevado
    del ....... 90 C3

Huize ....... 34 D5
Huld =
    Ulaanjirem .. 35 B5
Hull = Kingston
    upon Hull .. 11 E6
Hull ......... 71 D3
Hulun Nur ... 35 B6
Humaitá ..... 91 E6
Humber → ... 11 E6
Humboldt ... 69 C9
Humboldt → .. 72 F4
Hunan □ ..... 35 D6
Hungary ■ .. 16 E4
Ḥüngnam .... 35 C7
Hunsrück .... 14 D4
Huntington .. 76 E4
Huntington
    Beach .... 78 D3
Huntly ...... 10 C5
Huntsville ... 82 B4
Hupeh =
    Hubei □ ... 35 C6
Huron, L. .... 76 B4
Hutchinson .. 80 A5
Hwang Ho =
    Huang He → 35 C6
Hwange ..... 59 B5
Hyargas Nuur .. 34 B4
Hyderabad, India 43 L11
Hyderabad,
    Pakistan .. 42 G6
Hyères ...... 13 E7
Hyères, Îs. d' .. 13 E7

# I

Ialomiţa → ... 22 B6
Iaşi ......... 17 E8
Ibadan ...... 53 G6
Ibagué ...... 90 C3
Ibarra ...... 90 C3
Ibiá ........ 93 F4
Ibiapaba, Sa. da 92 C5
Ibiza = Eivissa . 19 C6
Ibotirama ... 93 E5
Ica ......... 91 F3
Içá → ....... 90 D5
İçel = Mersin .. 46 C3
Iceland ■ .... 8 B2
Ichihara ..... 33 F7
Ichinomiya .. 33 F5
Idaho □ ..... 73 D7
Idaho Falls ... 73 E8
Idar-Oberstein .. 14 D4
Idlib ........ 46 D4
Ife ......... 53 G6
Igarapava ... 93 G4
Iglésias ..... 21 E2
Igloolik ..... 70 B2
Iguaçu →
    Chesterfield
    Inlet ..... 68 B10
Iglulik = Igloolik 70 B2
Iguaçu → .... 94 B6
Iguaçu, Cat. del 94 B6
Iguala ...... 84 D5
Iguassu =
    Iguaçu → .. 94 B6
Iguatu ...... 92 D6
Iisalmi ...... 8 C11
IJsselmeer ... 14 B3
Ikaluktutiak .. 68 B9
Ikparjuk = Arctic
    Bay ....... 70 A2
Ilagan ...... 36 A2
Ilâm ........ 46 D6
Ile → ....... 29 E8
Île-de-France □ 13 B5
Ilebo ....... 56 E4
Ilesha ...... 53 G6
Ilhéus ...... 93 E6
Ili = Ile → .... 29 E8
Iligan ...... 36 C2

Illampu =
    Ancohuma,
    Nevada .... 91 G5
Illapel ...... 94 C2
Iller → ...... 14 D5
Illimani, Nevado 91 G5
Illium = Troy .. 23 E6
Ilmen, Ozero .. 24 B3
Iloilo ....... 36 B2
Ilorin ....... 53 G6
Imabari ..... 33 F3
Imandra, Ozero 28 C4
Imperatriz ... 92 D4
Imphal ...... 41 E9
In Salah ..... 52 C6
Inari ........ 8 B11
Inarijärvi .... 8 B11
Ince Burun ... 46 B3
Inch'ŏn ..... 35 C7
Incomáti → ... 59 D6
Indalsälven → . 8 C9
Independence .. 75 F7
India ■ ..... 43 J10
Indiana □ ... 76 D3
Indianapolis .. 76 E2
Indigirka → ... 31 B12
Indira Gandhi
    Canal .... 42 F8
Indonesia ■ . 39 E4
Indore ...... 43 H9
Indre → ..... 12 C4
Indus → ..... 43 G5
İnebolu ...... 46 B3
Ingolstadt ... 15 D6
Ingraj Bazar .. 40 E7
Inland Sea ... 33 F3
Inn → ....... 15 D7
Inner Hebrides . 10 C3
Inner
    Mongolia =
    Nei Monggol
    Zizhiqu □ .. 35 B6
Innsbruck ... 15 E6
Inowrocław .. 16 B4
Insein ....... 41 J11
International
    Falls ...... 75 A8
Inukjuak .... 70 C3
Inuvik ...... 68 B6
Invercargill .. 65 G3
Invergordon .. 10 C4
Inverness ... 10 C4
Inverurie .... 10 C5
Ionian Is. =
    Iónioi Nísoi . 23 E3
Ionian Sea ... 21 F6
Iónioi Nísoi .. 23 E3
Iowa □ ...... 75 D8
Iowa City .... 75 E9
Ipameri ..... 93 F4
Ipatinga ..... 93 F5
Ipin = Yibin .. 35 D5
Ipoh ........ 38 D2

Ipswich,
    Australia .. 63 A5
Ipswich, U.K. . 11 E7
Iqaluit ...... 70 B4
Iquique ..... 91 H4
Iquitos ...... 90 D4
Iráklion ..... 23 G5
Iran ■ ...... 44 C3
Irapuato ..... 84 C4
Iraq ■ ...... 46 D5
Ireland ■ ... 11 E3
Irian Jaya =
    Papua □ ... 37 E5
Iringa ....... 57 F7
Irish Republic =
    Ireland ■ .. 11 E3
Irish Sea ..... 11 E4
Irkutsk ...... 30 D8
Iron Gate =
    Portile de Fier 22 B4
Ironwood .... 75 B9
Irrawaddy → .. 41 K10

Irtysh → ..... 28 C7
Irunea =
    Pamplona .. 19 A5
Irvine ....... 10 D4
Isar → ...... 15 D7
Isère → ...... 13 D6
Isfahan =
    Eşfahān ... 44 C2
Ishinomaki .. 32 D7
Iskenderun .. 46 C4
Islamabad ... 42 C8
Island L. ..... 69 C10
Islay ....... 10 D3
Isle of Wight □ 11 F6
Ismail = Izmayil 17 F9
Ismâ'ilîya ... 47 E3
Isparta ..... 46 C2
Israel ■ .... 46 E3
Issoire ...... 13 D5
Issyk-Kul,
    Ozero = Ysyk-
    Köl ...... 29 E8
İstanbul .... 22 D7
İstanbul Boğazı 22 D7
Istra ....... 20 B4
İstres ....... 13 E6
Istria = Istra .. 20 B4
Itaberaba ... 93 E5
Itabira ...... 93 F5
Itabuna ..... 93 E6
Itajaí ....... 94 B7
Italy ■ ..... 20 C4
Itaperuna ... 93 G5
Itapicuru → ... 93 E6
Ivanava ..... 17 B7
Ivano-Frankivsk 17 D7
Ivanovo =
    Ivanava ... 17 B7
Ivanovo ..... 24 B5
Ivory Coast ■ . 53 G4
Ivujivik ..... 70 B3
Iwaki ....... 33 E7
Iwakuni ..... 33 F3
Iwo ......... 53 G6
Izhevsk ..... 28 D6
Izmayil ..... 17 F9
İzmir ....... 23 E6
İzmit = Kocaeli . 25 E2
İznik Gölü ... 23 D7
Izumi-Sano .. 33 F4

# J

Jabalpur ..... 43 H11
Jaboatão .... 92 D6
Jackson, Mich.,
    U.S.A. .... 76 C3
Jackson, Miss.,
    U.S.A. .... 81 C8
Jackson, Tenn.,
    U.S.A. .... 82 B3
Jacksonville .. 83 D7
Jacmel ...... 87 C5
Jacobabad ... 42 E6
Jacobina .... 93 E5
Jadotville =
    Likasi .... 57 G5
Jaén ........ 18 D4
Jaffa = Tel Aviv-
    Yafo ...... 46 D3
Jaffna ....... 43 Q12
Jahrom ...... 44 D3
Jaipur ....... 42 F9
Jakarta ...... 39 F3
Jalālābād ... 42 B7
Jalapa
    Enríquez =
    Xalapa .... 84 D5
Jalgaon ..... 43 J9
Jalna ....... 43 K9
Jalpaiguri ... 41 D7
Jaluit I. ..... 64 J11
Jamaica ■ .. 86 C4

Jamalpur,
Bangla. ..... 41  E7
Jamalpur, India  40  E6
Jambi .......... 39  E2
James ➤ ...... 74  D6
James B. ...... 71  C2
Jamestown,
N. Dak., U.S.A. 74  B5
Jamestown,
N.Y., U.S.A.  .. 77  C6
Jammu ....... 42  C9
Jammu &
Kashmir ☐ .. 42 B10
Jamnagar .... 43  H7
Jamshedpur .. 40  F6
Janesville .... 75 D10
Januária ..... 93  F5
Jaora ......... 43  H9
Japan ■ ...... 33  F5
Japan, Sea of . 32  D4
Japen = Yapen  37  E5
Japurá ➤ ..... 90  D5
Jargalant =
Hovd ....... 34  B4
Jarvis I. ...... 65 K15
Jäsk ......... 44  E4
Jauja ......... 91  F3
Jaunpur ...... 40  E4
Java = Jawa .. 39  F3
Java Sea ..... 39  F3
Jawa ......... 39  F3
Jaya, Puncak .. 37  E5
Jebel, Bahr el ➤ 55  G5
Jedburgh ..... 10  D5
Jedda = Jiddah 47  G4
Jelenia Góra .. 16  C2
Jelgava ...... 24  B1
Jena ......... 15  C6
Jequié ....... 93  E5
Jequitinhonha . 93  F5
Jequitinhonha ➤
........... 93  F6
Jérémie ...... 86  C5
Jerez de la
Frontera ... 18  D2
Jerid, Chott el =
Djerid, Chott . 52  B7
Jersey ....... 11  G5
Jersey City ... 77  D8
Jerusalem .... 47  E3
Jesselton = Kota
Kinabalu ... 38  C5
Jessore ...... 41  F7
Jhang Maghiana 42  D8
Jhansi ....... 43 G11
Jhelum ....... 42  C8
Jhelum ➤ .... 42  D8
Jiamusi ...... 35  B8
Ji'an ......... 35  D6
Jiangmen ..... 35  D6
Jiangsu ☐ .... 35  C6
Jiangxi ☐ .... 35  D6
Jiaxing ...... 35  C7
Jiayi = Chiai .. 35  D7
Jibuti =
Djibouti ■ ... 49  E3
Jiddah ....... 47  G4
Jihlava ➤ .... 16  D3
Jilin .......... 35  B7
Jilong = Chilung 35  D7
Jima ......... 55  G6
Jiménez ...... 84  B4
Jinan ......... 35  C6
Jingdezhen ... 35  D6
Jinggu ....... 34  D5
Jinhua ....... 35  D6
Jining,
Nei Monggol Zizhiqu,
China ...... 35  B6
Jining,
Shandong,
China ...... 35  C6
Jinja ......... 57  D6
Jinzhou ...... 35  B7
Jiujiang ..... 35  D6
Jixi .......... 35  B8

Jizzakh ...... 29  E7
João Pessoa . 92  D7
Jodhpur ...... 42  F8
Jogjakarta =
Yogyakarta .. 39  F4
Johannesburg . 59  D5
Johnson City . 83  A6
Johnstown ... 77  D6
Johor Baharu . 39  D2
Joinville ..... 94  B7
Joliet ........ 76  D1
Joliette ...... 71  D3
Jolo ......... 36  C2
Jonesboro ... 81  B8
Jönköping ... 9  D8
Jonquière .... 71  D3
Joplin ....... 81  A6
Jordan ■ .... 47  E4
Jos ......... 53  G7
Jotunheimen .. 8  C7
Jowzjān ☐ ... 45  B6
Juan de Fuca
Str. ....... 72
Juan Fernández,
Arch. de ... 89  G3
Juàzeiro ..... 93  D5
Juàzeiro do
Norte ...... 92  D6
Juba = Giuba ➤ 49  G3
Jubbulpore =
Jabalpur ... 43 H11
Juchitán ..... 85  D5
Jugoslavia =
Serbia &
Montenegro ■ 22  B3
Juiz de Fora .. 93  G5
Juliaca ...... 91  G4
Julianehåb =
Qaqortoq .. 70  B6
Jullundur .... 42  D9
Jumna =
Yamuna ➤ .. 40  E3
Junagadh .... 43  J7
Jundiaí ...... 94  A7
Juneau ...... 69  C6
Junggar Pendi . 34  B3
Junín ....... 94  C4
Jura = Jura, Mts.
du ......... 13  C7
Jura =
Schwäbische
Alb ........ 14  D5
Jura ......... 10  D4
Jura, Mts. du . 13  C7
Juruá ➤ ..... 90  D5
Juruena ➤ ... 91  E7
Jutland =
Jylland .... 9  D7
Juventud, I. de
la ......... 86  B3
Jylland ...... 9  D7
Jyväskylä ... 8 C11

# K

K2 ......... 42 B10
Kaapstad = Cape
Town ...... 58  E3
Kabardino-
Balkaria ☐ .. 25  E5
Kábul ....... 42  B6
Kabwe ...... 59  A5
Kachchh, Gulf of 43  H6
Kachchh, Rann
of ......... 43  G6
Kachin ☐ .... 41 D11
Kaçkar ...... 25  E5
Kadiyevka =
Stakhanov .. 25  D4
Kadoma ..... 59  B5
Kaduna ...... 53  F7
Kaesŏng ..... 35  C7
Kafue ➤ ..... 59  B5
Kaga Bandoro . 56  C3

Kagoshima ... 33  H2
Kahoolawe ... 78 H12
Kahramanmaraş 46  C4
Kai, Kepulauan 37  F4
Kaieteur Falls .. 90  B7
Kaifeng ...... 35  C6
Kainji Res. .... 53  F6
Kairouan .... 54  A1
Kaiserslautern . 14  D4
Kaitaia ...... 64  A5
Kajaani ...... 8 C11
Kajabbi ...... 61  D6
Kakamega .... 57  D6
Kakinada .... 40  J4
Kalaallit
Nunaat =
Greenland ☑ 66  C9
Kalahari ..... 58  C4
Kalamazoo ... 76  C3
Kalemie ..... 57  F5
Kalgan =
Zhangjiakou . 35  B6
Kalgoorlie-
Boulder .... 60  G3
Kalimantan ... 39  E4
Kalinin = Tver . 24  B4
Kaliningrad .. 24  C1
Kalispell ..... 73  B6
Kalisz ....... 16  C4
Kalmar ...... 9  D9
Kalmykia ☐ .. 25  D6
Kaluga ...... 24  C4
Kalutara ..... 43 R11
Kama ➤ ..... 29  D6
Kamchatka,
Poluostrov . 31 D13
Kamchatka
Pen. =
Kamchatka,
Poluostrov . 31 D13
Kamina ..... 57  F5
Kamloops ... 69  C7
Kampala .... 57  D6
Kampong Saom 38  B2
Kampuchea =
Cambodia ■ . 38  B2
Kamyanets-
Podilskyy ... 17  D8
Kamyshin ... 24  C6
Kananga .... 56  F4
Kanash ..... 24  B6
Kanazawa ... 33  E5
Kanchenjunga . 40  D7
Kanchipuram . 43 N11
Kandahar =
Qandahār .. 42  D4
Kandalaksha . 8 B12
Kandi ....... 53  F6
Kandy ...... 43 R12
Kangaroo I. .. 62  C2
Kangiqliniq =
Rankin Inlet . 68 B10
Kangiqsualujjuaq
........... 70  C4
Kangiqsujuaq . 70  B3
Kangiqtugaapik =
Clyde River . 70  A4
Kangirsuk ... 70  C4
Kaniapiskau =
Caniapiscau ➤
........... 70  C4
Kaniapiskau, L. =
Caniapiscau,
L. de ...... 71  C4
Kanin,
Poluostrov . 28  C5
Kanin Nos, Mys 28  C5
Kankakee ... 76  D2
Kankan ..... 53  F4
Kankendy =
Xankändi ... 25  F6
Kano ........ 53  F7
Kanpur ..... 40  D3
Kansas ☐ .... 74  F5
Kansas City,

Kansas City,
Mo., U.S.A. .. 75  F7
Kansu =
Gansu ☐ .... 34  C5
Kaohsiung ... 35  D7
Kaolack ..... 53  F2
Kapiri Mposhi . 59  A5
Kāpisā ☐ .... 45  C7
Kaposvár .... 16  E3
Kaptai L. .... 41  F9
Kapuas ➤ ... 39  E3
Kara Bogaz Gol,
Zaliv =
Garabogazköl
Aylagy ..... 29  E6
Kara Kalpak
Republic =
Qoraqalpoghistan ☐
........... 29  E6
Kara Kum .... 29  F6
Kara Sea .... 28  B8
Karabük .... 46  B3
Karachi ...... 43  G5
Karaganda =
Qaraghandy . 29  E8
Karakalpakstan =
Qoraqalpoghistan ☐
........... 29  E6
Karakoram Ra. . 42 B10
Karaman .... 46  C3
Karamay .... 34  B3
Karbalā' ..... 47  D6
Karelia ☐ .... 8 C12
Kariba, L. .... 59  B5
Kariba Dam .. 59  B5
Karimata, Selat 39  E3
Karl-Marx-
Stadt =
Chemnitz ... 15  C7
Karlskrona ... 9  D9
Karlsruhe .... 14  D5
Karlstad ..... 9  D8
Karnal ...... 42 E10
Karnaphuli
Res. = Kaptai
L. .......... 41  F9
Karnataka ☐ .. 43 N10
Kärnten ☐ ... 15  E7
Kars ......... 46  B5
Karshi = Qarshi 29  F7
Karwar ...... 43  M9
Kasai ➤ ..... 56  E3
Kasaragod ... 43  N9
Kasba L. .... 68  B9
Kāshān ..... 44  C2
Kashgar = Kashi 34  C2
Kashi ....... 34  C2
Kasongo .... 57  E5
Kassalâ ..... 55  E6
Kassel ...... 14  C5
Kastamonu .. 46  B3
Kasur ....... 42  D9
Katanga ☐ ... 57  F4
Kathmandu =
Katmandu .. 40  D5
Katihar ..... 40  E6
Katima Mulilo . 58  B4
Katmandu ... 40  D5
Katowice .... 16  C4
Katsina ..... 53  F7
Kattegat .... 9  D8
Kauai ....... 78 G11
Kaunas ..... 24  C1
Kavála ...... 22  D5
Kavīr, Dasht-e  44  C3
Kawagoe .... 33  F6
Kawaguchi ... 33  F6
Kawardha ... 40  G3
Kawasaki ... 33  F6
Kawthoolei =
Kayin ☐ .... 41 H11
Kawthule =
Kayin ☐ .... 41 H11
Kayah ☐ .... 41 H11
Kayes ....... 53  F3
Kayin ☐ ..... 41 H11

Kayseri ...... 46  C3
Kazakhstan ■ . 29  E7
Kazan ....... 24  B6
Kebnekaise .. 8  B9
Kebri Dehar .. 49  F3
Kecskemét ... 16  E4
Kediri ....... 39  F4
Keelung =
Chilung .... 35  D7
Keetmanshoop 58  D3
Kefallinía .... 23  E3
Keflavík ..... 8  C1
Keighley ..... 11  E6
Kelang ...... 39  D2
Kells =
Ceanannus
Mor ....... 11  E3
Kelowna .... 69  D8
Keluang ..... 39  D2
Kem ........ 28  C4
Kemerovo ... 29  D9
Kemi ....... 8 B10
Kemi älv =
Kemijoki ➤ . 8 B10
Kemijoki ➤ .. 8 B10
Kemp Land ... 96  A9
Kendari ..... 37  E2
Kenitra ...... 52  B4
Kennewick ... 72  C4
Kenogami ➤ . 71  C2
Kenosha .... 76  C2
Kent, Pte. ... 68  B9
Kentucky ☐ .. 76  F3
Kentville .... 71  D4
Kenya ■ .... 57  D7
Kenya, Mt. .. 57  E7
Kerala ☐ .... 43 P10
Kerch ...... 25  D4
Kericho ..... 57  E7
Kerinci ..... 39  E2
Kérkira ...... 23  E2
Kermadec Is. . 64 M13
Kermadec
Trench .... 65 N13
Kermān .... 44  D4
Kermänshäh =
Bākhtarān .. 46  D6
Kerrobert ... 69  C9
Kerulen ➤ ... 35  B6
Ketchikan ... 69  C6
Key West ... 86  B3
Khabarovsk . 31 E11
Khairpur .... 42  F6
Khakassia ☐ .. 30  D6
Khambhat ... 43  H8
Khambhat, G. of 43  J8
Khanewal ... 42  D7
Khaniá ...... 23  G5
Khanka, L. .. 32  A3
Khankendy =
Xankändi ... 25  F6
Kharagpur ... 40  F6
Kharg = Khārk,
Jazīreh-ye .. 47  E7
Khārk, Jazīreh-
ye ......... 47  E7
Kharkiv ..... 24  D4
Kharkov =
Kharkiv .... 24  D4
Khartoum = El
Khartûm ... 55  E5
Khaskovo ... 22  D5
Kherson .... 25  D3
Khíos ....... 23  E6
Khiuma =
Hiiumaa .... 24  B1
Khmelnytskyy . 17  D8
Khmer Rep. =
Cambodia ■ . 38  B2
Khodzent =
Khujand .... 29  E7
Khojak Pass .. 42  D5
Kholm ...... 45  B6
Khon Kaen .. 38  A2
Khorat = Nakhon
Ratchasima . 38  B2
Khorramābād . 46  D7

Khorrāmshahr . 47 E7
Khouribga .... 52 B4
Khudzhand =
  Khŭjand .... 29 E7
Khŭjand ..... 29 E7
Khulna ...... 41 F7
Khulna □ .... 41 F7
Khushab .... 42 C8
Khuzdar ..... 42 F5
Khvoy ....... 46 C6
Khyber Pass ... 42 B7
Kiangsi =
  Jiangxi □ .. 35 D6
Kiangsu =
  Jiangsu □ .. 35 C6
Kicking Horse
  Pass ...... 69 C8
Kiel ........ 14 A6
Kiel Canal =
  Nord-Ostsee-
  Kanal ..... 14 A5
Kielce ...... 16 C5
Kieler Bucht ... 14 A6
Kiev = Kyyiv .. 17 C10
Kigali ...... 57 E6
Kigoma-Ujiji .. 57 E5
Kikládhes .... 23 F5
Kikwit ...... 56 E3
Kilimanjaro ... 57 E7
Kilkenny .... 11 E3
Killarney .... 11 E2
Killeen ..... 80 D5
Kilmarnock ... 10 D4
Kilrush ..... 11 E2
Kimberley,
  Australia ... 60 D4
Kimberley,
  S. Africa ... 58 D4
Kimmirut .... 70 B4
Kinabalu,
  Gunong ... 38 C5
Kindia ...... 53 F3
Kindu ...... 57 E5
Kineshma .... 24 B5
King George I. . 96 A4
King George Is. 71 C2
King I. ...... 62 C3
King William I. . 68 B10
Kingait = Cape
  Dorset .... 70 B3
Kingaok =
  Bathurst Inlet 68 B9
Kings Canyon △ 78 B3
King's Lynn ... 11 E7
Kingston,
  Canada .... 71 D3
Kingston,
  Jamaica ... 86 C4
Kingston upon
  Hull ...... 11 E6
Kingstown ... 87 D7
Kingsville .... 80 F5
Kinsale ..... 11 F2
Kinshasa .... 56 E3
Kirghizia =
  Kyrgyzstan ■ 29 E8
Kiribati ■ .... 64 K12
Kırıkkale .... 46 C3
Kirin = Jilin .. 35 B7
Kirinyaga =
  Kenya, Mt. .. 57 E7
Kiritimati .... 65 J15
Kirkcaldy .... 10 C5
Kirkcudbright . 11 D4
Kirkland Lake .. 71 D2
Kırklareli .... 22 D6
Kirkūk ..... 46 D6
Kirkwall .... 10 B5
Kirov ...... 28 D5
Kirovabad =
  Gäncä .... 25 E6
Kirovohrad ... 25 D3
Kırşehir .... 46 C3
Kiruna ..... 8 B10
Kiryū ...... 33 E6
Kisangani .... 57 D5
Kishanganj ... 40 D7


Kishinev =
  Chişinău .... 17 E9
Kisii ....... 57 E6
Kislovodsk ... 25 E5
Kisumu ..... 57 E6
Kitakyūshū ... 33 G2
Kitale ...... 57 D7
Kitami ...... 32 B8
Kitchener .... 71 D2
Kitega = Gitega 57 E5
Kithira ..... 23 F4
Kitwe ...... 59 A5
Kivu, L. ..... 57 E5
Kiyev = Kyyiv . 17 C10
Kızıl Irmak → .. 25 E4
Kizlyar ..... 25 E6
Kizyl-Arvat =
  Gyzylarbat .. 29 F6
Kladno ..... 16 C2
Klagenfurt ... 15 E8
Klaipėda .... 24 B1
Klamath Falls . 72 E3
Klarälven → .. 9 C8
Klerksdorp ... 59 D5
Kluane L. .... 68 B6
Knossós .... 23 G5
Knoxville .... 83 B6
Koartac =
  Quaqtaq ... 70 B4
Kobdo = Hovd . 34 B4
Kōbe ...... 33 F4
København ... 9 D8
Koblenz ..... 14 C4
Kocaeli ..... 25 E2
Koch Bihar ... 41 D7
Kochi = Cochin 43 Q10
Kōchi ...... 33 G3
Kochiu = Gejiu . 34 D5
Kodiak ..... 69 C4
Kodiak I. .... 69 C4
Koforidua ... 53 G5
Kōfu ....... 33 F6
Kohat ...... 42 C7
Kohima ..... 41 E10
Kokand = Qŭqon 29 E8
Kokchetav =
  Kökshetaū .. 29 D7
Koko Kyunzu .. 41 K9
Kokomo ..... 76 D2
Kökshetaū ... 29 D7
Koksoak → ... 70 C4
Kola Pen. =
  Kolskiy
  Poluostrov . 8 B13
Kolar Gold
  Fields ..... 43 N11
Kolguyev,
  Ostrov .... 28 C5
Kolhapur .... 43 L9
Kolkata ..... 41 F7
Kollam = Quilon 43 Q10
Köln ....... 14 C4
Kolomna .... 24 B4
Kolomyya ... 17 D7
Kolpino ..... 24 B3
Kolskiy
  Poluostrov . 8 B13
Kolwezi ..... 57 G5
Kolyma → .... 31 C13
Komatsu .... 33 E5
Komi □ ..... 28 C6
Kommunarsk =
  Alchevsk ... 25 D4
Kommunizma,
  Pik ....... 29 F8
Kompong Cham 38 B3
Kompong Som =
  Kampong
  Saom .... 38 B2
Konārhā □ ... 42 B7
Königsberg =
  Kaliningrad . 24 C1
Konin ...... 16 B4
Konosha .... 28 C5
Konotop .... 24 C3
Konstanz .... 14 E5


Konya ....... 46 C3
Kootenay L. ... 69 D8
Korçë ....... 23 D3
Kordestan =
  Kurdistan ... 46 D5
Kordofân .... 55 F4
Kordestān □ .. 46 D6
Korea, North ■ 35 C7
Korea, South ■ 35 C7
Korea Bay .... 35 C7
Korea Strait ... 35 C7
Korhogo ..... 53 G4
Korinthiakós
  Kólpos .... 23 E4
Kórinthos ... 23 F4
Köriyama .... 33 E7
Koror ...... 36 C4
Kŏrŏs → ..... 16 E5
Korosten .... 17 C9
Kortrijk ..... 14 C2
Kos ........ 23 F6
Kosciuszko, Mt. 63 C4
Košice ..... 16 D5
Kosovo □ .... 22 C3
Kôstî ...... 55 F5
Kostroma .... 24 B5
Koszalin .... 16 A3
Kota ....... 43 G9
Kota Baharu .. 38 C2
Kota Kinabalu . 38 C5
Kotabumi .... 39 E2
Kotelnich .... 24 B6
Kotka ...... 9 C11
Kotlas ..... 28 C5
Kotri ...... 42 G6
Kotuy → ..... 30 B8
Kotzebue .... 69 B3
Kovel ...... 17 C7
Kovrov ..... 24 B5
Kozhikode =
  Calicut .... 43 P9
Kra, Isthmus of =
  Kra, Kho Khot 38 B1
Kra, Kho Khot 38 B1
Kragujevac ... 22 B3
Krajina ..... 20 B6
Krakatau =
  Rakata, Pulau 39 F3
Kraków ..... 16 C4
Kramatorsk ... 25 D4
Krasnodar ... 25 D4
Krasnoturinsk . 28 D7
Krasnovodsk =
  Türkmenbashi 29 E6
Krasnoyarsk .. 30 D7
Krasnyy Luch . 25 D4
Krefeld ..... 14 C4
Kremenchuk .. 24 D3
Krishna → .... 40 K3
Kristiansand .. 9 D7
Kristiansund .. 8 C7
Kriti ....... 23 G5
Krivoy Rog =
  Kryvyy Rih .. 25 D3
Kronshtadt ... 24 B2
Kroonstad ... 59 D5
Kropotkin .... 25 D5
Krung Thep =
  Bangkok ... 38 B2
Kruševac .... 22 C3
Krymskyy
  Pivostriv ... 25 D3
Kryvyy Rih ... 25 D3
Ksar el Kebir .. 52 B4
Ksar es Souk =
  Er Rachidia . 52 B5
Kuala Lumpur . 39 D2
Kuala
  Terengganu . 38 C2
Kuangchou =
  Guangzhou . 35 D6
Kuantan ..... 39 D2
Kuching ..... 39 D4
Kucing =
  Kuching ... 39 D4
Kudymkar ... 28 D6


Kueiyang =
  Guiyang ... 35 D5
Kufra Oasis = Al
  Kufrah .... 54 D3
Kugaaruk = Pelly
  Bay ...... 70 B2
Kugluktuk .... 68 B8
Kuji ....... 32 C8
Kuldja = Yining 34 B3
Kŭlob ...... 29 F7
Kulsary ..... 29 E6
Kulyab = Kŭlob 29 F7
Kuma → ..... 25 E6
Kumagaya ... 33 E6
Kumamoto ... 33 G2
Kumanovo ... 22 C3
Kumasi ..... 53 G5
Kumayri =
  Gyumri ... 25 E5
Kumbakonam . 43 P11
Kungrad =
  Qŭnghirot .. 29 E6
Kungur ..... 29 D6
Kunlun Shan . 34 C3
Kunming .... 34 D5
Kuopio ..... 8 C11
Kuqa ...... 34 B3
Kür → ...... 25 E6
Kura = Kür → . 25 E6
Kurdistan ... 46 D5
Kure ...... 33 F3
Kurgan ..... 29 D7
Kuril Is. =
  Kurilskiye
  Ostrova ... 31 E12
Kurilskiye
  Ostrova ... 31 E12
Kurnool ..... 43 L11
Kursk ...... 24 C4
Kuruktag .... 34 B3
Kurume ..... 33 G2
Kushiro ..... 32 B9
Kushtia ..... 41 F7
Kuskokwim B. . 69 C3
Kütahya ..... 46 C2
Kutaïsi ..... 25 E6
Kutaraja =
  Banda Aceh . 38 C1
Kutch, Gulf of =
  Kachchh, Gulf
  of ....... 43 H6
Kutch, Rann of =
  Kachchh, Rann
  of ....... 43 G6
Kuujjuaq .... 70 C4
Kuwait = Al
  Kuwayt ... 47 E7
Kuwait ■ .... 47 E6
Kuybyshev =
  Samara ... 24 C7
Kuybyshevskoye
  Vdkhr. .... 28 B6
Kuzey Anadolu
  Dağları .... 46 B3
Kuznetsk .... 24 C6
Kwangchow =
  Guangzhou . 35 D6
Kwangju .... 35 C7
Kwango → ... 56 E3
Kwangsi-
  Chuang =
  Guangxi
  Zhuangzu
  Zizhiqu □ .. 35 D5
Kwangtung =
  Guangdong □ 35 D6
Kweichow =
  Guizhou □ .. 35 D5
Kwekwe ..... 59 B5
Kyoga, L. .... 57 D6
Kyōto ...... 33 F4
Kyrenia ..... 46 D3
Kyrgyzstan ■ . 29 E8
Kyūshū ..... 33 G2
Kyyiv ...... 17 C10
Kyzyl Kum ... 29 E7
Kyzyl-Orda =
  Qyzylorda .. 29 E7


# L

La Ceiba ..... 85 D7
La Coruña = A
  Coruña .... 18 A1
La Crosse .... 75 D9
La Grange .... 82 C5
La Habana ... 86 B3
La Mancha ... 19 C4
La Palma .... 52 C2
La Paz, Bolivia . 91 G5
La Paz, Mexico 84 C2
La Plata ..... 94 D5
La Quiaca .... 94 A3
La Rioja ..... 94 B3
La Rioja □ ... 19 A4
La Roche-sur-
  Yon ...... 12 C3
La Rochelle ... 12 C3
La Romana ... 87 C6
La Serena .... 94 B2
La Spézia .... 20 B2
La Tortuga ... 87 D6
La Tuque .... 71 D3
La Vega ..... 87 C5
Labe = Elbe → . 14 B5
Labé ...... 53 F3
Labrador .... 71 C4
Lac la Biche .. 69 C8
Lac la Martre =
  Wha Ti .... 68 B8
Laccadive Is. =
  Lakshadweep
  Is. ....... 26 H11
Lacombe .... 69 C8
Ladoga, L. =
  Ladozhskoye
  Ozero .... 8 C12
Ladozhskoye
  Ozero .... 8 C12
Ladysmith ... 59 D5
Lae ....... 61 B8
Lafayette .... 81 D7
Lafia ...... 53 G7
Laghmān □ ... 45 C7
Laghouat .... 52 B6
Lagos, Nigeria . 53 G6
Lagos, Portugal 18 D1
Lahn → ..... 14 C4
Lahore ..... 42 D9
Lahti ...... 8 C11
Lahtis = Lahti . 8 C11
Lairg ...... 10 B4
Laizhou ..... 35 C6
Lake Charles .. 81 D7
Lake City .... 83 D6
Lake Harbour =
  Kimmirut ... 70 B4
Lakeland .... 83 E7
Lakewood ... 76 D5
Lakshadweep Is. 26 H11
Lambaréné ... 56 E2
Lamon B. .... 36 B2
Lancaster, U.K. 11 D5
Lancaster,
  U.S.A. .... 77 D7
Lancaster Sd. .. 70 A2
Lanchow =
  Lanzhou ... 35 C5
Landes ..... 12 D3
Land's End ... 11 F4
Langres ..... 13 C6
Langres, Plateau
  de ....... 13 C6
Langsa ..... 38 D1
Languedoc ... 13 E5
Lannion ..... 12 B2
Lansing ..... 76 C3
Lanzarote ... 52 C3
Lanzhou .... 35 C5
Laoag ...... 36 A2
Laois □ ..... 11 E3
Laon ...... 13 B5
Laos ■ ..... 38 A3
Lappland .... 8 B10
Laptev Sea ... 30 B10
Laramie ..... 74 E2

Laredo ....... 80 F4
Lárisa ........ 23 E4
Larnaca ....... 46 D3
Larne ......... 11 D4
Larrimah ...... 60 D5
Larvik ........ 9 D8
Las Cruces .... 79 D9
Las Palmas .... 52 C2
Las Vegas ..... 78 B5
Lashio ........ 41 F11
Lassen Pk. .... 72 F3
Lastoursville . 56 E2
Latacunga ..... 90 D3
Latakia = Al
  Lādhiqīyah .. 46 D3
Latina ........ 20 D4
Latium = Lazio □ 20 C4
Latvia ■ ...... 24 B1
Launceston .... 62 D4
Laurel ........ 81 D9
Lausanne ...... 14 E4
Laval ......... 12 B3
Lawrence ...... 75 F7
Lawton ........ 80 B4
Lazio □ ....... 20 C4
Le Creusot .... 13 C6
Le Havre ...... 12 B4
Le Mans ....... 12 C4
Le Mont-St-
  Michel ...... 12 B3
Le Puy-en-Velay 13 D5
Le Touquet-
  Paris-Plage . 12 A4
Leamington
  Spa = Royal
  Leamington
  Spa ........ 11 E6
Leavenworth ... 75 F7
Lebanon ■ ..... 46 D3
Lebu .......... 94 D2
Lecce ......... 23 D2
Leeds ......... 11 E6
Leeuwarden .... 14 B3
Leeuwin, C. ... 60 G2
Leeward Is. ... 87 C7
Leganés ....... 18 B4
Legazpi ....... 36 B2
Leghorn =
  Livorno ..... 20 C3
Legnica ....... 16 C3
Leicester ..... 11 E6
Leiden ........ 14 B3
Leine → ....... 14 B5
Leinster □ .... 11 E3
Leipzig ....... 15 C7
Leitrim ....... 11 D2
Leizhou Bandao 35 D6
Léman, L. ..... 13 C7
Lena → ........ 30 B10
Leninabad =
  Khŭjand .... 29 E7
Leninakan =
  Gyumri .... 25 E5
Leningrad =
  Sankt-
  Peterburg .. 24 B3
Lens .......... 13 A5
Leodhas = Lewis 10 B3
León, Mexico .. 84 C4
León, Nic. .... 85 E7
León, Spain ... 18 A3
Lérida = Lleida 19 B6
Lerwick ....... 10 A6
Les Cayes ..... 86 C5
Les Sables-
  d'Olonne ... 12 C3
Lesbos = Lésvos 23 E6
Leskovac ...... 22 C3
Lesotho ■ ..... 59 D5
Lesser Antilles 87 D7
Lesser Sunda Is. 37 F2
Lésvos ........ 23 E6
Leszno ........ 16 C3
Lethbridge .... 69 D8
Leti, Kepulauan 37 F3
Leticia ....... 90 D4
Letterkenny ... 11 D3

Leuven ........ 14 C3
Lévis ......... 71 D3
Levkás ........ 23 E3
Levkôsia =
  Nicosia ..... 46 D3
Lewis ......... 10 B3
Lewisporte .... 71 D5
Lewiston, Idaho,
  U.S.A. ...... 72 C5
Lewiston, Maine,
  U.S.A. ...... 77 B10
Lexington ..... 76 E3
Leyte □ ....... 36 B2
Lhasa ......... 34 D4
Lhazê ......... 34 D3
L'Hospitalet de
  Llobregat ... 19 B7
Lianyungang ... 35 C6
Liaoning □ .... 35 B7
Liaoyuan ...... 35 B7
Liard → ....... 68 B7
Libau = Liepãja 24 B1
Liberal ....... 80 A3
Liberec ....... 16 C2
Liberia ■ ..... 53 G4
Līblya, Sahrâ' . 54 C4
Libourne ...... 12 D3
Libreville .... 56 D1
Libya ■ ....... 54 C2
Libyan Desert =
  Līblya, Sahrâ' 54 C4
Liechtenstein ■ 14 E5
Liège ......... 14 C3
Liegnitz =
  Legnica ..... 16 C3
Lienyünchiangshih =
  Lianyungang . 35 C6
Liepãja ....... 24 B1
Liffey → ...... 11 E3
Lifford ....... 11 D3
Liguria □ ..... 20 D2
Ligurian Sea .. 20 C2
Lijiang ....... 34 D5
Likasi ........ 57 G5
Lille ......... 13 A5
Lillehammer ... 8 C8
Lilongwe ...... 59 A6
Lima, Peru .... 91 F3
Lima, U.S.A. .. 76 D3
Limassol ...... 46 D3
Limbe ......... 56 D1
Limeira ....... 93 G4
Limerick ...... 11 E2
Limfjorden .... 9 D7
Límnos ........ 23 E5
Limoges ....... 12 D4
Limón ......... 86 E3
Limousin □ .... 12 D4
Limoux ........ 12 E5
Limpopo → ..... 59 D6
Linares, Chile . 94 D2
Linares, Mexico 84 C5
Linares, Spain . 18 C4
Lincoln, U.K. .. 11 E6
Lincoln, U.S.A. 75 E6
Lindesnes ..... 9 D7
Lingga,
  Kepulauan .. 39 E2
Linhai ........ 35 D7
Linhares ...... 93 F5
Linköping ..... 9 D9
Linxia ........ 34 C5
Linz .......... 15 D8
Lion, G. du ... 13 E6
Lipa .......... 36 B2
Lipetsk ....... 24 C4
Lippe → ....... 14 C4
Lisboa ........ 18 C1
Lisbon = Lisboa 18 C1
Lisburn ....... 11 D3
Lisichansk =
  Lysychansk . 25 D4
Lisieux ....... 12 B4
Liski ......... 24 C4
Lismore ....... 63 A5
Listowel ...... 11 E2
Litani → ...... 46 D3

Lithuania ■ ... 24 B1
Little
  Missouri → .. 74 B3
Little Rock ... 81 B7
Liuwa Plain ... 58 A4
Liuzhou ....... 35 D5
Liverpool,
  Canada ...... 71 D4
Liverpool, U.K. 11 E5
Livingstone ... 59 B5
Livorno ....... 20 C3
Ljubljana ..... 20 A5
Llanelli ...... 11 F4
Llano Estacado 80 C2
Llanos ........ 90 C4
Lleida ........ 19 B6
Lloret de Mar . 19 B7
Llullaillaco,
  Volcán ...... 94 A3
Lobatse ....... 59 D5
Lobito ........ 58 A2
Locarno ....... 13 C8
Loch Garman =
  Wexford ..... 11 E3
Loches ........ 12 C4
Łódź .......... 16 C4
Lofoten ....... 8 B9
Logan ......... 73 F8
Logan, Mt. .... 68 B5
Logroño ....... 19 A4
Lohardaga ..... 40 F5
Loir → ........ 12 C3
Loire → ....... 12 C2
Loja .......... 90 D3
Lombárdia □ ... 20 B2
Lomblen ....... 37 F2
Lombok ........ 39 F5
Lomé .......... 53 G6
Lomond, L. .... 10 C4
Łomża ......... 16 B6
London ........ 11 F6
Londonderry ... 11 D3
Londonderry, C. 60 C4
Londrina ...... 94 A6
Long Beach .... 78 D3
Long I.,
  Bahamas .... 86 B4
Long I., U.S.A. 77 D9
Long Xuyen .... 38 B3
Longford ...... 11 E3
Longreach ..... 61 E7
Longview, Tex.,
  U.S.A. ...... 81 C6
Longview,
  Wash., U.S.A. 72 C2
Lons-le-Saunier 13 C6
Lop Nur ....... 34 B4
Lopez, C. ..... 56 E1
Lorain ........ 76 D4
Loralai ....... 42 D6
Lorca ......... 19 D5
Lorestān □ .... 46 D6
Lorient ....... 12 C2
Lorraine □ .... 13 B7
Los Alamos .... 79 C9
Los Andes ..... 94 C2
Los Angeles,
  Chile ...... 94 D2
Los Angeles,
  U.S.A. ..... 78 C3
Los Mochis .... 84 B3
Los Roques Is. . 90 A5
Lot → ......... 12 D4
Lota .......... 94 D2
Louis Trichardt 59 C5
Louis XIV, Pte. . 71 C3
Louisiade Arch. 61 C9
Louisiana □ ... 81 D8
Louisville .... 76 E3
Lourdes ....... 12 E3
Louth ......... 11 E6
Louvain =
  Leuven ..... 14 C3
Lowell ........ 77 C10
Lower
  California =
  Baja California 84 A1

Lower Hutt .... 65 D6
Lower Saxony =
  Niedersachsen □
  ............. 14 B5
Lower
  Tunguska =
  Tunguska,
  Nizhnyaya → 30 C7
Lowestoft ..... 11 E7
Loyalty Is. =
  Loyauté, Îs. . 64 M11
Loyang =
  Luoyang ..... 35 C6
Loyauté, Îs. .. 64 M11
Lualaba → ..... 57 D5
Luanda ........ 56 F2
Luangwa → ..... 59 A6
Luanshya ...... 59 A5
Luapula → ..... 57 F5
Lubbock ....... 80 C3
Lübeck ........ 15 B6
Lubero = Luofu 57 E5
Lublin ........ 17 C6
Lubumbashi .... 59 A5
Lucena ........ 36 B2
Lucerne =
  Luzern ...... 13 C8
Lucknow ....... 40 D3
Lüda = Dalian . 35 C7
Lüderitz ...... 58 D3
Ludhiana ...... 42 D9
Ludwigshafen .. 14 D5
Lufkin ........ 81 D6
Luga .......... 24 B2
Lugano ........ 13 C8
Lugansk =
  Luhansk ..... 25 D4
Lugo .......... 18 A2
Luhansk ....... 25 D4
Luimneach =
  Limerick .... 11 E2
Lule älv → .... 8 B10
Luleå ......... 8 B10
Lüneburger
  Heide ...... 14 B6
Lunéville ..... 13 B7
Luni → ........ 42 G8
Luofu ......... 57 E5
Luoyang ....... 35 C6
Lurgan ........ 11 D3
Lusaka ........ 59 B5
Luta = Dalian . 35 C7
Luton ......... 11 F6
Łutsel'e ...... 68 B8
Lutsk ......... 17 C7
Luxembourg .... 13 B7
Luxembourg ■ .. 14 D4
Luxor = El Uqsur 54 C5
Luzern ........ 13 C8
Luzhou ........ 35 D5
Luziânia ...... 93 F4
Luzon ......... 36 A2
Lviv .......... 17 D7
Lvov = Lviv ... 17 D7
Lyakhovskiye,
  Ostrova .... 31 B12
Lyallpur =
  Faisalabad . 42 D8
Lynchburg ..... 77 F6
Lynn Lake ..... 69 C9
Lyon .......... 13 D6
Lyonnais ...... 13 D6
Lysychansk .... 25 D4
Lyubertsy ..... 24 B4

## M

Ma'ān ......... 47 E3
Ma'anshan ..... 35 C6
Maas → ........ 14 C3
Maastricht .... 13 A6
McAllen ....... 80 F4
Macao = Macau 35 D6
Macapá ........ 92 B3

Macau, Brazil . 92 D6
Macau, China .. 35 D6
M'Clintock Chan. 68 A9
McComb ........ 81 D8
MacDonnell
  Ranges ...... 60 E5
Macedonia =
  Makedhonía □ 23 D4
Macedonia ■ ... 22 D3
Maceió ........ 93 D6
Macgillycuddy's
  Reeks ...... 11 F2
Mach .......... 42 E5
Machakos ...... 57 E7
Machala ....... 90 D3
Machilipatnam . 40 J3
Mackay ........ 61 E8
Mackay, L. .... 60 E4
Mackenzie → ... 68 B6
Mackenzie Mts. 68 B6
McKinley, Mt. . 69 B4
McMurdo Sd. .. 96 B15
Mâcon, France . 13 C6
Macon, U.S.A. . 83 C6
Madagascar ■ .. 59 J9
Madang ........ 61 B8
Madeira ....... 52 B2
Madeira → ..... 90 D7
Madhya
  Pradesh □ .. 43 H10
Madison ....... 75 D10
Madiun ........ 39 F4
Madras =
  Chennai .... 43 N12
Madras = Tamil
  Nadu □ ..... 43 P10
Madre de
  Dios → ..... 91 F5
Madre de Dios, I. 95 G1
Madre
  Occidental,
  Sierra ..... 84 B3
Madrid ........ 18 B4
Madurai ....... 43 Q11
Maebashi ...... 33 E6
Mafia □ ....... 57 F7
Magadan ....... 31 D13
Magallanes,
  Estrecho de . 95 G2
Magangué ...... 90 B4
Magdalena → ... 90 A4
Magdeburg ..... 15 B6
Magelang ...... 39 F4
Magellan's Str. =
  Magallanes,
  Estrecho de . 95 G2
Maggiore, Lago 20 B2
Magnetic Pole
  (South) .... 96 A13
Magnitogorsk .. 29 D6
Magosa =
  Famagusta .. 46 D3
Magwe ......... 41 G10
Mahābād ....... 46 C6
Mahajanga ..... 59 H9
Mahakam → ..... 39 E5
Mahalapye ..... 59 C5
Mahallāt ...... 44 C2
Mahanadi → .... 40 G6
Maharashtra □ . 43 J9
Mahdia ........ 54 A1
Mahesana ...... 43 H8
Mahilyow ...... 17 B10
Mahón = Maó .. 19 C8
Maí-Ndombe, L. 56 E3
Maidstone ..... 11 F7
Maiduguri ..... 55 F1
Maijdi ........ 41 F8
Main → ........ 14 D5
Maine ......... 12 C3
Mainland,
  Orkney, U.K. . 10 B5
Mainland, Shet.,
  U.K. ....... 10 A6
Mainz ......... 14 C5
Maiquetía ..... 90 A5

# Majorca

Majorca =
Mallorca ..... 19 C7
Makale ..... 37 E1
Makarikari =
  Makgadikgadi
  Salt Pans .. 59 C5
Makasar = Ujung
  Pandang ... 37 F1
Makasar, Selat . 37 E1
Makasar, Str.
  of = Makasar,
  Selat ..... 37 E1
Makedhonía □ . 23 D4
Makedonija =
  Macedonia ■ 22 D3
Makgadikgadi
  Salt Pans .. 59 C5
Makhachkala .. 25 E6
Makkah ..... 47 G4
Makran Coast
  Range ..... 42 G4
Makurdi ..... 53 G7
Malabar Coast . 43 P9
Malabo = Rey
  Malabo ..... 56 D1
Malacca, Str. of 38 D1
Málaga ..... 18 D3
Malagasy Rep. =
  Madagascar ■ 59 J9
Malakâl ..... 55 G5
Malang ..... 39 F4
Malanje ..... 56 F3
Mälaren ..... 9 D9
Malatya ..... 46 C4
Malawi ■ ..... 59 A6
Malawi, L. =
  Nyasa, L. ... 59 A6
Malay Pen. ... 38 C2
Malåyer ..... 46 D7
Malaysia ■ ... 38 D4
Malden I. ..... 65 K15
Maldives ■ ... 26 J11
Maldonado ... 94 C6
Malegaon ..... 43 J9
Mali ■ ..... 53 E5
Malin Hd. ..... 10 D3
Malindi ..... 57 E8
Malines =
  Mechelen ... 14 C3
Mallaig ..... 10 C4
Mallorca ..... 19 C7
Mallow ..... 11 E2
Malmö ..... 9 D8
Malpelo, I. de .. 90 C2
Malta ■ ..... 21 G5
Maluku ..... 37 E3
Maluku □ ..... 37 E3
Maluku Sea =
  Molucca Sea 37 E2
Malvinas, Is. =
  Falkland Is. ☒ 95 G5
Mamoré → ..... 91 F5
Man ..... 53 G4
Man, I. of ..... 11 D4
Manaar, G. of =
  Mannar, G. of 43 Q11
Manado ..... 37 D2
Managua ..... 85 E7
Manama = Al
  Manämah ... 44 E2
Manaos =
  Manaus ..... 90 D7
Manas ..... 34 B3
Manaus ..... 90 D7
Manchester,
  U.K. ..... 11 E5
Manchester,
  U.S.A. ..... 77 C10
Mand → ..... 9 D7
Mandalay ..... 41 F11
Mandla ..... 40 F3
Mandsaur ..... 43 G9
Mandvi ..... 43 H6
Mangalore ..... 43 N9
Mangnai ..... 34 C4
Mangole ..... 37 E3
Manica ..... 59 B6

Manicoré ..... 91 E6
Manicouagan → 71 D4
Manihiki ..... 65 L14
Manila ..... 36 B2
Manipur □ ..... 41 E9
Manisa ..... 23 E6
Manitoba □ ... 69 C10
Manitoba, L. .. 69 C10
Manitowoc ... 76 B2
Manizales ..... 90 B3
Mannar ..... 43 Q11
Mannar, G. of . 43 Q11
Mannheim ..... 14 D5
Manokwari ... 37 E4
Manosque ..... 13 E6
Mansel I. ..... 70 B2
Mansfield, U.K. 11 E6
Mansfield,
  U.S.A. ..... 76 D4
Manta ..... 90 D2
Mantes-la-Jolie 12 B4
Mántova ..... 20 B3
Manuel Alves → 93 E4
Manzai ..... 42 C7
Manzanillo,
  Cuba ..... 86 B4
Manzanillo,
  Mexico ..... 84 D4
Manzhouli ..... 35 B6
Mao ..... 19 C8
Maoming ..... 35 D6
Mapam Yumco . 40 B3
Maputo ..... 59 D6
Maquan He =
  Brahmaputra →
  ..... 41 F7
Maquinchao ... 95 E3
Mar Chiquita, L. 94 C4
Mar del Plata .. 94 D5
Marabá ..... 92 D4
Maracaibo ..... 90 A4
Maracaibo, L. de 90 B4
Maracay ..... 90 A5
Maradi ..... 53 F7
Marajó, I. de .. 92 C4
Maranhão = São
  Luís ..... 92 C5
Maranhão □ ... 92 D4
Marañón → ... 90 D4
Maraş =
  Kahramanmaraş
  ..... 46 C4
Marbella ..... 18 D3
Marche ..... 12 C4
Mardan ..... 42 B8
Mardin ..... 46 C5
Margarita, I. de 90 A6
Margate ..... 11 F7
Margilan ..... 29 E8
Märgow, Dasht-
  e ..... 42 D3
Mari El □ ..... 24 B6
Mariana Trench 64 H9
Maribor ..... 20 A5
Marie Byrd Land 96 B18
Mariecourt =
  Kangiqsujuaq 70 B3
Mariental ..... 58 C3
Marília ..... 93 G3
Marion ..... 81 A9
Maritimes, Alpes 13 D7
Maritsa =
  Évros → ..... 22 D6
Mariupol ..... 25 D4
Marka = Merca 49 G3
Markham, Mt. . 96 C15
Marmara Denizi 22 D7
Marmaris ..... 23 F7
Marne → ..... 12 B5
Marquises, Is. . 65 K17
Marrakech ..... 52 B4
Marree ..... 62 A2
Marsá Matrûh . 54 B4
Marseille ..... 13 E6
Marshall ..... 81 C6

Marshall Is. ■ . 64 J12
Martaban ..... 41 J11
Martaban, G. of 41 J11
Martigues ..... 13 E6
Martinique ☒ .. 87 D7
Marwar ..... 42 G8
Mary ..... 29 F7
Maryborough =
  Port Laoise .. 11 E3
Maryborough .. 63 A5
Maryland □ ... 77 E7
Marzûq ..... 54 C1
Masan ..... 35 C7
Masandam, Ra's 44 E4
Masaya ..... 85 E7
Masbate ..... 36 B2
Mascara ..... 52 A6
Maseru ..... 59 D5
Mashhad ..... 44 B4
Masjed
  Soleyman .. 47 E7
Mask, L. ..... 11 E2
Mason City ... 75 D8
Masqat ..... 45 C4
Massachusetts □
  ..... 77 C9
Massena ..... 77 B8
Massif Central . 13 D5
Masvingo ..... 59 C6
Matadi ..... 56 F2
Matagalpa ..... 85 E7
Matagami, L. .. 71 D3
Matamoros,
  Coahuila,
  Mexico ..... 84 B4
Matamoros,
  Tamaulipas,
  Mexico ..... 84 B5
Matane ..... 71 D4
Matanzas ..... 86 B3
Mataró ..... 19 B7
Matehuala ..... 84 C4
Matera ..... 21 D6
Mathura ..... 42 F10
Mati ..... 36 C3
Mato Grosso □ 93 E3
Mato Grosso,
  Planalto do .. 93 F3
Mato Grosso do
  Sul □ ..... 93 F3
Matrûh ..... 45 F4
Matsue ..... 33 F3
Matsumoto ... 33 E6
Matsusaka ... 33 F5
Matsuyama ... 33 G3
Mattagami → . 71 C2
Mattancheri .. 43 Q10
Maturín ..... 90 B6
Maubeuge ..... 13 A5
Maudin Sun ... 41 K10
Maui ..... 78 H12
Maulamyaing =
  Moulmein ... 41 J11
Maun ..... 58 B4
Mauritania ■ .. 53 E3
Mauritius ■ ... 51 H9
Mawlamyine =
  Moulmein ... 41 J11
Mayaguana ... 87 B5
Mayagüez ..... 87 C6
Maykop ..... 25 E5
Mayo ..... 68 B6
Mazagán = El
  Jadida ..... 52 B4
Mázandarán □ . 44 B3
Mazâr-e Sharîf . 45 B6
Mazatlán ..... 84 C3
Mazyr ..... 17 C9
Mbabane ..... 59 D6
Mbaïki ..... 56 D3
Mbala ..... 57 F6
Mbale ..... 57 D6
Mbandaka ..... 56 D3
Mbanza Ngungu 56 F2

Mbeya ..... 57 F6
Mbini = Río
  Muni □ ..... 56 D2
Mbuji-Mayi ... 56 F4
Mead, L. ..... 78 B5
Mecca = Makkah 47 G4
Mechelen ..... 14 C3
Mecklenburg .. 15 B6
Medan ..... 39 D1
Médéa ..... 52 A6
Medellín ..... 90 B3
Medford ..... 72 E2
Medicine Bow
  Ra. ..... 73 F10
Medicine Hat .. 69 C8
Medina = Al
  Madînah ... 47 F4
Mediterranean
  Sea ..... 50 C5
Médoc ..... 12 D3
Medvezhyegorsk 28 C4
Meekatharra .. 60 F2
Meerut ..... 42 E10
Meghalaya □ .. 41 E8
Meiktila ..... 41 G10
Meizhou ..... 35 D6
Mejillones ..... 94 A2
Mekhtar ..... 42 D6
Meknès ..... 52 B4
Mekong → ... 38 C3
Mekvari = Kür → 25 E6
Melaka ..... 39 D2
Melanesia ..... 64 K10
Melbourne ... 63 C3
Mélèzes → ... 70 C3
Melfort ..... 69 C9
Melilla ..... 19 E4
Melitopol ..... 25 D4
Melun ..... 13 B5
Melville ..... 69 C9
Melville I. ..... 60 C5
Melville Pen. .. 70 B2
Memel =
  Klaipeda .. 24 B1
Memphis ..... 82 B3
Mende ..... 13 D5
Mendocino, C. . 72 F1
Mendoza ..... 94 C3
Mengzi ..... 34 D5
Menominee ... 76 B2
Menorca ..... 19 C7
Mentawai,
  Kepulauan .. 39 E1
Merca ..... 49 G3
Merced ..... 78 B2
Mercedes,
  Corrientes,
  Argentina .. 94 B5
Mercedes,
  San Luis,
  Argentina .. 94 C3
Mercedes,
  Uruguay .... 94 C5
Mercy, C. ..... 70 B4
Mérida, Mexico 85 C7
Mérida, Spain . 18 C2
Mérida,
  Venezuela .. 90 B4
Meridian ..... 82 C3
Mersin ..... 46 C3
Merthyr Tydfil . 11 F5
Meru ..... 57 D7
Mesa ..... 79 D7
Meshed =
  Mashhad ... 44 B4
Mesopotamia =
  Al Jazirah ... 46 D5
Messina ..... 21 E5
Messina, Str. di 21 E5
Meta → ..... 90 B5
Metlakatla ..... 69 C6
Metz ..... 13 B7
Meuse → ..... 14 C3
Mexiana, I. ... 92 C4
Mexicali ..... 84 A1
México ..... 84 D5

Mexico ■ ..... 84 C4
Mexico, G. of . 85 B7
Meymaneh ... 42 B4
Mezen → ..... 28 C5
Miami ..... 83 G7
Miami Beach .. 83 G7
Miändowáb ... 46 C6
Miäneh ..... 46 C6
Mianwali ..... 42 C7
Miass ..... 29 D7
Michigan □ ... 76 C3
Michigan, L. .. 76 C2
Michurinsk ... 24 C5
Micronesia,
  Federated
  States of ■ .. 64 J10
Middelburg ... 58 E5
Middlesbrough 11 D6
Midi, Canal
  du → ..... 12 E4
Midland ..... 80 D3
Mieres ..... 18 A3
Mikonos ..... 23 F5
Milan = Milano 20 B2
Milano ..... 20 B2
Mildura ..... 62 B3
Milford Haven . 11 F4
Milford Sd. ... 65 F2
Millau ..... 13 D5
Millennium I. =
  Caroline I. .. 65 K15
Millinocket ... 77 B11
Milton Keynes . 11 E6
Milwaukee ... 76 C2
Min Jiang →,
  Fujian, China 35 D6
Min Jiang →,
  Sichuan,
  China ..... 35 D5
Minas ..... 94 C5
Minas Gerais □ 93 F4
Mindanao ..... 36 C2
Mindanao Sea =
  Bohol Sea .. 36 C2
Mindanao
  Trench ..... 36 B3
Mindoro ..... 36 B2
Mindoro Str. .. 36 B2
Minho =
  Miño → ..... 18 B1
Minna ..... 53 G7
Minneapolis .. 75 C8
Minnesota □ .. 75 B7
Miño → ..... 18 B1
Minorca =
  Menorca ... 19 C7
Minot ..... 74 A4
Minsk ..... 24 C2
Miramichi ..... 71 D4
Mirim, L. ..... 94 C6
Mirpur Khas .. 42 G6
Mirzapur ..... 40 E4
Mishan ..... 35 B8
Miskolc ..... 16 D5
Misool ..... 37 E4
Mişrâtah ..... 54 B2
Missinaibi → .. 71 C2
Mississippi □ .. 81 C9
Mississippi → . 81 E9
Mississippi River
  Delta ..... 81 E9
Missoula ..... 73 C7
Missouri □ ... 75 F8
Missouri → ... 75 F9
Mistassini, L. . 71 C3
Misurata =
  Mişrâtah ... 54 B2
Mitchell ..... 74 D5
Mitchell → ... 61 D7
Mito ..... 33 E7
Mittimatalik =
  Pond Inlet .. 70 A3
Mitú ..... 90 C4
Mitumba, Mts. . 57 F5
Miyakonojō ... 33 H2
Miyazaki ..... 33 H2

Miyet, Bahr el =
 Dead Sea ... 47 E3
Mizoram □ .. 41 F9
Mjøsa ......... 8 C8
Mo i Rana ... 8 B8
Mobaye .... 56 D4
Mobile ....... 82 D3
Mobutu Sese
 Seko, L. =
 Albert, L. .. 57 D6
Moçambique . 59 H8
Moçâmedes =
 Namibe .... 58 B2
Mocoa ...... 90 C3
Módena ..... 20 B3
Modesto .... 78 B2
Mogadishu =
 Muqdisho .. 49 G4
Mogador =
 Essaouira .. 52 B4
Mogi das Cruzes 94 A7
Mogilev =
 Mahilyow .. 17 B10
Moisie → ... 71 C4
Mojave Desert . 78 C4
Moldavia =
 Moldova ■ .. 17 E9
Molde ........ 8 C7
Moldova ■ .. 17 E9
Mollendo ..... 91 G4
Molokai .... 78 H12
Molopo → .... 58 D4
Molotov = Perm 29 D6
Molucca Sea .. 37 E2
Moluccas =
 Maluku .... 37 E3
Mombasa .... 57 E7
Mompós ..... 90 B4
Mona Passage . 87 C6
Monaco ■ ... 13 E7
Monastir =
 Bitola ..... 22 D3
Mönchengladbach
 .......... 14 C4
Monclova .... 84 B4
Monghyr =
 Munger .... 40 E6
Mongibello =
 Etna ....... 21 F5
Mongolia ■ .. 35 B5
Mongu ....... 58 B4
Monroe ...... 82 D4
Monrovia .... 53 G3
Mons ........ 14 C2
Mont-de-Marsan 12 E3
Mont-St-Michel,
 Le ........ 12 B3
Montana □ ... 73 C9
Montargis ... 13 C5
Montauban .. 12 D4
Montbéliard .. 13 C7
Montceau-les-
 Mines ..... 13 C6
Monte Azul .. 93 F5
Monte-Carlo .. 20 C7
Monte Caseros 94 C5
Montego Bay .. 86 C4
Montélimar .. 13 D6
Montemorelos . 84 B5
Montenegro □ . 22 C2
Monterey .... 78 B2
Monteria .... 90 B3
Monterrey ... 84 B4
Montes Claros 93 F5
Montevideo .. 94 C5
Montgomery .. 82 C4
Montluçon ... 13 C5
Montpellier .. 13 E5
Montréal .... 71 D3
Montrose, U.K. 10 C5
Montrose,
 U.S.A. ..... 79 A9
Montserrat ☑ . 87 C7
Monywa ..... 41 F10
Monza ....... 20 B2
Monze, C. ... 43 G5
Moose Jaw .. 69 C9

Moosomin ... 69 C9
Moosonee ... 71 C2
Mopti ....... 53 F5
Mora ......... 8 C8
Moradabad .. 42 E11
Moratuwa ... 43 R11
Morava →,
 Serbia & M. . 22 B3
Morava →,
 Slovak Rep. . 16 D3
Moravian Hts. =
 Českomoravská
 Vrchovina ... 16 D2
Moray Firth ... 10 C5
Morden ..... 69 D10
Mordvinia □ .. 24 C5
Moree ....... 63 A4
Morelia ..... 84 D4
Morena, Sierra 18 C3
Morgan City .. 81 E8
Morioka .... 32 D7
Morlaix ..... 12 B2
Morocco ■ ... 52 B4
Morogoro ... 57 F7
Morón ...... 86 B4
Morotai .... 37 D3
Morphou .... 46 D3
Morrinhos ... 93 F4
Moscos Is. ... 41 L11
Moscow =
 Moskva ... 24 B4
Moscow .... 72 C5
Mosel → ... 13 A7
Moselle =
 Mosel → ... 13 A7
Moshi ...... 57 E7
Moskva .... 24 B4
Mosselbaai .. 58 E4
Mossoró ... 92 D6
Most ....... 16 C1
Mostaganem . 52 A6
Mostar ..... 20 C6
Mosul = Al
 Mawşil .... 46 C5
Motihari .... 40 D5
Moulins .... 13 C5
Moulmein .. 41 J11
Moundou ... 55 G2
Mount Gambier 62 C3
Mount Isa ... 61 E6
Mount Lofty Ra. 62 B2
Moyen Atlas .. 52 B4
Mozambique =
 Moçambique 59 H8
Mozambique ■ 59 B7
Mozambique
 Chan. ..... 51 H8
Mozdok .... 25 E5
Mozyr = Mazyr 17 C9
Mpanda .... 57 F6
Mu Us Shamo . 35 C5
Muar ....... 39 D2
Mubarraz = Al
 Mubarraz .. 47 F7
Mucuri .... 93 F6
Mudanjiang .. 35 B7
Mufulira .... 59 A5
Muğla ...... 23 F7
Muine =
 Muynak ... 29 E6
Mukden =
 Shenyang .. 35 B7
Muktsar .... 42 D9
Mulde → .... 15 C7
Mulhacén ... 18 D4
Mulhouse ... 13 C7
Mull ....... 10 C4
Mullingar ... 11 E3
Multan ..... 42 D7
Mumbai .... 43 K8
Muna ....... 37 F2
München ... 15 D6
München-
 Gladbach =
 Mönchengladbach
 .......... 14 C4
Muncie ..... 76 D3

Mundo Novo .. 93 E5
Munger ..... 40 E6
Munich =
 München ... 15 D6
Münster .... 14 C4
Munster □ ... 11 E2
Muqdisho ... 49 G4
Murashi .... 24 B6
Murchison → . 60 F1
Murcia ..... 19 C5
Murcia □ .... 19 D5
Mureş → .... 22 A3
Müritz ..... 15 B7
Murmansk ... 8 B12
Murom ..... 24 B5
Muroran .... 32 B7
Murray → ... 62 C2
Murrumbidgee →
 .......... 62 B3
Murwara .... 40 F3
Muş ........ 46 C5
Mûsa, Gebel .. 47 E3
Muscat =
 Masqat .... 45 F4
Muscat &
 Oman =
 Oman ■ ... 48 C6
Musgrave
 Ranges .... 60 F5
Musina .... 59 C6
Muskogee ... 81 B6
Mutare .... 59 B6
Muynak ..... 29 E6
Muzaffarnagar . 42 E10
Mwanza .... 57 E6
Mweru, L. ... 57 F5
My Tho .... 38 B3
Myanmar =
 Burma ■ ... 41 G11
Myingyan ... 41 G10
Myitkyina ... 41 E11
Mykolayiv ... 25 D3
Mymensingh .. 41 E8
Mysore =
 Karnataka □ . 43 N10
Mysore ..... 43 N10
Mytishchi ... 24 B4

# N

Na Hearadh =
 Harris .... 10 C3
Naab → .... 15 D7
Naberezhnyye
 Chelny ... 29 D6
Nabeul .... 54 A1
Nāblus =
 Nābulus ... 46 D3
Nābulus .... 46 D3
Nacogdoches . 81 D6
Nacozari .... 84 A3
Nadiad ..... 43 H8
Nafud Desert =
 An Nafūd ... 47 E5
Naga ....... 36 B2
Nagaland □ ... 41 E10
Nagano ..... 33 E6
Nagaoka .... 33 E6
Nagappattinam 43 P11
Nagasaki .... 33 G1
Nagaur ..... 42 F8
Nagercoil ... 43 Q10
Nagoya .... 33 F5
Nagpur .... 43 J11
Naha ....... 35 D7
Nain ....... 70 C4
Nairn ...... 10 C5
Nairobi .... 57 E7
Najafābād ... 44 C2
Najd ....... 47 F5
Najibabad ... 42 E11
Nakhichevan
 Rep. =
 Naxçıvan □ . 25 F6

Nakhon
 Ratchasima . 38 B2
Nakhon Sawan 38 A2
Nakhon Si
 Thammarat . 38 C2
Nakina ..... 71 C2
Nakuru ..... 57 E7
Nalchik .... 25 E5
Nam Co .... 34 C4
Nam-Phan .. 38 B3
Namak,
 Daryācheh-ye 44 C3
Namaland ... 58 C3
Namangan ... 29 E8
Namib Desert . 58 C2
Namibe ..... 58 B2
Namibia ■ ... 58 C3
Nampa ..... 72 E5
Namp'o .... 35 C7
Nampula ... 59 B7
Namur ..... 14 C3
Nanaimo ... 69 D7
Nanchang ... 35 D6
Nanchong ... 35 C5
Nancy ...... 13 B7
Nanda Devi ... 42 D11
Nanded ..... 43 K10
Nandurbar ... 43 J9
Nanga Parbat . 42 B9
Nangarhār □ . 42 B7
Nanjing .... 35 C6
Nanking =
 Nanjing ... 35 C6
Nanning ... 35 D5
Nanping ... 35 D6
Nansei-Shotō =
 Ryūkyū-rettō 35 D7
Nantes .... 12 C3
Nantucket I. .. 77 D10
Nanuque ... 93 F5
Nanyang ... 35 C6
Nanyuki ... 57 D7
Napa ....... 72 G2
Napier ..... 64 C7
Naples = Nápoli 21 D5
Naples ..... 83 F7
Napo → .... 90 D4
Nápoli .... 21 D5
Narayanganj . 41 F8
Narbonne ... 13 E5
Narmada → .. 43 J8
Narodnaya .. 28 C7
Narva ...... 24 B2
Narvik ..... 8 B9
Naryan-Mar .. 28 C6
Naryn ...... 24 B2
Naser, Buheirat
 en ........ 54 D5
Nashville ... 82 A4
Nasik ...... 43 K8
Nasirabad ... 42 F9
Nassau ..... 86 A4
Nasser, L. =
 Naser,
 Buheirat en 54 D5
Natal ...... 92 D6
Nataschquan . 71 C4
Nataschquan → 71 C4
Natchez .... 81 D8
Nathḍwāra ... 40 G8
Natitingou ... 53 F6
Natron, L. ... 57 E7
Natuna Besar,
 Kepulauan . 39 D3
Naujaat =
 Repulse Bay . 70 B2
Nauru ■ .... 64 K11
Navarino, I. .. 95 H3
Navarra □ ... 19 A5
Navojoa .... 84 B3
Navsari .... 43 J8
Nawabshah .. 42 F6
Naxçıvan □ .. 25 F6
Náxos ..... 23 F5
Nazas → .... 84 B4
Nazilli .... 23 F7
Ndjamena ... 55 F1
Ndola ..... 59 A5
Neagh, Lough . 11 D3

Near Is. ..... 69 C1
Neath ...... 11 F5
Nebitdag ... 29 F6
Nebraska □ .. 74 E5
Neckar → ... 14 D5
Necochea ... 94 D5
Neemuch =
 Nimach .... 43 G9
Neepawa ... 69 C10
Negapatam =
 Nagappattinam
 .......... 43 P11
Negele .... 49 F2
Negombo ... 43 R11
Negrais C. =
 Maudin Sun . 41 K10
Negro →,
 Argentina .. 95 E4
Negro →, Brazil 90 D6
Negros .... 36 C2
Nei Monggol
 Zizhiqu □ .. 35 B6
Neijiang ... 35 D5
Neiva ...... 90 C3
Nejd = Najd .. 47 F5
Nellore .... 43 M11
Nelson, Canada 69 D8
Nelson, N.Z. .. 65 D5
Nelson → ... 69 C10
Neman =
 Nemunas → . 24 B1
Nemunas → .. 24 B1
Nemuro .... 32 B9
Nenagh .... 11 E2
Nenjiang ... 35 B7
Nepal ■ .... 40 D5
Ness, L. ... 10 C4
Netherlands ■ . 14 B3
Netherlands
 Antilles ☑ .. 87 D6
Nettilling L. .. 70 B3
Neuquén ... 94 D3
Neva → .... 24 B3
Nevada □ ... 72 G5
Nevers .... 13 C5
Nevinnomyssk 25 E5
New Amsterdam 90 B7
New Bedford .. 77 D10
New Britain,
 Papua N. G. . 64 K10
New Britain,
 U.S.A. .... 77 D9
New
 Brunswick □ 71 D4
New
 Caledonia ☑ . 64 M11
New Castile =
 Castilla-La
 Mancha □ .. 18 C4
New Delhi ... 42 E10
New Glasgow . 71 D4
New
 Hampshire □ 77 C10
New Haven ... 77 D9
New Hebrides =
 Vanuatu ■ . 64 L11
New Ireland .. 64 K10
New Jersey □ . 77 E9
New London .. 77 D9
New Mexico □ 79 C5
New Orleans .. 81 E8
New Plymouth 64 C6
New Providence
 I. ........ 86 A4
New Siberian
 Is. =
 Novosibirskiye
 Ostrova ... 31 B12
New South
 Wales □ ... 63 B4
New York .... 77 D9
New York □ .. 77 C8
New Zealand ■ 64 D7
New → .... 77 D8
Newark .... 77 D9
Newburgh ... 77 D8
Newbury ... 11 F6
Newcastle ... 63 B5

Newcastle-upon-
  Tyne ....... 11 D6
Newfoundland
  and
  Labrador □ .. 71 C5
Newman ...... 60 E2
Newport,
  I. of W., U.K. . 11 F6
Newport, Newp.,
  U.K. ....... 11 F5
Newport, U.S.A. 77 D10
Newport News 77 F7
Newquay ..... 11 F4
Newry ....... 11 D3
Neyshābūr ... 44 B4
Nezhin = Nizhyn 24 C3
Ngaoundéré .. 56 C2
Ngoring Hu .. 34 C4
Nha Trang ... 38 B3
Niagara Falls,
  Canada ..... 71 D3
Niagara Falls,
  U.S.A. ...... 77 C6
Niamey ...... 53 F6
Nias ........ 39 D1
Nicaragua ■ .. 85 E7
Nicaragua, L. de 85 E7
Nice ........ 13 E7
Nicobar Is. ... 27 J13
Nicosia ...... 46 D3
Nicoya, Pen. de 85 F7
Niedersachsen □
  ........... 14 B5
Niemen =
  Nemunas → . 24 B1
Nieuw Nickerie 92 A2
Niğde ....... 46 C3
Niger ■ ...... 53 E7
Niger → ...... 53 G7
Nigeria ■ ..... 53 G7
Niigata ...... 33 E6
Niihau ...... 78 H10
Nijmegen .... 14 C3
Niklayev =
  Mykolayiv ... 25 D3
Nikopol ...... 25 D3
Nīl, Nahr en → 54 B5
Nīl el Abyaḍ → 55 E5
Nīl el Azraq → . 55 E5
Nile = Nīl, Nahr
  en → ....... 54 B5
Nimach ...... 43 G9
Nîmes ....... 13 E6
Nimrūz □ ..... 45 D5
Nīnawá ...... 46 C5
Nineveh =
  Nīnawá ..... 46 C5
Ningbo ...... 35 D7
Ningxia Huizu
  Zizhiqu □ ... 35 C5
Niobrara → ... 74 D5
Niort ....... 12 C3
Nipawin ..... 69 C9
Nipigon, L. ... 71 D2
Niquelândia .. 93 E4
Niš ........ 22 C3
Nistru =
  Dnister → .. 17 E10
Niterói ...... 93 G5
Niue ........ 65 L14
Nivernais .... 13 C5
Nizamabad ... 43 K11
Nizhnevartovsk 29 C8
Nizhniy
  Novgorod ... 24 B5
Nizhniy Tagil .. 29 D6
Nizhyn ...... 24 C3
Nkongsamba .. 56 D1
Noakhali =
  Maijdi ...... 41 F8
Nobeoka .... 33 G2
Nogales, Mexico 84 A2
Nogales, U.S.A. 79 E7
Noirmoutier, Î.
  de ........ 12 C2
Nola ........ 56 D3
Nome ....... 69 B3

Noranda =
  Rouyn-
  Noranda .... 71 D3
Nord-Ostsee-
  Kanal ...... 14 A5
Nordfriesische
  Inseln ...... 14 A5
Nordkapp ..... 8 A11
Nordrhein-
  Westfalen □ . 14 C4
Norfolk ...... 11 F7
Norfolk I. .... 64 M11
Norilsk ...... 30 C6
Norman ...... 80 B5
Norman Wells . 68 B7
Normandie ... 12 B4
Normanton ... 61 D7
Norrköping ... 9 D9
Norrland .... 8 C9
Norseman .... 60 G3
North Battleford 69 C9
North Bay .... 71 D3
North C. ..... 64 A5
North Cape =
  Nordkapp .... 8 A11
North Carolina □ 83 B7
North Channel . 11 D4
North Dakota □ 74 B4
North East
  Frontier
  Agency =
  Arunachal
  Pradesh □ .. 41 C10
North Frisian
  Is. =
  Nordfriesische
  Inseln ...... 14 A5
North I. ...... 64 B5
North Korea ■ . 35 C7
North Minch .. 10 B4
North Ossetia □ 25 E5
North Platte .. 74 E4
North Platte → 74 E4
North Rhine
  Westphalia =
  Nordrhein-
  Westfalen □ . 14 C4
North
  Saskatchewan →
  ........... 69 C8
North Sea ... 10 D8
North
  Sporades =
  Vóriai
  Sporádhes .. 23 E4
North
  Thompson → 69 C7
North Uist ... 10 C3
North West C. . 60 E1
North West
  Frontier □ ... 42 B8
North West
  Highlands ... 10 C4
North West
  River ...... 71 C4
Northampton .. 11 E6
Northern Circars 40 J4
Northern
  Ireland □ ... 11 D3
Northern
  Marianas ☑ . 64 H9
Northern
  Territory □ .. 60 D5
Northumberland
  Str. ....... 71 C4
Northwest
  Territories □ . 68 B9
Norton Sd. ... 69 B3
Norway ■ .... 8 C8
Norway House 69 C10
Norwegian Sea 6 B5
Norwich ..... 11 E7
Nossob → .... 58 D4
Notre Dame B. . 71 D5
Notre-Dame-de-
  Koartac =
  Quaqtaq ... 70 B4

Notre-Dame-
  d'Ivugivic =
  Ivujivik ..... 70 B3
Nottaway → ... 71 C3
Nottingham ... 11 E6
Nouâdhibou ... 52 D2
Nouâdhibou,
  Ras ....... 52 D2
Nouakchott ... 53 E2
Nouméa ..... 64 M11
Nouveau
  Comptoir =
  Wemindji ... 71 C3
Nouvelle-
  Calédonie =
  New
  Caledonia ☑ . 64 M11
Nova Casa Nova 93 D5
Nova Friburgo . 93 G5
Nova Iguaçu .. 93 G5
Nova Lima ... 93 F5
Nova Lisboa =
  Huambo .... 58 A3
Nova Scotia □ . 71 D4
Nova Venécia . 93 F5
Novara ...... 20 B2
Novaya Zemlya 28 B6
Novgorod .... 24 B3
Novi Sad .... 22 B2
Novo Remanso 93 D5
Novocherkassk 25 D5
Novokuybyshevsk
  ........... 24 C6
Novokuznetsk . 29 D9
Novomoskovsk 24 C4
Novorossiysk . 25 E4
Novoshakhtinsk 25 D4
Novosibirsk ... 29 D9
Novosibirskiye
  Ostrova ... 31 B12
Novotroitsk .. 29 D6
Nubian Desert =
  Nûbîya, Es
  Sahrâ en .. 54 D5
Nûbîya, Es
  Sahrâ en .. 54 D5
Nueltin L. ... 68 B10
Nueva Rosita . 84 B4
Nuevitas .... 86 B4
Nuevo Laredo . 84 B5
Nuku'alofa ... 65 M13
Nukus ...... 29 E6
Nullarbor Plain 60 G4
Numazu ..... 33 F6
Nunap Isua ... 70 C6
Nuneaton .... 11 E6
Nunivak I. ... 69 B3
Nuremberg =
  Nürnberg ... 15 D6
Nürnberg ... 15 D6
Nuuk ....... 70 B5
Nyahururu ... 57 D7
Nyainqentanglha
  Shan ...... 34 C4
Nyâlâ ...... 55 F3
Nyasa, L. .... 59 A6
Nyíregyháza .. 17 E5
Nyoman =
  Nemunas → . 24 B1
Nysa ....... 16 C3
Nysa → ...... 16 B2

# O

Oahe, L. ..... 74 C4
Oahu ....... 78 H12
Oak Ridge ... 83 A5
Oakland .... 78 B1
Oates Land .. 96 A15
Oaxaca ..... 84 D5
Ob → ....... 28 C7
Oba ........ 71 D2
Oban ....... 10 C4
Oberhausen .. 14 C4

Obi ........ 37 E3
Óbidos ...... 92 C2
Obihiro ..... 32 B8
Obozerskiy ... 28 C5
Obskaya Guba . 28 C8
Ocala ....... 83 E6
Occidental,
  Cordillera ... 90 C3
Oceanside ... 78 D4
Odawara ..... 33 F6
Odense ...... 9 D8
Oder → ...... 15 B8
Odesa ...... 25 D3
Odessa ...... 80 D2
Odintsovo ... 24 B4
Odra = Oder → 15 B8
Offa ........ 53 G6
Offenbach ... 14 C5
Ōgaki ...... 33 F5
Ogbomosho .. 53 G6
Ogden ...... 73 F7
Ogdensburg .. 77 B8
Ogooué → .... 56 E1
Ohio □ ...... 76 D4
Ohio → ...... 76 F1
Ohře → ...... 16 C2
Ohridsko Jezero 23 D3
Oise → ...... 12 B5
Ōita ........ 33 G2
Ojos del Salado,
  Cerro ...... 94 B3
Oka → ...... 28 D5
Okanogan → .. 72 B4
Okara ...... 42 D8
Okavango Delta 58 B4
Okayama .... 33 F3
Okazaki ..... 33 F5
Okeechobee, L. 83 F7
Okefenokee
  Swamp .... 83 D6
Okhotsk, Sea of 31 D12
Oki-Shotō ... 33 E3
Okinawa-Jima . 35 D7
Oklahoma □ .. 80 B5
Oklahoma City . 80 B5
Oktyabrsk ... 29 E6
Öland ...... 9 D9
Olavarría .... 94 D4
Old Castile =
  Castilla y
  León □ ..... 18 A3
Old Crow .... 68 B6
Oldenburg ... 14 B5
Oldham ..... 11 E5
Olekminsk ... 31 C10
Olenek → .... 30 B10
Oléron, Î. d' .. 12 D3
Olifants =
  Elefantes → . 59 C6
Ólimbos, Óros . 23 D4
Ollagüe ..... 91 H5
Olomouc ... 16 D3
Olsztyn ..... 16 B5
Olt → ...... 22 C5
Olympia ..... 72 C2
Olympic Mts. .. 72 C2
Olympus, Mt. =
  Ólimbos, Óros 23 D4
Omagh ...... 11 D3
Omaha ..... 75 E7
Oman ■ ..... 48 C6
Oman, G. of .. 45 E4
Omdurmân .. 55 E5
Ometepec ... 84 D5
Omsk ...... 29 D8
Ōmuta ...... 33 G2
Ondangwa ... 58 B3
Onega, L. =
  Onezhskoye
  Ozero .... 8 C13
Onezhskoye
  Ozero .... 8 C13
Onitsha ..... 53 G7
Ontario □ .... 71 D2
Ontario, L. ... 77 C7
Oostende .... 14 C2

Ootacamund =
  Udagamandalam
  ........... 43 P10
Opava ...... 16 D3
Opole ...... 16 C3
Oporto = Porto 18 B1
Oradea ...... 17 E5
Öræfajökull .. 8 C2
Oral =
  Zhayyq → .. 29 E6
Oral ........ 24 C7
Oran ....... 52 A5
Orange,
  Australia .... 63 B4
Orange, France 13 D6
Orange → .... 58 D3
Orange, C. ... 92 B3
Orangeburg .. 83 C7
Oranje =
  Orange → .. 58 D3
Oraşul Stalin =
  Braşov ..... 17 F7
Ordos = Mu Us
  Shamo .... 35 C5
Ordu ....... 46 B4
Ordzhonikidze =
  Vladikavkaz . 25 E5
Ore Mts. =
  Erzgebirge .. 15 C7
Örebro ...... 9 D9
Oregon □ .... 72 E3
Orekhovo-
  Zuyevo .... 24 B4
Orel ....... 24 C4
Orenburg .... 29 D6
Orense =
  Ourense ... 18 A2
Orhon Gol → .. 35 A5
Oriental,
  Cordillera ... 90 B4
Orinoco → .... 90 B6
Orissa □ ..... 40 G5
Oristano .... 21 E3
Orizaba ..... 84 D5
Orizaba, Pico de 84 D5
Orkney Is. ... 10 B5
Orlando ..... 83 E7
Orléanais ... 12 C4
Orléans ..... 12 C4
Ormara ...... 42 G4
Ormoc ...... 36 B2
Örnsköldsvik . 8 C9
Orol Dengizi =
  Aral Sea ... 29 E6
Orsha ...... 24 C3
Orsk ....... 29 D6
Orümiyeh .... 46 C6
Orümiyeh,
  Daryächeh-ye 46 C6
Oruro ...... 91 G5
Oruzgân □ ... 42 C5
Ōsaka ...... 33 F4
Ösel = Saaremaa 24 B1
Oshawa ..... 71 D3
Oshkosh .... 53 G6
Osijek ...... 20 B7
Osipenko =
  Berdyansk .. 25 D4
Oskarshamn .. 9 D9
Öskemen ... 29 D9
Oslo ....... 9 D8
Oslofjorden .. 9 D8
Osmaniye ... 46 C4
Osnabrück ... 14 B5
Osorno ..... 95 E2
Ossa, Mt. .... 62 D4
Ostend =
  Oostende ... 14 C2
Österdalälven . 8 C8
Östersund ... 8 C8
Ostfriesische
  Inseln ..... 14 B4
Ostrava ..... 16 D4
Ostrołęka ... 16 B5
Ostrów
  Wielkopolski 16 C3

Ostrowiec-
Świętokrzyski  16  C5
Oswego ......... 77  C7
Otago □ ....... 65  F3
Otaru ........... 32  B7
Otjiwarongo ... 58  C3
Otranto, Str. of  23  D2
Ōtsu ............ 33  F4
Ottawa ......... 71  D3
Ottawa Is. ...... 70  C2
Ottumwa ....... 75  E8
Ouachita Mts. . 81  B6
Ouagadougou . 53  F5
Ouahran = Oran  52  A5
Oubangi → ..... 56  E3
Oudtshoorn .... 58  E4
Ouessant, Î. d' . 12  B1
Ouezzane ...... 52  B4
Oujda .......... 52  B5
Oulu ........... 8  B11
Oulujärvi ...... 8  C11
Oulujoki → .... 8  B11
Ourense ....... 18  A2
Ouro Prêto .... 93  G5
Outer Hebrides  10  C3
Outjo .......... 58  C3
Ovalle ......... 94  C2
Ovamboland .. 58  B3
Oviedo ........ 18  A3
Owambo =
Ovamboland  58  B3
Owen Sound .. 71  D2
Owen Stanley
Ra. ........... 61  B8
Owo ........... 53  G7
Owyhee → .... 72  E5
Oxford ........ 11  F6
Oxnard ........ 78  C3
Oxus =
Amudarya → .. 29  E6
Oyama ........ 33  E6
Oyo ........... 53  G6
Ozark Plateau . 81  A8

## P

Paarl ......... 58  E3
Pabna ........ 41  E7
Pacaraima, Sa.  90  C6
Pacasmayo ... 91  E3
Pachuca ...... 84  C5
Padang ....... 39  E2
Padangsidempuan
.............. 39  D1
Paderborn .... 14  C5
Pádova ....... 20  B3
Padua = Pádova  20  B3
Paducah ...... 76  F1
Pagadian ..... 36  C2
Pagalu =
Annobón .... 51  G4
Paint Hills =
Wemindji ... 71  C3
Painted Desert  79  C7
País Vasco □ .. 19  A4
Paisley ........ 10  D4
Paita .......... 90  E2
Pakistan ■ .... 42  E7
Paktiā □ ...... 42  C6
Pakxe ......... 38  A3
Palanpur ...... 43  G8
Palapye ....... 59  C5
Palau ■ ....... 36  C4
Palawan ...... 38  C5
Palembang ... 39  E2
Palencia ...... 18  A3
Palermo ...... 21  E4
Palestine ..... 81  D6
Palghat ....... 43  P10
Pali .......... 42  G8
Palk Strait .... 43  Q11
Palma de
Mallorca ... 19  C7
Palmares .... 92  D6

Palmas, C. ... 53  H4
Palmeira dos
Índios ....... 93  D6
Palmer ....... 69  B5
Palmer Land . 96  B3
Palmerston
North ....... 64  D6
Palmira ...... 90  C3
Palmyra =
Tudmur .... 46  D4
Palopo ....... 37  E2
Palu, Indonesia  37  E1
Palu, Turkey .. 46  C5
Pamiers ...... 12  E4
Pamir ........ 29  F8
Pamlico Sd. .. 83  B10
Pampa ....... 80  B3
Pampas → ... 94  D4
Pamplona .... 19  A5
Panaji ....... 43  M8
Panamá ..... 85  F9
Panamá ■ .... 86  E4
Panamá, G. de . 86  E4
Panama Canal . 86  E4
Panama City . 82  D5
Panay ....... 36  B2
Pančevo ..... 22  B3
Panevėžys ... 24  B1
Pangfou =
Bengbu .... 35  C6
Pangkalpinang  39  E3
Pangnirtung .. 70  B4
Panjim = Panaji  43  M8
Pannirtuuq =
Pangnirtung . 70  B4
Pantar ....... 37  F2
Pante Macassar  37  F2
Pantelleria ... 21  F3
Paoting =
Baoding .... 35  C6
Paot'ou =
Baotou ..... 35  B6
Papantla ..... 84  C5
Papeete ...... 65  L16
Papua □ ..... 37  E5
Papua New
Guinea ■ ... 61  B8
Pará = Belém .  92  C4
Pará □ ...... 92  C3
Paracatu .... 93  F4
Paracel Is. ... 38  A4
Paraguaçu → . 93  E6
Paraguaná, Pen.
de .......... 90  A4
Paraguarí ... 94  B5
Paraguay ■ .. 94  A5
Paraguay → .. 94  B5
Paraíba = João
Pessoa ..... 92  D7
Paraíba □ .... 92  D6
Parakou ..... 53  G6
Paramaribo .. 92  A2
Paraná,
Argentina .. 94  C4
Paraná, Brazil . 93  E4
Paraná □ ..... 94  A6
Paraná → .... 94  C5
Paranaguá ... 94  B7
Paranaíba → . 93  G3
Parananjanrinia =
.............. 94  A6
Parbhani ..... 43  K10
Pardo → ..... 93  F6
Pardubice ... 16  C2
Parecis, Serra
dos ........ 91  F7
Parepare ..... 37  E1
Parima, Serra . 90  C6
Parintins .... 92  C2
Pariparit Kyun . 41  K9
Paris, France . 12  B5
Paris, U.S.A. . 81  C6
Park Range ... 73  G10
Parkersburg .. 76  E5
Parma ....... 20  B3
Parnaguá .... 93  E5
Parnaíba ..... 92  C5

Parnaíba → ... 92  C5
Parnassós ... 23  E4
Pärnu ....... 24  B1
Parry Sound . 71  D3
Paru → ...... 92  C3
Parván □ .... 42  B6
Pasadena, Calif.,
U.S.A. .... 78  C3
Pasadena, Tex.,
U.S.A. .... 81  E6
Pasco, Cerro de  91  F3
Passau ...... 15  D7
Passo Fundo . 94  B6
Passos ...... 93  G4
Pastaza → ... 90  D3
Pastu ....... 90  C3
Patagonia ... 95  F3
Patan ....... 43  H8
Paterson .... 77  D8
Pathankot ... 42  C9
Pathein =
Bassein .... 41  J10
Patna ....... 40  E5
Patos, L. dos . 94  C6
Patos de Minas  93  F4
Pátrai ....... 23  E3
Patras = Pátrai . 23  E3
Patrocínio ... 93  F4
Pau ......... 12  E3
Paulistana ... 92  D5
Paulo Afonso . 93  D6
Pavia ........ 20  B2
Pavlodar .... 29  D8
Pavlohrad ... 25  D4
Pavlovo ..... 24  B5
Pawtucket ... 77  D10
Payakumbuh . 39  E2
Payne Bay =
Kangirsuk .. 70  C4
Paysandú ... 94  C5
Paz, B. de la . 84  C2
Pazardzhik ... 22  C5
Peace → ..... 68  C8
Pechenga ... 28  C4
Pechora → ... 28  C6
Pechorskaya
Guba ....... 28  C6
Pecos → ..... 80  E3
Pécs ........ 16  E4
Pedra Azul ... 93  F5
Pedro Afonso . 93  D4
Peel → ...... 68  B6
Pegu ........ 41  J11
Pegu Yoma .. 41  H10
Peip'ing =
Beijing .... 35  C6
Peipus, L. =
Chudskoye,
Ozero ..... 24  B2
Peixe ....... 93  E4
Pekalongan .. 39  F3
Pekanbaru ... 39  D2
Pekin ....... 75  E10
Peking = Beijing  35  C6
Peleng ...... 37  E2
Pelly → ...... 68  B6
Pelly Bay .... 70  B2
Peloponnese =
Pelopónnisos □
.............. 23  F4
Pelopónnisos □  23  F4
Pelotas ...... 94  C6
Pelvoux, Massif
du ......... 13  D7
Pematangsiantar  39  D1
Pemba I. ..... 57  F7
Pembroke,
Canada .... 71  D3
Pembroke, U.K. . 11  F4
Penang = Pinang  38  C2
Penas, G. de . 95  F2
Pench'i = Benxi . 35  B7
Pend Oreille, L. 72  C5
Pendleton ... 72  D4
Penedo ...... 93  E6
Peninsular
Malaysia □ .. 39  D2

Penmarch, Pte.
de .......... 12  C1
Pennines .... 11  D5
Pennsylvania □  77  D7
Penong ...... 60  G5
Pensacola ... 82  D4
Pensacola Mts.  96  C4
Penticton ... 69  D8
Pentland Firth . 10  B5
Penza ....... 24  C6
Penzance .... 11  F4
Peoria ....... 75  E10
Perabumulih . 39  E2
Perdido, Mte. . 19  A6
Perdu, Mt. =
Perdido, Mte.  19  A6
Pereira ...... 90  C3
Pergamino ... 94  C4
Péribonka → . 71  D3
Périgueux ... 12  D4
Perm ........ 29  D6
Pernambuco =
Recife ..... 92  D7
Perpignan ... 13  E5
Persepolis ... 44  D3
Persia = Iran ■ . 44  C3
Persian Gulf =
Gulf, The ... 44  E2
Perth, Australia  60  G2
Perth, U.K. ... 10  C5
Peru ■ ....... 90  C3
Perúgia ..... 20  C4
Pervomaysk .. 25  D3
Pervouralsk .. 29  D6
Pescara ..... 20  C5
Peshawar ... 42  B7
Pesqueira ... 92  D6
Petah Tiqwa . 46  D3
Peterborough,
Canada .... 71  D3
Peterborough,
U.K. ....... 11  E6
Peterhead ... 10  C6
Petersburg,
Alaska, U.S.A.  69  C6
Petersburg, Va.,
U.S.A. .... 77  F7
Petitsikapau L. . 71  C4
Peto ........ 85  C7
Petrograd =
Sankt-
Peterburg .. 24  D3
Petrolândia .. 93  D6
Petrolina ... 93  D5
Petropavl ... 29  D7
Petropavlovsk-
Kamchatskiy  31  D13
Petrópolis ... 93  G5
Petrozavodsk . 8  C12
Pforzheim ... 14  D5
Phalodi ..... 42  F8
Phan Rang ... 38  B3
Philadelphia . 77  E8
Philippines ■ . 36  B2
Philippopolis =
Plovdiv .... 22  C5
Phitsanulok .. 38  A2
Phnom Penh . 38  B2
Phoenix ..... 79  D7
Phra Nakhon Si
Ayutthaya .. 38  B2
Phuket ...... 38  C1
Piacenza .... 20  B2
Piatra Neamţ . 17  E8
Piauí □ ...... 92  D5
Picardie .... 13  B5
Pichilemu ... 94  C2
Picton ....... 65  D6
Piedmont =
Piemonte □ . 20  B1
Piedras Negras  84  B4
Piemonte □ .. 20  B1
Pietermaritzburg  59  D6
Pilar ........ 94  B5
Pilcomayo → . 94  B5
Pilibhit ..... 42  E11
Pilica → ..... 16  C5

Pilsen = Plzeň . 16  D1
Pimentel .... 91  E3
Pinang ...... 38  C2
Pinar del Río . 86  B3
Pindos Óros . 23  E3
Pindus Mts. =
Pindos Óros . 23  E3
Pine Bluff ... 81  B7
Pine Point .. 68  B8
Pinega → .... 28  C5
Pingdong ... 35  D7
Pingliang ... 35  C5
Pingxiang ... 35  D5
Pinsk ....... 17  B8
Piotrków
Trybunalski . 16  C4
Piracicaba ... 94  A7
Piraeus =
Piraiévs ... 23  F4
Piraiévs .... 23  F4
Piraora ...... 93  F5
Pirineos =
Pyrénées .. 19  A6
Pirmasens ... 14  D4
Pisa ........ 20  C3
Pisagua .... 91  G4
Pishan ...... 34  C2
Pistóia ..... 20  C3
Pitcairn I. ... 65  M17
Piteå ....... 8  B10
Piteşti ...... 22  B5
Pittsburg ... 81  A6
Pittsburgh .. 77  D5
Piura ....... 90  E2
Placentia ... 71  D5
Placentia B. . 71  D5
Plainview ... 80  B3
Plata, Río de la  94  C5
Plauen ...... 15  C7
Plenty, B. of . 64  B7
Pleven ...... 22  C5
Płock ....... 16  B4
Ploieşti ..... 22  B6
Plovdiv ..... 22  C5
Plymouth ... 11  F4
Plzeň ....... 16  D1
Po → ....... 20  B4
Po Hai = Bo Hai  35  C6
Pocatello ... 73  E7
Poços de Caldas  93  G4
Podgorica ... 22  C2
Podolsk .... 24  B4
Pohnpei .... 64  J10
Pointe-à-Pitre  87  C7
Pointe-Noire . 56  E2
Poitiers ..... 12  C4
Poitou ...... 12  C3
Pokrovsk =
Engels ..... 24  C6
Poland ■ ... 16  B5
Polatsk .... 24  B2
Polesye = Pripet
Marshes ... 17  B9
Poltava ..... 24  D3
Polynésia .. 65  L15
Polynésie
française =
French
Polynesia ☑ . 65  M16
Ponape =
Pohnpei ... 64  J10
Ponca City .. 80  A5
Ponce ...... 87  C6
Pond Inlet .. 70  A3
Pondicherry . 43  P11
Ponta Grossa . 94  B6
Pontarlier ... 13  C7
Pontchartrain L. 81  D8
Ponte Nova . 93  G5
Pontevedra . 18  A1
Pontiac .... 76  C4
Pontianak ... 39  E3
Pontine Mts. =
Kuzey
Anadolu
Dağları .... 46  B3

**Pontivy**

| | | |
|---|---|---|
| Pontivy | 12 | B2 |
| Poole | 11 | F6 |
| Poona = Pune | 43 | K8 |
| Poopó, L. de | 91 | G5 |
| Popayán | 90 | C3 |
| Poplar Bluff | 81 | A8 |
| Popocatépetl, Volcán | 84 | D5 |
| Porbandar | 43 | J6 |
| Porcupine → | 69 | B5 |
| Pori | 8 | C10 |
| Port Alberni | 69 | D7 |
| Port Arthur | 81 | E7 |
| Port-au-Prince | 87 | C5 |
| Port Augusta | 62 | B2 |
| Port-Cartier | 71 | C4 |
| Port Elizabeth | 59 | E5 |
| Port Etienne = Nouâdhibou | 52 | D2 |
| Port-Gentil | 56 | E1 |
| Port Harcourt | 53 | H7 |
| Port Harrison = Inukjuak | 70 | C3 |
| Port Hawkesbury | 71 | D4 |
| Port Hedland | 60 | E2 |
| Port Huron | 76 | C4 |
| Port Lairge = Waterford | 11 | E3 |
| Port Laoise | 11 | E3 |
| Port Lincoln | 62 | B2 |
| Port Louis | 51 | J9 |
| Port Macquarie | 63 | B5 |
| Port Moresby | 61 | B8 |
| Port Nolloth | 58 | D3 |
| Port Nouveau-Québec = Kangiqsualujjuaq | 70 | C4 |
| Port of Spain | 87 | D7 |
| Port Pirie | 62 | B2 |
| Port Radium = Echo Bay | 68 | B8 |
| Port Safaga = Bûr Safâga | 54 | C5 |
| Port Said = Bûr Sa'îd | 54 | B5 |
| Port Shepstone | 59 | E6 |
| Port Stanley = Stanley | 95 | G5 |
| Port Sudan = Bûr Sûdân | 55 | E6 |
| Port Talbot | 11 | F5 |
| Portadown | 11 | D3 |
| Portage la Prairie | 69 | D10 |
| Portile de Fier | 22 | B4 |
| Portland, Maine, U.S.A. | 77 | C10 |
| Portland, Oreg., U.S.A. | 72 | D2 |
| Porto | 18 | B1 |
| Pôrto Alegre | 94 | C6 |
| Pôrto Esperança | 91 | G7 |
| Pôrto Nacional | 93 | E4 |
| Porto-Novo | 53 | G6 |
| Pôrto Seguro | 93 | F6 |
| Pôrto-Vecchio | 13 | F8 |
| Pôrto Velho | 91 | E6 |
| Portree | 10 | C3 |
| Portsmouth, U.K. | 11 | F6 |
| Portsmouth, U.S.A. | 77 | F7 |
| Porttipahtan tekojärvi | 8 | B11 |
| Portugal ■ | 18 | C1 |
| Posadas | 94 | B5 |
| Posse | 93 | E4 |
| Potchefstroom | 59 | D5 |
| Potenza | 21 | D5 |
| Poti | 25 | E5 |
| Potomac → | 77 | E7 |
| Potosí | 91 | G5 |
| Potsdam | 15 | B7 |
| Poughkeepsie | 77 | D9 |
| Powder → | 74 | B2 |
| Powell, L. | 79 | B7 |
| Poyang Hu | 35 | D6 |
| Poznań | 16 | B3 |
| Prado | 93 | F6 |
| Prague = Praha | 16 | C2 |
| Praha | 16 | C2 |
| Prata | 93 | F4 |
| Prato | 20 | C3 |
| Praya | 39 | F5 |
| Presidencia Roque Saenz Peña | 94 | B4 |
| Presidente Prudente | 93 | G3 |
| Prespansko Jezero | 23 | D3 |
| Presque Isle | 77 | A11 |
| Preston | 11 | E5 |
| Pretoria | 59 | D5 |
| Prieska | 58 | D4 |
| Priluki = Pryluky | 24 | C3 |
| Prince Albert | 69 | C9 |
| Prince Albert Pen. | 68 | A8 |
| Prince Albert Sd. | 68 | A8 |
| Prince Charles I. | 70 | B3 |
| Prince Charles Mts. | 96 | B10 |
| Prince Edward I. □ | 71 | D4 |
| Prince of Wales I., Canada | 68 | A10 |
| Prince of Wales I., U.S.A. | 69 | C6 |
| Pripet → Prypyat → | 17 | C10 |
| Pripet Marshes | 17 | B9 |
| Priština | 22 | C3 |
| Privas | 13 | D6 |
| Privolzhskaya Vozvyshennost | 24 | C6 |
| Prizren | 22 | C3 |
| Progreso | 85 | C7 |
| Prome | 41 | H10 |
| Propriá | 93 | E6 |
| Provence | 13 | E6 |
| Providence | 77 | D10 |
| Providencia, I. de | 86 | D3 |
| Provins | 13 | B5 |
| Provo | 73 | F8 |
| Prut → | 17 | F9 |
| Pruzhany | 24 | C3 |
| Prypyat → | 17 | C10 |
| Pskov | 24 | B2 |
| Puducherri = Pondicherry | 43 | P11 |
| Puebla | 84 | D5 |
| Pueblo | 74 | F2 |
| Puerto Aisén | 95 | F2 |
| Puerto Barrios | 85 | D7 |
| Puerto Cabello | 90 | A5 |
| Puerto Cabezas | 86 | D3 |
| Puerto Carreño | 90 | B5 |
| Puerto Cortés | 85 | D7 |
| Puerto Deseado | 95 | F3 |
| Puerto La Cruz | 90 | A6 |
| Puerto Madryn | 95 | E3 |
| Puerto Maldonado | 91 | F5 |
| Puerto Montt | 95 | E2 |
| Puerto Plata | 87 | C5 |
| Puerto Princesa | 36 | C1 |
| Puerto Rico ☑ | 87 | C6 |
| Puerto Suárez | 91 | G7 |
| Puerto Wilches | 90 | B4 |
| Puget Sound | 72 | C2 |
| Pukapuka | 65 | L14 |
| Pullman | 72 | C5 |
| Pune | 43 | K8 |
| Punjab □, India | 42 | D9 |
| Punjab □, Pakistan | 42 | D8 |
| Puno | 91 | G4 |
| Punta Arenas | 95 | G2 |
| Puralia = Puruliya | 40 | F6 |
| Puri | 40 | H5 |
| Purnia | 40 | E6 |
| Puruliya | 40 | F6 |
| Purus → | 90 | D6 |
| Pusan | 35 | C7 |
| Puttalam | 43 | Q11 |
| Putumayo → | 90 | D5 |
| Puy-de-Dôme | 13 | D5 |
| Pwllheli | 11 | E4 |
| Pyatigorsk | 25 | E5 |
| Pyè = Prome | 41 | H10 |
| P'yŏngyang | 35 | C7 |
| Pyrénées | 19 | A6 |

**Q**

| | | |
|---|---|---|
| Qâ'emshahr | 44 | B3 |
| Qahremänshahr = Bäkhtarän | 46 | D6 |
| Qaidam Pendi | 34 | C4 |
| Qamani'tuaq = Baker Lake | 68 | B10 |
| Qandahär | 42 | D4 |
| Qaqortoq | 70 | B6 |
| Qaraghandy | 29 | E8 |
| Qarqan He → | 34 | C3 |
| Qarshi | 29 | F7 |
| Qatar ■ | 44 | E2 |
| Qattâra, Munkhafed el | 54 | C4 |
| Qattâra Depression = Qattâra, Munkhafed el | 54 | C4 |
| Qazaqstan = Kazakhstan ■ | 29 | E7 |
| Qazvin | 46 | C7 |
| Qena | 54 | C5 |
| Qeqertarsuaq | 70 | B5 |
| Qeshm | 44 | E4 |
| Qiqiktarjuaq | 70 | B4 |
| Qilian Shan | 34 | C4 |
| Qingdao | 35 | C7 |
| Qinghai □ | 34 | C4 |
| Qinghai Hu | 34 | C5 |
| Qinhuangdao | 35 | C6 |
| Qinzhou | 35 | D5 |
| Qiqihar | 35 | B7 |
| Qitai | 34 | B3 |
| Qom | 44 | C2 |
| Qomolangma Feng = Everest, Mt. | 40 | C6 |
| Qondūz | 45 | B7 |
| Qoraqalpoghistan □ | 29 | E6 |
| Quan Long = Ca Mau | 38 | C3 |
| Quang Ngai | 38 | A3 |
| Quanzhou | 35 | D6 |
| Quaqtaq | 70 | B4 |
| Québec | 71 | D3 |
| Québec □ | 71 | D3 |
| Queen Charlotte Is. | 68 | C6 |
| Queen Charlotte Sd. | 69 | C7 |
| Queen Elizabeth Is. | 66 | B9 |
| Queen Maud G. | 68 | B9 |
| Queen Maud Land = Dronning Maud Land | 96 | B7 |
| Queensland □ | 61 | E7 |
| Queenstown, N.Z. | 65 | F3 |
| Queenstown, S. Africa | 59 | E5 |
| Queimadas | 93 | E6 |
| Quelimane | 59 | B7 |
| Quelpart = Cheju do | 35 | C7 |
| Querétaro | 84 | C4 |
| Quetta | 42 | D5 |
| Quezon City | 36 | B2 |
| Qui Nhon | 38 | B3 |
| Quibdó | 90 | B3 |
| Quiberon | 12 | C2 |
| Quilán, C. | 95 | E2 |
| Quilon | 43 | Q10 |
| Quilpie | 63 | A3 |
| Quimper | 12 | B1 |
| Quincy | 75 | F9 |
| Quito | 90 | D3 |
| Qûnghirot | 29 | E6 |
| Qûqon | 29 | E8 |
| Quseir | 54 | C5 |
| Quzhou | 35 | D6 |
| Qyzylorda | 29 | E7 |

**R**

| | | |
|---|---|---|
| Raahe | 8 | C10 |
| Raba | 37 | F1 |
| Rabat | 52 | B4 |
| Rabaul | 64 | K10 |
| Räbigh | 47 | G4 |
| Race, C. | 71 | D5 |
| Rach Gia | 38 | B3 |
| Racine | 76 | C2 |
| Radom | 16 | C5 |
| Rae | 68 | B8 |
| Rae Bareli | 40 | D3 |
| Rae Isthmus | 70 | B2 |
| Rafaela | 94 | C4 |
| Rafsanjän | 44 | D4 |
| Ragusa | 21 | F5 |
| Rahimyar Khan | 42 | E7 |
| Raichur | 43 | L10 |
| Raigarh | 40 | G4 |
| Rainier, Mt. | 72 | C3 |
| Raipur | 40 | G3 |
| Raj Nandgaon | 40 | G3 |
| Rajahmundry | 40 | J3 |
| Rajapalaiyam | 43 | Q10 |
| Rajasthan □ | 42 | F8 |
| Rajasthan Canal = Indira Gandhi Canal | 42 | F8 |
| Rajkot | 43 | H7 |
| Rajshahi | 41 | E7 |
| Rakata, Pulau | 39 | F3 |
| Raleigh | 83 | B8 |
| Ramgarh | 40 | F5 |
| Râmnicu Vâlcea | 17 | F7 |
| Rampur | 42 | E11 |
| Ramree I. | 41 | H9 |
| Rancagua | 94 | C2 |
| Ranchi | 40 | F5 |
| Randers | 9 | D8 |
| Rangoon | 41 | J11 |
| Rangpur | 41 | E7 |
| Rankin Inlet | 68 | B10 |
| Rapa | 65 | M16 |
| Rapid City | 74 | C3 |
| Rarotonga | 65 | M14 |
| Ra's al Khaymah | 44 | E4 |
| Rasht | 46 | C7 |
| Rat Islands | 69 | C1 |
| Ratangarh | 42 | E9 |
| Ratlam | 43 | H9 |
| Ratnagiri | 43 | L8 |
| Raurkela | 40 | F5 |
| Ravenna | 20 | B4 |
| Ravi → | 42 | D7 |
| Rawalpindi | 42 | C8 |
| Rawändüz | 46 | C6 |
| Rawlins | 73 | F10 |
| Rawson | 95 | E3 |
| Ray, C. | 71 | D5 |
| Raz, Pte. du | 12 | B1 |
| Ré, Î. de | 12 | C3 |
| Reading, U.K. | 11 | F6 |
| Reading, U.S.A. | 77 | D8 |
| Recife | 92 | D7 |
| Reconquista | 94 | B5 |
| Red →, La., U.S.A. | 81 | D8 |
| Red →, N. Dak., U.S.A. | 74 | A6 |
| Red Deer | 69 | C8 |
| Red Sea | 48 | C2 |
| Redcar | 11 | D6 |
| Redding | 72 | F2 |
| Redditch | 11 | E6 |
| Redon | 12 | C2 |
| Ree, L. | 11 | E3 |
| Regensburg | 15 | D7 |
| Reggâne = Zaouiet Reggâne | 52 | C6 |
| Réggio di Calábria | 21 | E5 |
| Réggio nell'Emília | 20 | B3 |
| Regina | 69 | C9 |
| Reichenbach | 15 | C7 |
| Reigate | 11 | F6 |
| Reims | 13 | B6 |
| Reina Adelaida, Arch. | 95 | G2 |
| Reindeer L. | 69 | C9 |
| Rennes | 12 | B3 |
| Reno | 72 | G4 |
| Republican → | 74 | F6 |
| Repulse Bay | 70 | B2 |
| Resht = Rasht | 46 | C7 |
| Resistencia | 94 | B5 |
| Resolution I. | 70 | B4 |
| Réthimnon | 23 | G5 |
| Réunion ☑ | 51 | J9 |
| Revelstoke | 69 | C8 |
| Revillagigedo, Is. de | 84 | D2 |
| Rewa | 40 | E3 |
| Rey Malabo | 56 | D1 |
| Reykjavík | 8 | C1 |
| Reynosa | 84 | B5 |
| Rhein → | 14 | C4 |
| Rheine | 14 | B4 |
| Rheinland-Pfalz □ | 14 | C4 |
| Rhine = Rhein → | 14 | C4 |
| Rhineland-Palatinate = Rheinland-Pfalz □ | 14 | C4 |
| Rhode Island □ | 77 | D10 |
| Rhodes = Ródhos | 23 | F7 |
| Rhodope Mts. = Rhodopi Planina | 22 | D5 |
| Rhodopi Planina | 22 | D5 |
| Rhön | 14 | C5 |
| Rhondda | 11 | F5 |
| Rhône → | 13 | E6 |
| Rhône □ | 13 | E6 |
| Riau, Kepulauan | 39 | D2 |
| Ribeirão Prêto | 93 | G4 |
| Riberalta | 91 | F5 |
| Richland | 72 | C4 |
| Richmond | 77 | F7 |
| Riga | 24 | B1 |
| Riga, G. of | 24 | B1 |
| Rigestán | 42 | D4 |
| Rigolet | 70 | C5 |
| Rijeka | 20 | B5 |
| Rímini | 20 | B4 |
| Rimouski | 71 | D4 |
| Río Branco | 91 | E5 |
| Río Cuarto | 94 | C4 |
| Río de Janeiro | 93 | G5 |
| Río de Janeiro □ | 93 | G5 |
| Río Gallegos | 95 | G3 |
| Río Grande, Brazil | 94 | C6 |
| Río Grande, U.S.A. | 81 | F5 |
| Río Grande de Santiago → | 84 | C3 |
| Río Grande do Norte □ | 92 | D6 |

Rio Grande do
  Sul □ ... 94 B6
Rio Muni □ ... 56 D2
Riobamba ... 90 D3
Riohacha ... 90 A4
Rivera ... 94 C5
Riverside ... 78 D4
Rivière-du-Loup 71 D4
Rivne ... 17 C8
Riyadh = Ar
  Riyāḍ ... 47 F6
Rize ... 46 B5
Roanne ... 13 C6
Roanoke ... 77 F6
Robson, Mt. ... 69 C8
Roca, C. da ... 18 C1
Rocha ... 94 C6
Rochefort ... 12 D3
Rochester,
  Minn., U.S.A. 75 C8
Rochester, N.Y.,
  U.S.A. ... 77 C7
Rock Hill ... 83 B7
Rock Island ... 75 E9
Rock Springs .. 73 F9
Rockford ... 75 D10
Rockhampton .. 61 E9
Rocky Mount .. 83 B9
Rocky Mts. ... 68 C7
Rodez ... 13 D5
Ródhos ... 23 F7
Roes Welcome
  Sd. ... 70 B2
Rohri ... 42 F6
Rojo, C. ... 84 C5
Roma, Australia 63 A4
Roma, Italy ... 20 D4
Romania ■ ... 22 B5
Romans-sur-
  Isère ... 13 D6
Rome = Roma . 20 D4
Rome ... 82 B5
Romorantin-
  Lanthenay .. 12 C4
Roncador, Serra
  do ... 93 E3
Rondônia □ → 91 F6
Ronge, L. la ... 69 C9
Ronne Ice Shelf 96 B3
Roosevelt → .. 91 E6
Roosevelt I. .. 96 B16
Roraima □ ... 90 C6
Roraima, Mt. .. 90 B6
Rosario,
  Argentina .. 94 C4
Rosario, Mexico 84 C3
Rosario de la
  Frontera ... 94 B3
Roscommon .. 11 E2
Roseau ... 87 C7
Roseburg ... 72 E2
Rosenheim ... 15 E7
Rosetown ... 69 C9
Roseville ... 72 G3
Roslavl ... 24 C3
Ross Ice Shelf . 96 C16
Ross Sea ... 96 B15
Rosslare ... 11 E3
Rossosh ... 24 C4
Rostock ... 15 A7
Rostov ... 25 D4
Roswell ... 80 C1
Rotherham ... 11 E6
Rotorua ... 64 C7
Rotterdam ... 14 C3
Rotuma ... 64 L12
Roubaix ... 13 A5
Rouen ... 12 B4
Round Mt. ... 63 B5
Roussillon ... 13 E5
Rouyn-Noranda 71 D3
Rovaniemi ... 8 B11
Rovno = Rivne . 17 C8
Rovuma =
  Ruvuma → . 57 G8
Roxas ... 36 B2

Royal
  Leamington
  Spa ... 11 E6
Royan ... 12 D3
Rub' al Khālī .. 48 D4
Rufiji → ... 57 F7
Rugby ... 11 E6
Rügen ... 15 A7
Ruhr → ... 14 C4
Rum = Rhum .. 10 C3
Rumania =
  Romania ■ .. 22 B5
Ruoqiang ... 34 C3
Rupert → ... 71 C3
Rupert House =
  Waskaganish 71 C3
Ruse ... 22 C5
Rustavi ... 25 E6
Rustenburg ... 59 D5
Ruvuma → ... 57 G8
Ruwenzori ... 57 D5
Rwanda ■ ... 57 E6
Ryazan ... 24 C4
Rybinsk ... 24 B4
Rybinskoye
  Vdkhr. ... 24 B4
Ryūkyū Is. =
  Ryūkyū-rettō 35 D7
Ryūkyū-rettō .. 35 D7
Rzeszów ... 16 C5
Rzhev ... 24 B3

**S**

Saale → ... 15 C6
Saar → ... 13 B7
Saarbrücken .. 14 D4
Saaremaa ... 24 B1
Sabadell ... 19 B7
Sabah □ ... 38 C5
Sabhah ... 54 C1
Sabinas ... 84 B4
Sabinas Hidalgo 84 B4
Sable, C.,
  Canada ... 71 D4
Sable, C., U.S.A. 86 A3
Sable I. ... 71 D5
Sachsen □ ... 15 C7
Sachsen-
  Anhalt □ ... 15 C7
Sacramento ... 72 G3
Sacramento → . 72 G3
Sacramento Mts. 79 D10
Sadd el Aali ... 54 D5
Sado ... 32 E6
Safi ... 52 B4
Saginaw ... 76 C4
Saglouc = Salluit 70 B3
Sagua la Grande 86 B3
Sahara ... 52 D6
Saharanpur ... 42 E10
Saharien, Atlas 52 B6
Sahiwal ... 42 D8
Sa'īdābād =
  Sīrjān ... 44 D3
Saidpur ... 41 E7
Saigon = Thanh
  Pho Ho Chi
  Minh ... 38 B3
St. Andrews ... 10 C5
St. Cloud ... 75 C7
St-Augustin .. 71 C5
St. Augustine .. 83 E7
St. Austell ... 11 F4
St-Brieuc ... 12 B2
St. Catharines . 77 C6
St. Christopher-
  Nevis = St.
  Kitts &
  Nevis ■ ... 87 C7
St. Cloud ... 75 C7
St. Croix ... 87 C7
St-Dizier ... 13 B6
St. Elias, Mt. .. 68 B5
St-Étienne ... 13 D6

St-Flour ... 13 D5
St-Gaudens ... 12 E4
St. George's .. 87 D7
St. George's
  Channel ... 11 F3
St. Gotthard P. =
  San Gottardo,
  P. del ... 13 C8
St. Helena ... 51 H3
St. Helier ... 11 G5
St-Hyacinthe .. 71 D3
St. John ... 71 D4
St. John's,
  Antigua & B. 87 C7
St. John's,
  Canada ... 71 D5
St. Johns → .. 83 D7
St. Joseph ... 75 F7
St. Joseph, L. .. 71 C1
St. Kilda ... 10 C2
St. Kitts &
  Nevis ■ ... 87 C7
St. Lawrence → 71 D4
St. Lawrence,
  Gulf of ... 71 D4
St. Lawrence I. . 69 B2
St-Lô ... 12 B3
St. Louis,
  Senegal ... 53 E2
St. Louis, U.S.A. 75 F9
St. Lucia ■ ... 87 D7
St-Malo ... 12 B2
St-Marc ... 87 C5
St-Nazaire ... 12 C2
St-Omer ... 12 A5
St. Paul ... 75 C8
St. Peter Port . 11 G5
St. Petersburg =
  Sankt-
  Peterburg .. 24 B3
St. Petersburg . 83 F6
St-Pierre et
  Miquelon □ . 71 D5
St-Quentin ... 13 B5
St-Tropez ... 13 E7
St. Vincent, G. . 62 C2
St. Vincent & the
  Grenadines ■ 87 D7
Saintes ... 12 D3
Saintonge ... 12 D3
Saipan ... 64 H9
Sajama ... 91 G5
Sakakawea, L. . 74 B4
Sakarya ... 46 B2
Sakata ... 32 D6
Sakhalin ... 31 D12
Sala ... 9 G9
Salado →,
  La Pampa,
  Argentina .. 94 D3
Salado →,
  Santa Fe,
  Argentina .. 94 C4
Galālah ... 40 D5
Salamanca ... 18 B3
Salar de Uyuni 91 H5
Salaverry ... 91 E3
Salayar ... 37 F2
Saldanha ... 58 E3
Sale, Australia . 63 C4
Salé, Morocco . 52 B4
Salekhard ... 28 C7
Salem, India ... 43 P11
Salem, U.S.A. .. 72 D2
Salerno ... 21 D5
Salina ... 74 F6
Salina Cruz ... 85 D5
Salinas ... 78 B2
Salinas Grandes 94 C3
Salisbury =
  Harare ... 59 B6
Salisbury ... 11 F6
Saliq = Coral
  Harbour ... 70 B2
Salluit ... 70 B3
Salmon → ... 72 D5

Salmon River
  Mts. ... 73 D6
Salon-de-
  Provence ... 13 E6
Salonica =
  Thessaloníki . 23 D4
Salsk ... 25 D5
Salt Lake City . 73 F8
Salta ... 94 A3
Saltillo ... 84 B4
Salton Sea ... 78 D5
Salvador ... 93 E6
Salween → ... 41 J11
Salyan ... 25 F6
Salzburg ... 15 E7
Salzgitter ... 14 B6
Samangān □ ... 45 B7
Samar ... 36 B3
Samara ... 24 C7
Samarinda ... 39 E5
Samarkand =
  Samarqand . 29 F7
Samarqand ... 29 F7
Sambalpur ... 40 G5
Sambhal ... 42 E11
Sambhar ... 42 F9
Samoa ■ ... 65 L13
Sámos ... 23 F6
Samsun ... 46 B4
San Andrés, I. de 86 D3
San Andrés
  Tuxtla ... 85 D5
San Angelo ... 80 D3
San Antonio,
  Chile ... 94 C2
San Antonio,
  U.S.A. ... 80 E4
San Antonio
  Oeste ... 95 E4
San Bernardino 78 C4
San Bernardino
  Str. ... 36 B2
San Bernardo . 94 C2
San Carlos ... 36 B2
San Carlos de
  Bariloche ... 95 E2
San Cristóbal,
  Argentina .. 94 C4
San Cristóbal,
  Venezuela .. 90 B4
San Cristóbal de
  la Casas ... 85 D6
San Diego ... 78 D4
San Felipe ... 90 A5
San Fernando,
  Chile ... 94 C2
San Fernando,
  Trin. & Tob. . 87 D7
San Fernando,
  U.S.A. ... 78 C3
San Fernando de
  Apure ... 90 B5
San Francisco . 78 B1
San Francisco de
  Macorís ... 87 C5
San Gottardo, P.
  del ... 13 C8
San Ignacio ... 91 G6
San Joaquín → 91 A2
San Jorge, G. . 95 F3
San José,
  Costa Rica .. 86 E3
San Jose, Phil. . 36 B2
San Jose, U.S.A. 78 B2
San José de
  Chiquitos ... 91 G6
San José de
  Jáchal ... 94 C3
San José de
  Mayo ... 94 C5
San Juan,
  Argentina .. 94 C3
San Juan,
  Puerto Rico . 87 C6
San Juan → ... 86 D3
San Juan de los
  Morros ... 90 B5

San Juan Mts. . 79 B9
San Lorenzo,
  Mte. ... 95 F2
San Lucas, C. .. 84 C2
San Luis ... 94 C3
San Luis Obispo 78 C2
San Luis Potosí 84 C4
San Marino ■ . 20 C4
San Matías, G. . 95 E4
San Miguel ... 85 E7
San Miguel de
  Tucumán ... 94 B3
San Nicolás de
  los Arroyas . 94 C4
San Pedro de las
  Colonias ... 84 B4
San Pedro de
  Macorís ... 87 C6
San Pedro Sula 85 D7
San Rafael ... 94 C3
San Remo ... 20 C1
San Salvador .. 85 E7
San Salvador de
  Jujuy ... 94 A3
San Salvador I. . 86 B5
San Sebastián =
  Donostia-San
  Sebastián ... 19 A5
San Valentin,
  Mte. ... 95 F2
Sana' ... 49 D3
Sanandaj ... 46 D6
Sancti Spíritus . 86 B4
Sancy, Puy de . 13 D5
Sandakan ... 38 C5
Sanday ... 10 B5
Sandusky ... 76 D4
Sandy L. ... 69 C10
Sanford ... 83 E7
Sanford, Mt. .. 69 B5
Sanghe, Pulau . 37 D3
Sangli ... 43 L9
Sangre de Cristo
  Mts. ... 80 A1
Sanirajak ... 70 B2
Sankt Gallen .. 13 C8
Sankt Moritz .. 13 C8
Sankt-Peterburg 24 B3
Sanlúcar ... 56 E4
Sanliurfa ... 46 C4
Sanmenxia ... 35 C6
Santa Ana,
  El Salv. ... 85 E7
Santa Ana,
  U.S.A. ... 78 D4
Santa Barbara . 78 C3
Santa Catarina □ 94 B7
Santa Clara ... 86 B4
Santa Cruz,
  Bolivia ... 91 G6
Santa Cruz,
  U.S.A. ... 78 B1
Santa Cruz de
  Tenerife ... 52 C2
Santa Cruz Is. . 64 L11
Santa Fe,
  Argentina .. 94 C4
Santa Fe, U.S.A. 79 C10
Santa Inés, I. .. 95 G2
Santa Isabel =
  Rey Malabo . 56 D1
Santa Maria,
  Brazil ... 94 B6
Santa Maria,
  U.S.A. ... 78 C2
Santa Maria → 84 A3
Santa Marta ... 90 A4
Santa Marta,
  Sierra Nevada
  de ... 90 A4
Santa Maura =
  Levkás ... 23 E3
Santa Rosa,
  Argentina .. 94 D4
Santa Rosa,
  U.S.A. ... 72 G2
Santai ... 35 C5

# Santana do Livramento

Santana do
  Livramento . . 94 C5
Santander . . . . 18 A4
Santarém, *Brazil* 92 C3
Santarém,
  *Portugal* . . 18 C1
Santiago . . . . 94 C2
Santiago de
  Compostela . 18 A1
Santiago de
  Cuba . . . . . 86 C4
Santiago de los
  Caballeros . . 87 C5
Santiago del
  Estero . . . . 94 B4
Santo Domingo 87 C6
Santo Tomé de
  Guayana =
  Ciudad
  Guayana . . . 90 B6
Santorini = Thira 23 F5
Santos . . . . . 94 A7
São Bernardo do
  Campo . . . . 93 G4
São Borja . . . . 94 B5
São Carlos . . . 94 A7
São
  Francisco ➤ 93 E6
São João del Rei 93 G5
São João do
  Piauí . . . . . 92 D5
São José do Rio
  Prêto . . . . . 93 G4
São Lourenço . 93 G4
São Luís . . . . 92 C5
São Marcos = 93 F4
São Marcos, B.
  de . . . . . . 92 C5
São Mateus . . 93 F6
São Paulo . . . 94 A7
São Paulo ☐ . . 94 A7
São Roque, C.
  de . . . . . . 92 D6
São Tomé &
  Príncipe ■ . . 51 F4
Saône ➤ . . . . 13 D6
Sapporo . . . . 32 B7
Saqqez . . . . . 46 C6
Sar-e Pol . . . . 45 B6
Saragossa =
  Zaragoza . . 19 B5
Sarajevo . . . . 20 C7
Saransk . . . . 24 C6
Sarapul . . . . 29 D6
Sarasota . . . . 83 F6
Saratov . . . . . 24 C6
Sarawak ☐ . . . 39 D4
Sarda ➤ . . . . 40 D3
Sardegna ☐ . . 21 D2
Sardinia =
  Sardegna ☐ . 21 D2
Sargodha . . . . 42 C8
Sarh . . . . . . . 55 G2
Sāri . . . . . . . 44 B3
Sark . . . . . . . 11 G5
Sarlat-la-Canéda 12 D4
Sarmiento . . . 95 F3
Sarnia . . . . . . 71 D2
Sarre = Saar ➤ 13 B7
Sarreguemines . 13 B7
Sarthe ➤ . . . . 12 C3
Sasebo . . . . . 33 G1
Saskatchewan ☐ 69 C9
Saskatchewan
  ➤ . . . . . . . 69 C9
Saskatoon . . . 69 C9
Sássari . . . . . 21 D2
Sassnitz . . . . 15 A7
Satna . . . . . . 40 E3
Satpura Ra. . . . 43 J10
Satu Mare . . . 17 E6
Saudi Arabia ■ . 47 F6
Sault Ste. Marie,
  *Canada* . . 71 D2
Sault Ste. Marie,
  *U.S.A.* . . . . 76 A3
Saumur . . . . . 12 C3

Sava ➤ . . . . . 22 B3
Savage I. = Niue 65 L14
Savannah . . . . 83 C7
Savannah ➤ . . 83 C7
Savannakhet . . 38 A2
Save ➤ . . . . . 59 C6
Savoie ☐ . . . . 13 D7
Savona . . . . . 20 B2
Savoy =
  Savoie ☐ . . 13 D7
Sawatch Range 79 A9
Sawu . . . . . . 37 F2
Sawu Sea . . . 37 F2
Saxony =
  Sachsen ☐ . 15 C7
Saxony, Lower =
  Niedersachsen ☐
  . . . . . . . . 14 B5
Sayan,
  Zapadnyy . . 30 D7
Saydā . . . . . . 46 D3
Saynshand . . . 35 B6
Sázava ➤ . . . 16 D2
Scandinavia . . 8 D8
Scarborough . . 11 D6
Scebeli, Wabi ➤ 49 G3
Schaffhausen . 13 C8
Schefferville . . 71 C4
Schelde ➤ . . . 14 C3
Schenectady . . 77 C9
Schleswig . . . 14 A5
Schleswig-
  Holstein ☐ . . 14 A5
Schwäbische
  Alb . . . . . . 14 D5
Schwarzwald . . 14 D5
Schwerin . . . . 15 B6
Schwyz . . . . . 13 C8
Scilly, Isles of . 11 G3
Scotland ☐ . . . 10 C4
Scottsbluff . . . 74 E3
Scranton . . . . 77 D8
Scunthorpe . . . 11 E6
Scutari =
  Shkodër . . . 22 C2
Seattle . . . . . 72 C2
Sebastopol =
  Sevastopol . 25 E3
Sebha = Sabhah 54 C1
Şebinkarahisar 46 B4
Sebta = Ceuta . 18 E3
Sedalia . . . . . 75 F8
Sedan . . . . . . 13 B6
Ségou . . . . . . 53 F4
Segovia =
  Coco ➤ . . . 86 D3
Segovia . . . . . 18 B3
Sehore . . . . . 43 H10
Seine ➤ . . . . 12 B4
Seistan = Sīstān 45 D5
Sekondi-
  Takoradi . . . 53 H5
Selenga =
  Selenge
  Mörön ➤ . . 35 A5
Selenge
  Mörön ➤ . . 35 A5
Selkirk . . . . . 69 C10
Selkirk Mts. . . 69 C8
Selvas . . . . . 91 E5
Semarang . . . 39 F4
Semey . . . . . . 29 D9
Semipalatinsk =
  Semey . . . . 29 D9
Semnān . . . . 44 C3
Sena Madureira 91 E5
Sendai,
  *Kagoshima,
  Japan* . . . . 33 H2
Sendai, *Miyagi,
  Japan* . . . . 32 D7
Senegal ■ . . . 53 F3
Sénégal ➤ . . . 53 E2
Senge
  Khambab =
  Indus ➤ . . . 43 G5

Senhor-do-
  Bonfim . . . . 93 E5
Senja . . . . . . 8 B9
Senlis . . . . . . 13 B5
Sens . . . . . . . 13 B5
Seoul = Sôul . . 35 C7
Sept-Îles . . . . 71 C4
Sequoia △ . . . 78 B3
Seram . . . . . . 37 E3
Seram Sea . . . 37 E3
Serbia ☐ . . . . 22 C3
Serbia &
  Montenegro ■ 22 B3
Seremban . . . 39 D2
Sergipe ☐ . . . 93 E6
Sergiyev Posad 24 B4
Serov . . . . . . 28 D7
Serpukhov . . . 24 C4
Serrinha . . . . 93 E6
Sète . . . . . . . 13 E5
Sete Lagôas . . 93 F5
Sétif . . . . . . . 52 A7
Settat . . . . . . 52 B4
Setúbal . . . . . 18 C1
Sevana Lich . . 25 E6
Sevastopol . . . 25 E3
Severn ➤,
  *Canada* . . 71 C2
Severn ➤, *U.K.* 11 F5
Severnaya
  Zemlya . . . . 30 B7
Severodvinsk . 28 C4
Sevilla . . . . . . 18 D2
Seward . . . . . 69 B5
Seward
  Peninsula . . 69 B3
Seychelles ■ . 26 K9
Sfântu
  Gheorghe . . 17 F7
Sfax . . . . . . . 54 B1
Shaanxi ☐ . . . 35 C5
Shaba =
  Katanga ☐ . . 57 F4
Shabale =
  Scebeli,
  Wabi ➤ . . . 49 G3
Shache . . . . . 34 C2
Shahjahanpur . 42 F11
Shakhty . . . . 25 D5
Shaki . . . . . . 53 G6
Shām, Bādiyat
  ash . . . . . . 47 D4
Shamo = Gobi . 35 B6
Shamo, L. . . . 55 G6
Shan ☐ . . . . . 41 G12
Shandong ☐ . . 35 C6
Shanghai . . . . 35 C7
Shangqiu . . . . 35 C6
Shangrao . . . . 35 D6
Shangshui . . . 35 C6
Shannon ➤ . . 11 E2
Shansi =
  Shanxi ☐ . . 35 C6
Shantou . . . . . 35 D6
Shantung =
  Shandong ☐ . 35 C6
Shanxi ☐ . . . . 35 C6
Shaoguan . . . 35 D6
Shaoxing . . . . 35 C7
Shaoyang . . . 35 D6
Shaqrā' . . . . . 49 E4
Sharjah = Ash
  Shāriqah . . . 44 E3
Sharon . . . . . 76 D5
Sharya . . . . . 24 B6
Shashi . . . . . . 35 C6
Shasta, Mt. . . . 72 F2
Shatt al 'Arab ➤ 47 E7
Shawinigan . . 71 D3
Shcherbakov =
  Rybinsk ➤ . . 24 B4
Shebele =
  Scebeli,
  Wabi ➤ . . . 49 G3
Sheboygan . . . 76 C2
Sheffield . . . . 11 E6

Shenandoah ➤ 77 E7
Shensi =
  Shaanxi ☐ . . 35 C5
Shenyang . . . 35 B7
Shepparton . . . 63 C4
Sherbrooke . . 71 D3
Sheridan . . . . 73 D10
Sherman . . . . 81 C5
Shetland Is. . . 10 A6
Shibām . . . . . 49 D4
Shijiazhuang . . 35 C6
Shikarpur . . . . 42 F6
Shikoku ☐ . . . 33 G3
Shiliguri . . . . . 40 D7
Shillong . . . . . 41 E8
Shimoga . . . . 43 N9
Shimonoseki . . 33 G2
Shinyanga . . . 57 E6
Shiquan He =
  Indus ➤ . . . 43 G5
Shīrāz . . . . . . 44 D3
Shire ➤ . . . . . 59 B7
Shirwa, L. =
  Chilwa, L. . . 59 B7
Shivpuri . . . . . 43 G10
Shizuoka . . . . 33 F6
Shkodër . . . . 22 C2
Sholapur =
  Solapur . . . 43 L9
Shoshone Mts. 72 G5
Shreveport . . . 81 C7
Shrewsbury . . 11 E5
Shrirampur . . . 40 F7
Shuangyashan 35 B8
Shule . . . . . . 34 C2
Shumagin Is. . 69 C4
Shwebo . . . . . 41 F10
Shymkent . . . 29 E7
Si Kiang = Xi
  Jiang ➤ . . . 35 D6
Sialkot . . . . . . 42 C9
Siam =
  Thailand ■ . . 38 A2
Sian = Xi'an . . 35 C5
Šiauliai . . . . . 24 B1
Siberia . . . . . 30 C8
Siberut . . . . . 39 E1
Sibi . . . . . . . . 42 E5
Sibiu . . . . . . . 17 F7
Sibolga . . . . . 39 D1
Sibu . . . . . . . 39 D4
Sibuyan Sea . . 36 B2
Sichuan ☐ . . . 34 C5
Sicilia . . . . . . 21 F5
Sicily = Sicilia . 21 F5
Sicuani . . . . . 91 F4
Sidi-bel-Abbès . 52 A5
Sidon = Saydā . 46 D3
Sidra, G. of =
  Surt, Khalīj . . 54 B2
Siedlce . . . . . 17 B6
Siegen . . . . . 14 C5
Siena . . . . . . 20 C3
Sierra Leone ■ 53 G3
Sierra Nevada,
  *Spain* . . . . 18 D4
Sierra Nevada,
  *U.S.A.* . . . . 72 G3
Sihanoukville =
  Kampong
  Saom . . . . 38 B2
Sikar . . . . . . . 42 F9
Sikhote Alin,
  Khrebet . . . 32 A5
Sikkim ☐ . . . . 40 D7
Silesia = Śląsk . 16 C3
Silifke . . . . . . 46 C3
Siliguri =
  Shiliguri . . . 40 D7
Siling Co . . . . 34 C3
Simbirsk . . . . 24 C6
Simeulue . . . . 39 D1
Simferopol . . . 25 E3
Simla . . . . . . 42 D10
Simpson Desert 60 F6
Sinai = Es Sînâ' 54 C5

Sinai, Mt. =
  Mûsa, Gebel . 47 E3
Sind ☐ . . . . . 42 F6
Sindh = Sind ☐ 42 F6
Singapore ■ . . 39 D2
Singaraja . . . . 39 F5
Singkawang . . 39 D3
Singora =
  Songkhla . . . 38 C2
Sinkiang
  Uighur =
  Xinjiang
  Uygur
  Zizhiqu ☐ . . 34 B3
Sinop . . . . . . 46 B3
Sioux City . . . 75 D6
Sioux Falls . . . 74 D6
Sioux Lookout . 69 C10
Siping . . . . . . 35 B7
Siracusa . . . . 21 F5
Sirajganj . . . . 41 E7
Sirdaryo =
  Syrdarya ➤ . 29 E7
Sirjān . . . . . . 44 D3
Sirsa . . . . . . . 42 E9
Sīstān . . . . . . 45 D5
Sīstān,
  Daryācheh-ye 45 D5
Sitapur . . . . . 40 D3
Sitges . . . . . . 19 B6
Sitka . . . . . . . 69 C6
Sittwe . . . . . . 41 G9
Sivas . . . . . . 46 C4
Sivrihisar . . . . 46 C2
Siwa . . . . . . . 54 C4
Siwalik Range . 40 D4
Siwan . . . . . . 40 D5
Sjælland . . . . 9 D8
Skagerrak . . . 9 D7
Skagway . . . . 69 C6
Skeena ➤ . . . 68 C6
Skegness . . . 11 E7
Skellefte älv ➤ 8 C10
Skellefteå . . . 8 C10
Skiathos . . . . 23 E4
Skien . . . . . . 9 D7
Skikda . . . . . 52 A7
Skíros . . . . . . 23 E5
Skópelos . . . . 23 E4
Skopje . . . . . 22 C3
Skye . . . . . . . 10 C3
Skyros = Skíros 23 E5
Śląsk . . . . . . 16 C3
Slatina . . . . . 22 B5
Slave ➤ . . . . . 68 B8
Slavyansk =
  Slovyansk . . 25 D4
Sleeper Is. . . . 70 C2
Sligeach = Sligo 11 D2
Sligo . . . . . . . 11 D2
Sliven . . . . . . 22 C6
Slough . . . . . 11 F6
Slovak Rep. ■ . 16 D4
Slovakian Ore
  Mts. =
  Slovenské
  Rudohorie . . 16 D4
Slovenia ■ . . . 20 B5
Slovenské
  Rudohorie . . 16 D4
Slovyansk . . . 25 D4
Slutsk . . . . . . 17 B8
Smederevo . . . 22 B3
Smolensk . . . 24 C3
Smyrna = İzmir 23 E6
Snake ➤ . . . . 72 C4
Snake River
  Plain . . . . . 73 E7
Snøhetta . . . . 8 C7
Snowdon . . . . 11 E4
Snowdrift =
  Łutselk'e . . . 68 B8
Snowy ➤ . . . . 63 C4
Snowy Mts. . . 63 C4
Sobral . . . . . . 92 C5
Soc Trang . . . 38 C3
Soch'e = Shache 34 C2

Sochi ........ 25 E4
Société, Is. de la 65 L15
Society Is. =
  Société, Is. de
  la ........ 65 L15
Socotra ...... 49 E5
Söderhamn .. 8 C9
Sofia = Sofiya . 22 C4
Sofiya ....... 22 C4
Sognefjorden . 8 C7
Sohâg ....... 54 C5
Soissons .... 13 B5
Sokhumi .... 25 E5
Sokodé ...... 53 G6
Sokoto ...... 53 F7
Solapur ..... 43 L9
Solikamsk ... 28 D6
Solimões =
  Amazonas → 92 C3
Solingen .... 14 C4
Solomon Is. ■ . 64 K10
Solomon Sea .. 61 B9
Solon ....... 35 B7
Somali Rep. ■ . 49 F4
Sombrerete ... 84 C4
Somerset I. ... 68 A10
Somme → .... 12 A4
Songhua
  Jiang → ... 35 B8
Songkhla ... 38 C2
Songpan .... 34 C5
Sonora → ... 84 B2
Sonsonate ... 85 E7
Soochow =
  Suzhou ... 35 C7
Sopot ....... 16 A4
Sorel-Tracy ... 71 D3
Soria ....... 19 B4
Sorocaba .... 94 A7
Sørøya ..... 8 A10
Sosnowiec ... 16 C4
Sôul ....... 35 C7
Souris → ... 69 D10
Sousse ..... 54 A1
South Africa ■ 58 E4
South
  Australia □ .. 62 B2
South Bend .. 76 D2
South
  Carolina □ .. 83 C7
South China Sea 38 C4
South Dakota □ 74 C4
South East C. .. 62 D4
South I. ..... 65 E3
South Korea ■ 35 C7
South Magnetic
  Pole ..... 96 A13
South
  Nahanni → . 68 B7
South Orkney Is. 96 A4
South Platte → 74 E4
South Pole .. 96 C
South Ronaldsay 10 B5
South
  Saskatchewan →
  ......... 69 C9
South Shetland
  Is. ....... 96 A4
South Shields .. 11 D6
South Uist ... 10 C3
Southampton . 11 F6
Southampton I. 70 B2
Southend-on-
  Sea ..... 11 F7
Southern Alps . 65 E4
Southern Indian
  L. ....... 69 C10
Southern Ocean 96 A9
Southern
  Uplands ... 10 D5
Sovetsk .... 24 B1
Spain ■ ..... 18 C4
Spanish Town . 86 C4
Sparta = Spárti 23 F4
Spartanburg . 83 B7
Spárti ...... 23 F4

Spence Bay =
  Taloyoak ... 68 B10
Spencer G. ... 62 B2
Spey → ..... 10 C5
Spitzbergen =
  Svalbard □ .. 26 B5
Split ....... 20 C6
Spokane .... 72 C5
Spratly Is. ... 38 C4
Spree → .... 15 B7
Springfield, Ill.,
  U.S.A. ... 75 F10
Springfield,
  Mass., U.S.A. 77 C9
Springfield, Mo.,
  U.S.A. .... 81 A7
Springfield,
  Ohio, U.S.A. . 76 E4
Springfield,
  Oreg., U.S.A. 72 D2
Springs ..... 59 D5
Srbija =
  Serbia □ .... 22 C3
Srebrenica ... 20 B7
Sredinnyy
  Khrebet .... 31 D14
Sri Lanka ■ .. 43 R12
Srikakulam ... 40 H4
Srinagar .... 42 B9
Stafford ..... 11 E5
Stakhanov ... 25 D4
Stalingrad =
  Volgograd .. 25 D5
Staliníri =
  Tskhinvali ... 25 E5
Stalino =
  Donetsk .... 25 D4
Stalinogorsk =
  Novomoskovsk
  ......... 24 C4
Stamford .... 77 D9
Stanislav =
  Ivano-
  Frankivsk ... 17 D7
Stanley ..... 95 G5
Stanovoy
  Khrebet .... 31 D10
Stara Planina .. 22 C4
Stara Zagora .. 22 C5
Staraya Russa . 24 B3
Starbuck I. ... 65 K15
Staryy Oskol .. 24 C4
State College . 77 D7
Staten, I. =
  Estados, I. de
  Los ...... 95 G4
Stavanger ... 9 D7
Stavropol ... 25 D5
Stefanie L. =
  Chew Bahir . 55 H6
Steiermark □ .. 15 E8
Steinkjer .... 8 C8
Steornabhaigh =
  Stornoway .. 10 B3
Stepanakert =
  Xankändi ... 25 F6
Stepnoi = Elista 25 D5
Sterlitamak ... 29 D6
Stettin =
  Szczecin ... 16 B2
Stettler ..... 69 C8
Steubenville .. 76 D5
Stevenage ... 11 F6
Stewart → ... 68 B6
Stewart I. .... 65 G2
Steyr ....... 15 D8
Stillwater .... 80 A5
Stirling ..... 10 C5
Stockholm ... 9 D9
Stockport ... 11 E5
Stockton .... 78 B2
Stockton-on-
  Tees ..... 11 D6
Stoke-on-Trent 11 E5
Stonehaven ... 10 C5
Stora Lulevatten 8 B9
Storavan .... 8 B9

Store Bælt .... 9 D8
Stornoway ... 10 B3
Storsjön .... 8 C8
Storuman .... 8 B9
Stralsund .... 15 A7
Stranraer .... 11 D4
Strasbourg ... 13 B7
Stratford .... 77 C5
Strómboli .... 21 E5
Stronsay .... 10 B5
Stuttgart .... 14 D5
Styria =
  Steiermark □ 15 E8
Suakin ...... 55 E6
Subotica .... 16 E4
Suceava ..... 17 E8
Suchou =
  Suzhou ... 35 C7
Süchow =
  Xuzhou ... 35 C6
Sucre ....... 91 G5
Sudan ■ .... 55 E4
Sudbury ..... 71 D2
Südd ....... 55 G4
Sudeten Mts. =
  Sudety .... 16 C3
Sudety ..... 16 C3
Suez = El Suweis 54 C5
Suez, G. of =
  Suweis, Khalîg
  el ....... 54 C5
Sugluk = Salluit 70 B3
Şuḥār ....... 44 E4
Suihua ...... 35 B7
Sukhona → ... 28 C5
Sukhumi =
  Sokhumi ... 25 E5
Sukkur ..... 42 F6
Sulaiman Range 42 D6
Sulawesi □ ... 37 E2
Sulawesi Sea =
  Celebes Sea . 37 D2
Sullana ..... 90 D2
Sulu Arch. ... 36 C2
Sulu Sea .... 36 C2
Sumatera □ ... 39 D2
Sumatra =
  Sumatera □ . 39 D2
Sumba ...... 37 F1
Sumbawa .... 39 F5
Sumgait =
  Sumqayit ... 25 E6
Summerside .. 71 D4
Sumqayit ... 25 E6
Sumter ..... 83 C7
Sumy ....... 24 C3
Sunda, Selat . 39 F3
Sunda Str. =
  Sunda, Selat 39 F3
Sundarbans .. 41 G7
Sunderland .. 11 D6
Sundsvall ... 8 C9
Sungaipenuh . 39 E2
Sungari =
  Songhua
  Jiang → ... 35 B8
Superior .... 75 B8
Superior, L. .. 71 D2
Sugutra =
  Socotra .... 49 E5
Sür ........ 46 D3
Sura → ..... 24 B6
Surabaya .... 39 F4
Surakarta ... 39 F4
Surat ....... 43 J8
Surgut ..... 29 C8
Suriname ■ .. 92 B2
Surt ........ 54 B2
Surt, Khalîg ... 54 B2
Susquehanna → 77 F7
Sutherland Falls 65 F2
Sutlej → .... 42 E7
Suva ....... 64 L12
Suvorov Is. =
  Suwarrow Is. 65 L14
Suwałki .... 17 A6

Suwarrow Is. .. 65 L14
Suweis, Khalîg
  el ........ 54 C5
Suzhou ..... 35 C7
Svalbard □ ... 26 B5
Svealand □ .. 9 D9
Sverdlovsk =
  Yekaterinburg 29 D7
Swabian Alps =
  Schwäbische
  Alb ...... 14 D5
Swakopmund . 58 C2
Swan Hill .... 62 C3
Swansea .... 11 F5
Swatow =
  Shantou ... 35 D6
Swaziland ■ .. 59 D6
Sweden ■ ... 9 D9
Sweetwater .. 80 C3
Swellendam .. 58 E4
Swift Current . 69 C9
Swindon .... 11 F6
Switzerland ■ . 13 C8
Sydney,
  Australia ... 63 B5
Sydney, Canada 71 D4
Sydra, G. of =
  Surt, Khalîg .. 54 B2
Syktyvkar ... 28 C6
Sylhet ...... 41 E8
Syracuse .... 77 C7
Syrdarya → ... 29 E7
Syria ■ ..... 46 D4
Syrian Desert =
  Shâm, Bâdiyat
  ash ...... 47 D4
Syzran .... 24 C6
Szczecin ... 16 B2
Szechwan =
  Sichuan □ .. 34 C5
Szeged ..... 16 E5
Székesfehérvár . 16 E4
Szekszárd ... 16 E4
Szolnok .... 16 E5
Szombathely . 16 E3

# T

Tabas ....... 44 C4
Tablas I. .... 36 B2
Table B. ..... 58 E3
Table Mt. .... 58 E3
Tabora ...... 57 F6
Tabriz ...... 46 C6
Tacheng .... 34 B3
Tacloban .... 36 B2
Tacna ...... 91 G4
Tacoma .... 72 C2
Tacuarembó ... 94 C5
Tadzhikistan =
  Tajikistan ■ . 29 F8
Taegu ..... 35 C7
Taejon ..... 35 C7
Tafelbaai =
  Table B. .... 58 E3
Taguatinga .. 93 E5
Tagus = Tejo → 18 C1
Tahiti ...... 65 L16
Tahoe, L. ... 72 G3
Tahoua ..... 53 F7
Taibei = T'aipei 35 D7
T'aichung ... 35 D7
Taimyr
  Peninsula =
  Taymyr,
  Poluostrov .. 30 B7
Tain ...... 10 C4
T'ainan .... 35 D7
T'aipei ..... 35 D7
Taiping .... 39 D2
Taitao, Pen. de 95 F1
Taiwan ■ ... 35 D7
Taiyuan ... 35 C6

Taizhong =
  T'aichung ... 35 D7
Ta'izz ....... 49 E3
Tajikistan ■ .. 29 F8
Tajo = Tejo → . 18 C1
Tak ........ 38 A1
Takamatsu ... 33 F4
Takaoka .... 33 E5
Takapuna .... 64 B6
Takasaki .... 33 E6
Takhâr □ .... 45 B7
Taklamakan
  Shamo .... 34 C3
Talara ...... 90 D2
Talaud,
  Kepulauan . 36 D3
Talca ...... 94 D2
Talcahuano ... 94 D2
Taldyqorghan . 29 E8
Tallahassee ... 83 D5
Tallinn ..... 24 B1
Taloyoak ... 68 B10
Taltal ...... 94 B2
Tamale ..... 53 G5
Tamanrasset .. 52 D7
Tambov .... 24 C5
Tamil Nadu □ . 43 P10
Tammerfors =
  Tampere ... 8 C10
Tampa ...... 83 F6
Tampere .... 8 C10
Tampico .... 84 C5
Tamworth ... 63 B5
Tana →, Kenya 57 E8
Tana →,
  Norway .... 8 A11
Tana, L. .... 55 F6
Tanami Desert . 60 D5
Tanana → ... 69 B4
Tananarive =
  Antananarivo 59 H9
Tandil ...... 94 D5
Tanen Tong
  Dan = Dawna
  Ra. ...... 41 J12
Tanga ...... 57 F7
Tanganyika, L. 57 F5
Tanger =
  Tanger .... 52 A4
Tangshan ... 35 C6
Tanimbar,
  Kepulauan .. 37 F4
Tanjore =
  Thanjavur ... 43 P11
Tanjungbalai .. 39 D1
Tanjungkarang
  Telukbetung . 39 F3
Tanjungpandan 39 E3
Tanjungredeb . 39 D5
Tanta ...... 54 B5
Tantung =
  Dandong ... 35 B7
Tanzania ■ .. 57 F6
Taolanaro ... 59 K9
Tapa Shan =
  Daba Shan . 35 C5
Tapajós → ... 92 C3
Tapi → ..... 43 J8
Tarābulus,
  Lebanon ... 46 D3
Tarābulus, Libya 54 B1
Tarakan .... 39 D5
Taranaki □ ... 64 C6
Taranaki, Mt. .. 64 C6
Táranto .... 21 D6
Táranto, G. di . 21 D6
Taraz ...... 29 E8
Tarbagatay,
  Khrebet .... 29 E9
Tarbes ..... 12 E4
Tarcoola .... 62 B1
Taree ...... 63 B5
Tarfaya ..... 52 C3
Târgoviște ... 22 B5
Târgu-Jiu .... 17 F6

# Târgu Mureş

Târgu Mureş .. 17 E7
Tarija ........ 94 A4
Tarim Basin =
Tarim Pendi . 34 C3
Tarim He ➤ .. 34 C3
Tarim Pendi . 34 C3
Tarn ➤ ...... 12 D4
Tarnów ...... 16 C5
Taroudannt .. 52 B4
Tarragona .. 19 B6
Tarrasa =
Terrassa .. 19 B7
Tarsus ...... 46 C3
Tartu ........ 24 B2
Tashauz =
Dashhowuz . 29 E6
Tashi Chho
Dzong =
Thimphu .. 41 D7
Tashkent =
Toshkent .. 29 E7
Tasman Mts. .. 65 D5
Tasmania □ .. 62 D4
Tatarstan □ .. 29 D6
Tatra = Tatry . 16 D4
Tatry ........ 16 D4
Tatta ........ 43 G5
Tat'ung =
Datong .. 35 B6
Tatvan ...... 46 C5
Taubaté ...... 94 A7
Tauern ...... 15 E7
Taunton ...... 11 F5
Taunus ...... 14 C5
Taupo, L. .... 64 C6
Taurus Mts. =
Toros Dağları 46 C3
Tawau ........ 38 D5
Tay ➤ ........ 10 C5
Taymyr,
Poluostrov .. 30 B7
Taza ........ 52 B5
Tbilisi ...... 25 E5
Tchad = Chad ■ 55 E2
Tchad, L. .... 55 F1
Tébessa ...... 52 A7
Tedzhen = Tejen 29 F7
Tegal ........ 39 F3
Tegucigalpa .. 85 E7
Teheran =
Tehrān .. 44 C2
Tehrān ...... 44 C2
Tehuantepec . 85 D5
Tehuantepec, G.
de ........ 85 D5
Tehuantepec,
Istmo de .. 85 D6
Tejen ........ 29 F7
Tejo ➤ ...... 18 C1
Tekirdağ .... 22 D6
Tel Aviv-Yafo .. 46 D3
Tela ........ 85 D7
Telanaipura =
Jambi .. 39 E2
Teles Pires ➤ . 91 E7
Telford ...... 11 E5
Tellicherry .. 43 P9
Teluk Anson =
Teluk Intan . 39 D2
Teluk Betung =
Tanjungkarang
Telukbetung . 39 F3
Teluk Intan .. 39 D2
Tema ........ 53 G5
Tempe ........ 79 D7
Temple ...... 80 D5
Temuco ...... 94 D2
Tenerife .... 52 C2
Tengchong .. 34 D4
Tennessee □ .. 82 B4
Tennessee ➤ . 76 F1
Teófilo Otoni . 93 F5
Tepic ........ 84 C4
Téramo ...... 20 C4
Teresina .... 92 D5
Ternate ...... 37 D3
Terni ........ 20 C4

Ternopil ...... 17 D7
Terrassa .... 19 B7
Terre Haute .. 76 E2
Teruel ...... 19 B5
Tesiyn Gol ➤ .. 34 A4
Teslin ........ 68 B6
Tete ........ 59 B6
Tétouan ...... 52 A4
Tetovo ...... 22 C3
Teuco ➤ .... 94 B4
Teutoburger
Wald .. 14 B5
Tevere ➤ .... 20 D4
Texarkana .. 81 C6
Texas □ .... 80 D4
Texel ........ 14 B3
Tezpur ...... 41 D9
Thabana
Ntlenyana .. 59 D5
Thabazimbi .. 59 C5
Thailand ■ .. 38 A2
Thailand, G. of . 38 B2
Thala La =
Hkakabo Razi 41 C11
Thames ➤ .... 11 F7
Thane ........ 43 K8
Thanh Pho Ho
Chi Minh .. 38 B3
Thanjavur .. 43 P11
Thar Desert .. 42 F7
Thargomindah 63 A3
The Great
Divide = Great
Dividing Ra. . 61 E8
The Hague =
's-Gravenhage 14 B3
The Pas .... 69 C9
Thermaïkós
Kólpos .. 23 D4
Thermopylae P. 23 E4
Thessaloníki .. 23 D4
Thessaloníki,
Gulf of =
Thermaïkós
Kólpos .. 23 D4
Thetford .... 11 E7
Thetford Mines 71 D3
Thiers ...... 13 D5
Thiès ........ 53 F2
Thika ........ 57 E7
Thimphu .... 41 D7
Thionville .. 13 B7
Thira ........ 23 F5
Thiruvananthapuram =
Trivandrum . 43 Q10
Thomasville .. 83 D6
Thompson .. 69 C10
Thunder Bay .. 71 D2
Thüringer Wald 14 C6
Thurles ...... 11 E3
Thurso ...... 10 B5
Tian Shan .. 34 B3
Tianjin ...... 35 C6
Tianshui .... 35 C5
Tiaret ...... 52 A6
Tiber =
Tevere ➤ .. 20 D4
Tiberias, L. =
Yam Kinneret 46 D3
Tibesti ...... 54 D2
Tibet = Xizang
Zizhiqu □ .. 34 C3
Tiburón, I. .. 84 B2
Ticino ➤ .... 20 B2
Tien Shan = Tian
Shan .. 34 B3
Tientsin =
Tianjin .. 35 C6
Tierra del Fuego,
I. Gr. de .. 95 G3
Tiflis = Tbilisi . 25 E5
Tighina ...... 17 E9
Tigris = Dijlah,
Nahr ➤ .. 47 E6
Tijuana ...... 84 A1
Tikhoretsk .. 25 D5

Tikiraqjuaq =
Whale Cove . 68 B10
Tikrīt ...... 46 D5
Tiksi ........ 30 B10
Tilburg ...... 14 C3
Tilsit = Sovetsk 24 B1
Timaru ...... 65 F4
Timbuktu =
Tombouctou 53 E5
Timişoara .. 16 F5
Timmins .... 71 D2
Timor ........ 37 F2
Tinnevelly =
Tirunelveli . 43 Q10
Tinogasta .. 94 B3
Tipperary .. 11 E2
Tiranë ...... 22 D2
Tiraspol .... 17 E9
Tirebolu .... 25 E4
Tiree ........ 10 C3
Tîrgovişte =
Târgovişte .. 22 B5
Tîrgu-Jiu =
Târgu-Jiu .. 17 F6
Tirgu Mureş =
Târgu Mureş . 17 E7
Tirich Mir .. 42 A7
Tirol □ ...... 14 E6
Tiruchchirappalli 43 P11
Tirunelveli .. 43 Q10
Tiruppur .... 43 P10
Tisa ➤ ...... 22 B3
Tisdale ...... 69 C9
Tisza = Tisa ➤ .. 22 B3
Titicaca, L. .. 91 G5
Trå Li = Tralee . 11 E2
Titograd =
Podgorica .. 22 C2
Tizi-Ouzou .. 52 A6
Tjirebon =
Cirebon .. 39 F3
Tlaxiaco .... 84 D5
Tlemcen .... 52 B5
Toamasina .. 59 H9
Tobago ...... 87 D7
Tobermory .. 10 C3
Tobruk = Tubruq 54 B3
Tocantins □ .. 93 E4
Tocantins ➤ . 92 C4
Todos os
Santos, B. de 93 E6
Togliatti .... 24 C6
Togo ■ ...... 53 G6
Tojikiston =
Tajikistan ■ . 29 F8
Tokat ........ 46 B4
Tokelau Is. .. 65 K13
Tokushima .. 33 F4
Tokuyama .. 33 F2
Tōkyō ...... 33 F6
Tolbukhin =
Dobrich .. 22 C6
Toledo, Spain . 18 C3
Toledo, U.S.A. . 76 D4
Toliara ...... 59 J8
Tolima ...... 90 C3
Toluca ...... 84 D5
Tomakomai .. 32 B7
Tomaszów
Mazowiecki . 16 C4
Tombouctou .. 53 E5
Tomini, Teluk . 37 E2
Tomsk ...... 29 D9
Tonga ■ .... 65 L13
Tonga Trench . 65 L13
Tongareva .. 65 K15
Tongchuan .. 35 C5
Tonghua .... 35 B7
Tongking, G.
of = Tonkin, G.
of ........ 35 D5
Tongue ➤ .... 74 B2
Tonk ........ 42 F9
Tonkin, G. of . 35 D5
Tonle Sap .. 38 B2
Toowoomba .. 63 A5
Topeka ...... 75 F7

Topolobampo . 84 B3
Torbay □ .... 11 F5
Torino ...... 20 B1
Torne älv ➤ .. 8 B10
Torneå = Tornio 8 E12
Torneträsk .. 8 B9
Tornio ...... 8 E12
Toro, Cerro del 94 B3
Toronto .... 71 D3
Toros Dağları . 46 C3
Torre del Greco 21 D5
Torremolinos . 18 D3
Torrens, L. .. 62 B2
Torreón .... 84 B4
Tortosa .... 19 B6
Toruń ...... 16 B4
Toscana □ .. 20 C3
Toshkent .... 29 E7
Tottori ...... 33 F4
Toubkal, Djebel 52 B4
Touggourt .. 52 B7
Toul ........ 13 B6
Toulon ...... 13 E6
Toulouse .... 12 E4
Touraine .... 12 C4
Tourane = Da
Nang .. 38 A3
Tournai .... 14 C2
Tournon-sur-
Rhône .. 13 D6
Tours ........ 12 C4
Townsville .. 61 D8
Toyama .... 33 E5
Toyohashi .. 33 F5
Toyota ...... 33 F5
Tozeur ...... 54 B7
Trabzon .... 46 B5
Trafalgar, C. . 18 D2
Trail ........ 69 D8
Tralee ...... 11 E2
Trang ........ 38 C1
Transantarctic
Mts. .. 96 C3
Transilvania . 17 F7
Transilvanian
Alps = Carpaţii
Meridionali . 17 F7
Trápani .... 21 E4
Treinta y Tres . 94 C6
Trelew ...... 95 E3
Trent ➤ .... 11 E6
Trento ...... 20 A3
Trenton .... 77 D8
Tres Arroyos . 94 D4
Três Lagoas .. 93 G3
Tres Puntas, C. 95 F3
Tres Ríos .... 93 G5
Trichinopoly =
Tiruchchirappalli
........ 43 P11
Trichur .... 43 P10
Trier ........ 14 D4
Trieste ...... 20 B4
Trinidad, Bolivia 91 F6
Trinidad, Cuba . 86 B3
Trinidad, U.S.A. 80 A1
Trinidad &
Tobago ■ .. 87 D7
Trinity ➤ .... 81 E6
Trinity B. .... 71 D5
Tripoli =
Tarābulus,
Lebanon .. 46 D3
Tripoli =
Tarābulus,
Libya .. 54 B1
Tripura □ .... 41 F8
Trivandrum .. 43 Q10
Trois-Rivières . 71 D3
Trollhättan .. 9 D8
Tromsø ...... 8 B9
Tronador, Mte. 95 E2
Trondheim .. 8 C8
Trondheimsfjorden
........ 8 C8
Trout L. .... 68 B7

Troy, Turkey .. 23 E6
Troy, Ala.,
U.S.A. .. 82 D5
Troy, N.Y.,
U.S.A. .. 77 C9
Troyes ...... 13 B6
Trucial States =
United Arab
Emirates ■ .. 44 F3
Trujillo,
Honduras .. 85 D7
Trujillo, Peru . 91 E3
Trujillo,
Venezuela .. 90 B4
Truk ........ 64 J10
Truro, Canada . 71 D4
Truro, U.K. .. 11 F4
Tsangpo =
Brahmaputra ➤
........ 41 F7
Tselinograd =
Astana .. 29 D8
Tsetserleg .. 34 B5
Tsiigehtchic .. 68 B6
Tsimlyanskoye
Vdkhr. .. 25 D5
Tsinan = Jinan . 35 C6
Tsinghai =
Qinghai □ .. 34 C4
Tsingtao =
Qingdao .. 35 C7
Tskhinvali .. 25 E5
Tsuchiura .. 33 E7
Tsugaru Str. .. 32 C7
Tsumeb .... 58 B3
Tsushima .. 33 F1
Tuamotu Is. .. 65 L16
Tuamotu Ridge 65 M17
Tuapse ...... 25 E4
Tubarão .... 94 B7
Tubruq ...... 54 B3
Tubuai Is. .. 65 M16
Tucson ...... 79 D7
Tucumcari .. 80 B2
Tucupita .... 90 B6
Tucuruí ...... 92 C4
Tudmur .... 46 D4
Tuktoyaktuk .. 68 B6
Tula ........ 24 C4
Tulare ...... 78 B3
Tulcán ...... 90 C3
Tulcea ...... 17 F9
Tulita ...... 68 B7
Tullamore .. 11 E3
Tulle ........ 12 D4
Tulsa ........ 81 A6
Tumaco .... 90 C3
Tumbes .... 90 D2
Tumucumaque,
Serra .. 92 B3
Tunguska,
Nizhnyaya ➤ . 30 C6
Tunis ...... 54 A1
Tunisia ■ .. 54 A1
Tunja ...... 90 B4
Tupelo ...... 82 B3
Tupiza ...... 94 A3
Turfan = Turpan 34 B3
Turfan
Depression =
Turpan Hami . 34 B3
Turgutlu .... 23 E6
Turin = Torino . 20 B1
Turkana, L. .. 57 D7
Turkestan =
Türkistan .. 29 E7
Turkey ■ .... 46 C3
Türkistan .... 29 E7
Turkmenbashi . 29 E6
Turkmenistan ■ 29 F6
Turks & Caicos
Is. □ ...... 87 B5
Turku ...... 9 C10
Turneffe Is. .. 85 D7
Turpan ...... 34 B3
Turpan Hami .. 34 B3

Tuscaloosa ... 82 C4
Tuscany =
 Toscana □ .. 20 C3
Tuticorin ..... 43 Q11
Tutuila ...... 65 L13
Tuvalu ■ .... 64 K12
Tuxpan ...... 84 C5
Tuxtla Gutiérrez 85 D6
Tuz Gölü ..... 46 C3
Tuzla ......... 20 B7
Tver ......... 24 B4
Twin Falls .... 73 E6
Tychy ........ 16 C4
Tyler ........ 81 C6
Tyre = Sûr .... 46 D3
Tyrol = Tirol □ . 14 E6
Tyrrhenian Sea 21 E4
Tyumen ...... 29 D7
Tzaneen ...... 59 C6
Tzukong =
 Zigong ..... 35 D5

**U**

U.S.A. = United
 States of
 America ■ .. 67 F10
Uaupés → .... 90 C5
Ubá ......... 93 G5
Ubaitaba ..... 93 E6
Ubangi =
 Oubangi → . 56 E3
Ube ......... 33 G2
Uberaba ..... 93 F4
Uberlândia ... 93 F4
Ubon
 Ratchathani . 38 A2
Ucayali → .... 90 D4
Udagamandalam
 ........... 43 P10
Udaipur ...... 43 G8
Údine ........ 20 A4
Udmurtia □ ... 28 D6
Udon Thani ... 38 A2
Udupi ........ 43 N9
Uele → ....... 57 D4
Ufa ......... 29 D6
Uganda ■ .... 57 D6
Uíbhist a Deas =
 South Uist . 10 C3
Uíbhist a
 Tuath = North
 Uist ........ 10 C3
Uinta Mts. .... 73 F8
Uitenhage .... 59 E5
Ujjain ....... 43 H9
Ujung Pandang 37 F1
Ukhta ....... 28 C6
Ukraine ■ .... 25 D3
Ulaanbaatar ... 35 B5
Ulaangom .... 34 A4
Ulaanjirom ... 35 B5
Ulan Bator =
 Ulaanbaatar . 35 B5
Ulan Ude ..... 30 D8
Ulhasnagar ... 43 K8
Ullastay =
 Ulyasutay ... 34 B4
Ullapool ..... 10 C4
Ulm ......... 14 D5
Ulster □ ..... 11 D3
Ulungur He → . 34 B3
Uluru = Ayers
 Rock ....... 60 F5
Ulyanovsk =
 Simbirsk ... 24 C6
Ulyasutay .... 34 B4
Uman ........ 17 D10
Ume älv → ... 8 C10
Umeå ....... 8 C10
Umnak I. ..... 69 C3
Umtata ...... 59 E5
Umuarama ... 93 G3

Unalaska ..... 69 C3
Uncía ........ 91 G5
Ungava, Pén. d' 70 B3
Ungava B. .... 70 C4
Unimak I. ..... 69 C3
United Arab
 Emirates ■ .. 44 F3
United
 Kingdom ■ . 11 D5
United States of
 America ■ .. 67 F10
Unst ......... 10 A6
Upington ..... 58 D4
Upper Volta =
 Burkina
 Faso ■ ..... 53 F5
Uppsala ...... 9 D9
Uqsuqtuuq =
 Gjoa Haven . 68 B10
Ur .......... 47 E6
Ural =
 Zhayyq → .. 29 E6
Ural Mts. =
 Uralskie Gory 28 D6
Uralsk = Oral .. 24 C7
Uralskie Gory . 28 D6
Urbana ...... 76 D1
Urfa = Sanliurfa 46 C4
Urganch ...... 29 E7
Urmia =
 Orümiyeh .. 46 C6
Urmia, L. =
 Orümiyeh,
 Daryácheh-ye 46 C6
Urubamba → . 91 F4
Uruguai → .... 94 B6
Uruguaiana ... 94 B5
Uruguay ■ .... 94 C5
Uruguay → ... 94 C5
Ürümqi ...... 34 B3
Usakos ...... 58 C3
Ushant =
 Ouessant, Î. d' 12 B1
Ushuaia ...... 95 G3
Uspallata, P. de 94 C3
Ust-
 Kamenogorsk =
 Öskemen ... 29 E9
Ust Urt = Ustyurt
 Plateau ..... 29 E6
Ústí nad Labem 16 C2
Ustinov =
 Izhevsk .... 28 D6
Ustyurt Plateau 29 E6
Usu ......... 34 B3
Usumacinta → 85 D6
Usumbura =
 Bujumbura . 57 E5
Utah □ ...... 73 G8
Utica ........ 77 C8
Utrecht ...... 14 B3
Utsunomiya ... 33 E6
Uttar Pradesh □ 42 F11
Uttaradit ..... 38 A2
Uummannarsuaq =
 Nunap Isua . 70 C6
Uusikaupunki . 9 C10
Uvs Nuur .... 34 A4
Uyuni ....... 91 H5
Uzbekistan ■ . 29 E7
Uzhgorod =
 Uzhhorod .. 17 D6
Uzhhorod .... 17 D6

**V**

Vaal → ...... 58 D4
Vaasa ....... 8 C10
Vadodara .... 43 H8
Vadsø ....... 8 D13
Vaduz ....... 13 C8
Val-d'Or ..... 71 D3
Valahia ...... 22 B5

Valdai Hills =
 Valdayskaya
 Vozvyshennost
 ............ 24 B3
Valdayskaya
 Vozvyshennost
 ............ 24 B3
Valdés, Pen. ... 95 E4
Valdez ....... 69 B5
Valdivia ...... 95 D2
Valdosta ...... 83 D6
Valença ...... 93 E6
Valence ...... 13 D6
Valencia, Spain 19 C5
Valencia,
 Venezuela ... 90 A5
Valencia □ .... 19 C5
Valencia I. .... 11 F1
Valenciennes . 13 A5
Valera ....... 90 B4
Valladolid,
 Mexico ..... 85 C7
Valladolid, Spain 18 B3
Vallejo ....... 72 G2
Vallenar ...... 94 B2
Valletta ...... 21 G5
Valona = Vlorë . 23 D2
Valparaíso .... 94 C2
Van ......... 46 C5
Van, L. = Van
 Gölü ....... 46 C5
Van Gölü ..... 46 C5
Vancouver,
 Canada .... 69 D7
Vancouver,
 U.S.A. ..... 72 D2
Vancouver I. .. 69 D7
Vänern ...... 9 D8
Vännäs ...... 8 C9
Vannes ...... 12 C2
Vanrhynsdorp . 58 E3
Vanua Levu ... 64 L12
Vanuatu ■ .... 64 L11
Varanasi ..... 40 E4
Varangerfjorden 8 A11
Varberg ...... 9 D8
Vardak □ ..... 45 C7
Vardar → ....
Axiós → .... 23 D4
Varna ........ 22 C6
Vasa Barris → . 93 E6
Vascongadas =
 País Vasco □ 19 A4
Västerås ..... 9 D9
Västervik .... 9 D9
Vatican City ■ . 20 D4
Vättern ...... 9 D8
Vaupés =
 Uaupés → .. 90 C5
Vega ........ 8 B8
Vegreville .... 69 C8
Velhas → .... 93 F5
Velikiye Luki .. 24 B3
Vellore ...... 43 N11
Vendée □ .... 12 C3
Vendôme ..... 12 C4
Venézia ...... 20 B4
Venezuela ■ . 90 B5
Venezuela, G. de 90 A4
Vengurla ..... 43 M8
Venice = Venézia 20 B4
Ventoux, Mt. .. 13 D6
Ventspils ..... 24 B1
Veracruz ..... 84 D5
Veraval ...... 43 J7
Vercelli ...... 20 B2
Verdun ...... 13 B6
Vereeniging ... 59 D5
Verkhoyansk . 31 C11
Verkhoyanskiy
 Khrebet ..... 31 C10
Vermont □ .... 77 C9
Vernon, Canada 69 C8
Vernon, U.S.A. 80 B4
Verona ...... 20 B3
Versailles .... 12 B5
Vert, C. ...... 53 F2

Verviers ...... 14 C3
Vesoul ....... 13 C7
Vesterålen ... 8 B9
Vestfjorden ... 8 B8
Vesuvio ...... 21 D5
Vesuvius, Mt. =
 Vesuvio .... 21 D5
Veszprém .... 16 E3
Viangchan =
 Vientiane ... 38 A2
Vianópolis ... 93 F4
Vicenza ...... 20 B3
Vichy ........ 13 C5
Vicksburg .... 81 C8
Victoria ...... 69 D7
Victoria □ .... 62 C3
Victoria, L. ... 57 E6
Victoria de
 Durango =
 Durango .... 84 C4
Victoria Falls . 59 B5
Victoria I. .... 68 A8
Victoria Ld. ... 96 B14
Viedma, L. .... 95 F2
Vienna = Wien . 15 D9
Vienne ....... 13 D6
Vienne → ..... 12 C3
Vientiane .... 38 A2
Vierzon ...... 12 C5
Vietnam ■ .... 38 A3
Vigo ......... 18 A1
Vijayawada ... 40 J3
Vikna ........ 8 C8
Vila Velha .... 93 G5
Vilaine → ..... 12 C2
Vilhelmina ... 8 C9
Villa Bella .... 91 F5
Villa Bens =
 Tarfaya .... 52 C3
Villa Cisneros =
 Dakhla ..... 52 D2
Villa María .... 94 C4
Villach ...... 15 E7
Villahermosa . 85 D6
Villarrica .... 94 B5
Villavicencio . 90 C4
Villeneuve-sur-
 Lot ........ 12 D4
Vilnius ...... 24 C2
Vilyuy → ..... 31 C10
Vilyuysk ..... 31 C10
Viña del Mar .. 94 C2
Vindhya Ra. ... 43 H10
Vineland ..... 77 E8
Vinnitsa =
 Vinnytsya .. 17 D9
Vinnytsya .... 17 D9
Virden ....... 69 D9
Vire ......... 12 B3
Virgenes, C. .. 95 G3
Virgin Is. ..... 87 C7
Virginia □ .... 77 F6
Virginia Beach . 77 F8
Visalia ...... 78 B3
Visby ....... 9 D8
Vishakhapatnam 40 J4
Vistula =
 Wisła → .... 16 A4
Vitebsk =
 Vitsyebsk .. 24 B3
Viterbo ...... 20 C4
Viti Levu ..... 64 L12
Vitória ...... 93 G5
Vitória da
 Conquista ... 93 E5
Vitória-Gasteiz . 19 A4
Vitsyebsk .... 24 B3
Vizianagaram . 40 H4
Vladikavkaz ... 25 E5
Vladimir ..... 24 B5
Vladivostok ... 32 B2
Vlissingen .... 14 C2
Vlorë ....... 23 D2
Vltava → ..... 16 C2
Vogelkop =
 Doberai,
 Jazirah .... 37 E4

Vogelsberg ... 14 C5
Vohimena,
 Tanjon' i .... 59 K9
Voi ......... 57 E7
Vojvodina □ .. 22 B2
Volga → ..... 25 D6
Volga Hts. =
 Privolzhskaya
 Vozvyshennost
 ............ 24 C6
Volgodonsk ... 25 D5
Volgograd .... 25 D5
Vologda ...... 24 B4
Vólos ....... 23 E4
Volsk ........ 24 C6
Volta, L. ..... 53 G6
Volta Redonda . 93 G5
Volzhskiy .... 25 D5
Vóriai
 Sporádhes .. 23 E4
Vorkuta ...... 28 C7
Voronezh ..... 24 C4
Voroshilovgrad =
 Luhansk .... 25 D4
Voroshilovsk =
 Alchevsk ... 25 D4
Vosges ...... 13 B7
Vostok I. ..... 65 L15
Vrangelya,
 Ostrov ..... 31 B15
Vryburg ...... 58 D4
Vryheid ...... 59 D6
Vung Tau ..... 38 B3
Vyatka = Kirov . 28 D5
Vyazma ...... 24 B3
Vyborg ...... 28 C3
Vychegda → .. 28 C5
Vychodné
 Beskydy .... 17 D5
Vyshniy
 Volochek ... 24 B3

**W**

Waal → ...... 14 C3
Wabash → .... 76 F11
Waco ........ 80 D5
Wad Medani .. 55 F5
Waddington, Mt. 69 C7
Wadi Halfa .... 54 D5
Wager B. ..... 70 B2
Wagga Wagga . 63 C4
Wah ......... 42 C8
Waigeo ...... 37 E4
Waikato → .... 64 B6
Wakayama .... 33 F4
Wakkanai .... 32 A7
Wałbrzych .... 16 C3
Wales □ ..... 11 E4
Walgett ...... 63 A4
Walla Walla ... 72 C4
Walloahia =
 Valahia .... 22 B5
Wallis & Futuna,
 Is. ......... 64 L13
Walvis Bay ... 58 C2
Wanganui .... 64 C6
Warangal .... 43 L11
Wardha ...... 43 J11
Warrego → ... 63 B4
Warren ...... 76 C4
Warrington ... 11 E5
Warrnambool . 62 C3
Warsaw =
 Warszawa ... 16 B5
Warszawa .... 16 B5
Warta → ..... 16 B2
Wasatch Ra. .. 73 F8
Wash, The .... 11 E7
Washington ... 77 E7
Washington □ . 72 C3
Washington, Mt. 77 B10
Waskaganish .. 71 C3
Watampone ... 37 E2

Waterbury .... 77 D9
Waterford .... 11 E3
Waterloo .... 75 D8
Watertown .... 77 C8
Waterville .... 77 B11
Watford .... 11 F6
Watling I. = San
  Salvador I. . 86 B5
Watrous .... 69 C9
Watson Lake . 68 B7
Wau = Wâw .. 55 G4
Waukegan .... 76 C2
Waukesha .... 76 C1
Wausau .... 75 C10
Wauwatosa .. 76 C2
Wâw .... 55 G4
Waycross .... 83 D6
Wazirabad .... 42 C9
Weddell Sea .. 96 A4
Weifang .... 35 C6
Weipa .... 61 C7
Welkom .... 59 D5
Wellesley Is. .. 60 D6
Wellington .... 65 D6
Wellington, I. .. 95 F1
Wels .... 15 D8
Welshpool .... 11 E5
Wemindji .... 71 C3
Wenatchee .... 72 C3
Wenchow =
  Wenzhou .. 35 D7
Wensu .... 34 B3
Wenzhou .... 35 D7
Weser → .... 14 B5
West Bengal □ 40 F7
West Beskids =
  Západné
  Beskydy .. 16 D4
West Falkland . 95 G4
West Fjord =
  Vestfjorden . 8 B8
West Palm
  Beach .... 83 F7
West Virginia □ 76 E5
Western
  Australia □ .. 60 F3
Western Dvina =
  Daugava → .. 24 B1
Western Ghats 43 N9
Western
  Sahara ■ .. 52 D3
Western
  Samoa =
  Samoa ■ .. 65 L13
Westerwald .. 14 C4
Westland Bight 65 E4
Weston-super-
  Mare .... 11 F5
Westport,
  Ireland .... 11 E2
Westport, N.Z. 65 D4
Westray .... 10 B5
Wetar .... 37 F3
Wetaskiwin .. 69 C8
Wexford .... 11 E3
Weyburn .... 69 D9
Weymouth .... 11 F5
Wha Ti .... 68 B8
Whale → .... 70 C4
Whale Cove .. 68 B10
Whales, B. of .. 96 B16
Whangarei .... 64 A6
Wheeling .... 76 D5
White →, Ark.,
  U.S.A. .... 81 C8
White →, Ind.,
  U.S.A. .... 76 E2
White Nile = Nîl
  el Abyad → .. 55 E5
White Russia =
  Belarus ■ .. 24 C2
White Sea =
  Beloye More 8 B13
Whitehaven .. 11 D5
Whitehorse .. 68 B6

Whitney, Mt. .. 78 B3
Wholdaia L. .. 68 B9
Whyalla .... 62 B2
Wichita .... 80 A5
Wichita Falls .. 80 C4
Wick .... 10 B5
Wicklow Mts. .. 11 E3
Wien .... 15 D9
Wiener Neustadt 15 E9
Wiesbaden .... 14 C5
Wilhelm, Mt. .. 61 B8
Wilhelmshaven 14 B5
Wilkes-Barre .. 77 D8
Willemstad .... 87 D6
Williams Lake . 69 C7
Williamsburg .. 77 F7
Williamsport .. 77 D7
Williston .... 74 A3
Wilmington,
  Del., U.S.A. .. 77 E8
Wilmington,
  N.C., U.S.A. .. 83 B9
Winchester .... 11 F6
Wind River
  Range .... 73 E9
Windau =
  Ventspils .. 24 B1
Windhoek .... 58 C3
Windsor .... 71 D2
Winisk → .... 71 C2
Winnipeg .... 69 D10
Winnipeg, L. .. 69 C10
Winnipegosis L. 69 C9
Winona .... 75 C9
Winston-Salem 83 A7
Winterthur .... 13 C8
Winton .... 61 E7
Wisconsin □ .. 75 C10
Wisła → .... 16 A4
Witbank .... 59 D5
Wkra → .... 16 B5
Włocławek .... 16 B4
Wodonga =
  Albury-
  Wodonga .. 63 C4
Wolfsburg .... 15 B6
Wollaston Pen. 68 B8
Wollongong .. 63 B5
Wolverhampton 11 E5
Wônsan .... 35 C7
Woodroffe, Mt. 60 F5
Woods, L. of the 69 D10
Woodstock .... 71 D4
Worcester,
  S. Africa .. 58 E3
Worcester, U.K. 11 E5
Worcester,
  U.S.A. .... 77 C10
Workington .. 11 D5
Worms .... 14 D5
Worthing .... 11 F6
Wrangel I. =
  Vrangelya,
  Ostrov .... 31 B15
Wrangell .... 69 C6
Wrangell Mts. 69 B5
Wrath, C. .... 10 B4
Wrexham .... 11 E5
Wrigley .... 68 B7
Wrocław .... 16 C3
Wu Jiang → .. 35 D5
Wuhan .... 35 C6
Wuhsi = Wuxi .. 35 C7
Wuhu .... 35 C6
Wulumuchi =
  Ürümqi .... 34 B3
Wuppertal .... 14 C4
Würzburg .... 14 D5
Wutongqiao ... 34 D5
Wuwei .... 34 C5
Wuxi .... 35 C7
Wuyi Shan .... 35 D6
Wuzhong .... 35 C5
Wuzhou .... 35 D6
Wyndham .... 60 D4
Wyoming □ .... 73 E10

## X

Xainza .... 34 C3
Xalapa .... 84 D5
Xankändi .... 25 F6
Xi Jiang → .... 35 D6
Xiaguan .... 34 D5
Xiamen .... 35 D6
Xi'an .... 35 C5
Xiang Jiang → 35 D6
Xiangfan .... 35 C6
Xianggang =
  Hong Kong □ 35 D6
Xiangquan He =
  Sutlej → .... 42 E7
Xiangtan .... 35 D6
Xiao Hinggan
  Ling .... 35 B7
Xichang .... 34 D5
Xigazê .... 34 D3
Xing'an .... 35 D6
Xingu → .... 92 C3
Xining .... 34 C5
Xinjiang Uygur
  Zizhiqu □ .. 34 B3
Xinxiang .... 35 C6
Xique-Xique .. 93 E5
Xisha Qundao =
  Paracel Is. .. 38 A4
Xizang Zizhiqu □ 34 C3
Xuanhua .... 35 B6
Xuzhou .... 35 C6

## Y

Yablonovyy
  Khrebet .... 30 D9
Yacuiba .... 94 A4
Yakima .... 72 C3
Yakutat .... 69 C6
Yakutsk .... 31 C10
Yalong Jiang → 34 D5
Yalta .... 25 E3
Yam Ha Melah =
  Dead Sea .. 47 E3
Yam Kinneret . 46 D3
Yamagata .... 32 D7
Yamaguchi .... 33 F2
Yambol .... 22 C6
Yamethin .... 41 G11
Yamoussoukro 53 G4
Yamuna → .... 40 E3
Yamzho Yumco 34 D4
Yanbu 'al Baḥr . 47 F4
Yangon =
  Rangoon .... 41 J11
Yangquan .... 35 C6
Yangtse = Chang
  Jiang → .... 35 C7
Yangtze Kiang =
  Chang
  Jiang → .... 35 C7
Yanji .... 35 B7
Yangi .... 34 B3
Yantai .... 35 C6
Yaoundé .... 56 D2
Yapen .... 37 E5
Yaqui → .... 84 B2
Yaraka .... 61 E7
Yarkand =
  Shache .... 34 C2
Yarkhun → .... 42 A8
Yarlung Ziangbo
  Jiang =
  Brahmaputra →
    .... 41 F7
Yaroslavl .... 24 B4
Yathkyed L. .. 68 B10
Yatsushiro .... 33 G2
Yavari → .... 90 D4
Yazd .... 44 D3
Yazoo → .... 81 C8
Ye Xian =
  Laizhou .... 35 C6

Yekaterinburg . 29 D7
Yekaterinodar =
  Krasnodar .. 25 D4
Yelets .... 24 C4
Yelizavetgrad =
  Kirovohrad .. 25 D3
Yell .... 10 A6
Yellow Sea .... 35 C7
Yellowhead Pass 69 C8
Yellowknife .. 68 B8
Yellowstone △ . 73 D9
Yellowstone → 74 B3
Yemen ■ .... 49 E3
Yenbo = Yanbu
  'al Baḥr .... 47 F4
Yenisey → .... 28 B9
Yeola .... 43 J9
Yeovil .... 11 F5
Yerevan .... 25 E5
Yerushalayim =
  Jerusalem .. 47 E3
Yeu, Î. d' .... 12 C2
Yevpatoriya .. 25 D3
Yeysk .... 25 D4
Yezd = Yazd .. 44 D3
Yibin .... 35 D5
Yichang .... 35 C6
Yichun .... 35 B7
Yinchuan .... 35 C5
Yingkou .... 35 B7
Yining .... 34 B3
Yishan .... 35 D5
Yiyang .... 35 D6
Yogyakarta .. 39 F4
Yokkaichi .... 33 F5
Yokohama .... 32 F6
Yonago .... 33 F3
Yonkers .... 77 D9
Yonne → .... 13 B5
York, U.K. .... 11 E6
York, U.S.A. .. 77 E7
York, C. .... 61 C7
Yorkton .... 69 C9
Yosemite △ .. 78 B3
Yoshkar Ola .. 24 B6
Youghal .... 11 F3
Youngstown .. 76 D5
Yozgat .... 46 C3
Ysyk-Köl .... 29 E8
Yu Jiang → .. 35 D6
Yuan Jiang → 35 D5
Yuba City .... 72 G3
Yucatán □ .... 85 C7
Yucatán, Canal
  de .... 85 C7
Yucatán,
  Península de 85 D7
Yuci .... 35 C6
Yugoslavia =
  Serbia &
  Montenegro ■ 22 B3
Yukon → .... 69 B3
Yukon
  Territory □ .. 68 B6
Yuma .... 78 D5
Yumen .... 34 C4
Yungas .... 91 G5
Yunnan □ .... 34 D5
Yurimaguas .. 91 E3
Yushu .... 34 C4
Yuzhno-
  Sakhalinsk . 31 E12
Yvetot .... 12 B4

## Z

Zagorsk =
  Sergiyev
  Posad .... 24 B4
Zagreb .... 20 B6
Zagros, Kühhā-
  ye .... 44 C2
Zagros Mts. =
  Zāgros,
  Kühhā-ye .. 44 C2
Zähedän .... 45 D5
Zahlah .... 46 D3
Zaïre =
  Congo → .. 56 F2
Zakhodnaya
  Dzvina =
  Daugava → .. 24 B1
Zákinthos .... 23 F3
Zambeze → .. 59 B7
Zambezi =
  Zambeze → 59 B7
Zambia ■ .... 59 B5
Zamboanga .. 36 C2
Zamora, Mexico 84 D4
Zamora, Spain . 18 B3
Zamość .... 17 C6
Zanesville .... 76 E4
Zanján .... 46 C7
Zante =
  Zákinthos .. 23 F3
Zanzibar .... 57 F7
Zaouiet Reggâne 52 C6
Zap Suyu = Zâb
  al Kabir → .. 46 C5
Zapadnaya
  Dvina =
  Daugava → .. 24 B1
Západné
  Beskydy .. 16 D4
Zaporizhzhya .. 25 D4
Zaragoza .... 19 B5
Zaranj .... 42 D2
Zaria .... 53 F7
Zarzis .... 54 B1
Zaskar Mts. .. 42 C10
Zäwiyat al
  Baydā = Al
  Bayḍā .... 54 B3
Zeebrugge .... 14 C2
Zelenograd .. 24 B4
Zenica .... 20 B4
Zhambyl = Taraz 29 E8
Zhangjiakou .. 35 B6
Zhangye .... 34 C5
Zhangzhou .. 35 D6
Zhanjiang .... 35 D6
Zhanyi .... 34 D5
Zhaotong .... 34 D5
Zhayyq → .... 29 E6
Zhdanov =
  Mariupol .. 25 D4
Zhejiang □ .. 35 D7
Zhengzhou .. 35 C6
Zhezqazghan = 29 E7
Zhigansk .... 30 C10
Zhitomir =
  Zhytomyr .. 17 C9
Zhlobin .... 17 B10
Zhob .... 42 D6
Zhongdian .. 34 D4
Zhumadian .. 35 C6
Zhytomyr .... 17 C9
Zibo .... 35 C6
Zielona Góra .. 16 C2
Zigong .... 35 D5
Ziguinchor .. 53 F2
Zimbabwe ■ .. 59 B5
Zinder .... 53 F7
Zion △ .... 79 B6
Zlatoust .... 29 D6
Žlin .... 16 D3
Zonguldak .. 46 B2
Zrenjanin .... 22 B3
Zug .... 13 C8
Zugspitze .... 14 E6
Zunyi .... 35 D5
Zürich .... 13 C8
Zvishavane .. 59 C6
Zwickau .... 15 C7